The Price of Power
Being Chapters from the Secret History of the Imperial Court of Russia

by

William Le Queux

Double 9
BOOKS

The Price of Power
Being Chapters from the Secret History of the Imperial Court of Russia
by William Le Queux

ISBN: 978-93-59954-56-1

Published by

DOUBLE 9 BOOKS

2/13-B, Ansari Road
Daryaganj, New Delhi – 110002
info@double9books.com
www.double9books.com
Tel. 011-40042856

ABOUT THE AUTHOR

Anglo-French journalist and author William Tufnell Le Queux was born on July 2, 1864, and died on October 13, 1927. He was also a diplomat (honorary consul for San Marino), a traveler (in Europe, the Balkans, and North Africa), a fan of flying (he presided over the first British air meeting at Doncaster in 1909), and a wireless pioneer who played music on his own station long before radio was widely available. However, he often exaggerated his own skills and accomplishments. The Great War in England in 1897 (1894), a fantasy about an invasion by France and Russia, and The Invasion of 1910 (1906), a fantasy about an invasion by Germany, are his best-known works. Le Queux was born in the city. The man who raised him was English, and his father was French. He went to school in Europe and learned art in Paris from Ignazio (or Ignace) Spiridon. As a young man, he walked across Europe and then made a living by writing for French newspapers. He moved back to London in the late 1880s and managed the magazines Gossip and Piccadilly. In 1891, he became a parliamentary reporter for The Globe. He stopped working as a reporter in 1893 to focus on writing and traveling.

CONTENTS

Chapter One
The Madcap

"M'sieur Colin Trewinnard?"

"That is my name, Captain Stoyanovitch," I replied in surprise. "You know it quite well."

"The usual formality, *mon cher ami!*"

And the tall, handsome equerry in the white uniform of the Imperial Guard laughed lightly, clicked his heels together, and handed me a letter which I saw bore the Imperial cipher upon its black seal.

"From His Imperial Majesty the Emperor," he added in Russian.

I held my breath. Had the blow fallen?

With eager, trembling fingers I tore open the envelope and found therein a note in French, merely the words:

"His Imperial Majesty the Emperor commands Mr Colin Trewinnard to private audience to-day at 3:30 p.m.

"St. Petersburg, June 28th."

"Very well," I managed to reply. "Tell Colonel Polivanoff that—that I shall be there. Have a cigarette?" and I handed him the silver box of Bogdanoffs which were the common property of the staff of the Embassy.

Having flung himself into a big easy chair, he stretched out his long legs and lit up.

"Well," I said, leaning against the edge of the writing-table, "I suppose the Emperor returned from Odessa early this morning—eh?"

"Yes," replied the elegant officer, in English. "Thank Heaven, the journey is at last over. Ah! what a tour of the Empire! At Orel we held the great review, then on to Saratov, where there were more manoeuvres and a review. Afterwards we went down the Volga to Astrakhan to unveil the new statue to Peter the Great; then Kertch, more manoeuvres, and into the Crimea for a week's rest. Afterwards across to Odessa, and then, by a three nights' journey, back here to Petersburg. Faugh! How we all hate that armoured train!"

"But it is surely highly necessary, my dear Stoyanovitch," I said. "With this abominable wave of anarchism which has spread over Europe, it behoves the Secret Police to take every precaution for His Majesty's safety!"

"Ah! my dear friend," laughed the equerry. "I tell you it is not at all pleasant to travel when one expects every moment that the train will be blown up. One's sleeping-berth, though covered with a down quilt, is but a bed of torture in such conditions."

"Yes," I said. "But His Majesty—how does he bear it?"

"The Emperor has nerves of iron. He is the least concerned of any of us. But, *mon Dieu*! I would not be in his shoes for the wealth of all the Russias."

"What—more conspiracies?" I exclaimed.

"Conspiracies!" sighed the Captain. "*Mon Dieu*! A fresh one is discovered by the political police every week. Only the day before the Emperor left for the country he found among the Ministers' daily reports upon the table in his private cabinet an anonymous letter telling him that he will meet with a tragic end on the sixth of the present month. How this letter got there nobody knows. His Majesty is seldom out of temper, but I never saw him so furiously angry before."

"It is unfortunate," I said. "Apparently he cannot trust even his immediate *entourage*."

"Exactly," answered the dark-haired handsome man. "The constant reports of General Markoff regarding the revolutionists must be most alarming. And yet he preserves an outward calm that is truly remarkable. But, by the way," he added, "His Majesty, before I left the Palace with that letter, summoned me and gave me a message for you—a verbal one."

"Oh! What was that?"

"He told me to say that he sent to you a word—let me see, I wrote it down lest I should forget," and pulling down his left shirt cuff, he spelt:

"B-a-t-h-i-l-d-i-s."

"Thank you," I replied briefly.

"What does it mean? Is it some password?" Ivan Stoyanovitch asked with considerable curiosity.

"That's scarcely a fair question," I said in rebuke.

"Ah! of course," he replied, with a touch of sarcasm. "I ought not to have asked you. Pardon me, my friend. I forgot that you enjoy His Majesty's confidence—that—"

"Not at all," I protested. "I am but a humble attaché of a foreign Embassy. It is not likely that I am entrusted with the secrets of Russia."

"Not with those of Russia, but those of the Emperor personally. Dachkoff was discussing you at the Turf Club one night not long ago."

"That's interesting," I laughed. "And what had the old man to say?"

"Oh, nothing of a very friendly nature. But, you know, he never has a good word to say for anybody."

"Gamblers seldom have. I hear he lost ten thousand roubles to Prince Savinski at the Union the night before last."

"I heard it was more," and the long-legged equerry leaned back his head and watched the blue rings of cigarette smoke slowly ascend to the ceiling of the room, through the long window of which was a view across the Neva, with the grim Fortress of Peter and Paul opposite. "But," he went on, "we were speaking of these constant conspiracies. Though we have been back in Petersburg only a few hours, Markoff has already reported a desperate plot. The conspirators, it seems, had bored a tunnel and placed a mine under the Nevski, close to the corner of the Pushkinskaya, and it was arranged to explode it as the Emperor's carriage passed early this morning on the way from the Nicholas station. But Markoff—the ever-watchful Markoff—discovered the projected attempt only at eleven o'clock last night—two hours before we passed. There have been thirty-three arrests up to the present, including a number of girl students."

"Markoff is really a marvel," I declared. "He scents a conspiracy anywhere."

"And his spies are everywhere. Markoff takes a good deal of the credit, but it is his agents who do the real work. He has saved the Emperor's life on at least a dozen occasions."

I said nothing. I was thinking over the word—a very significant word—which the Emperor had sent me by his equerry. To me, that word meant a very great deal.

Our Ambassador, Sir Harding Lowe, being at home in England on leave, the Honourable Claude Saunderson, our Councillor of Embassy, was acting as Chargé d'Affaires. As far as we knew the political horizon was calm enough, save the dark little war cloud which perpetually hovers over the Balkans and grows darker each winter. The German negotiations with

Russia had been concluded, and the foreign outlook appeared more serene than it had been for many months.

Yet within the great Winter Palace there was unrest and trouble. Jealousy, hatred and all uncharitableness were rife amid the Tzar's immediate *entourage*, while the spirit of revolution was spreading daily with greater significance.

Within the past twelve months the two Prime Ministers, Semenoff and Mouravieff, had been assassinated by bombs, five governors of provinces had met with violent deaths, and eight chiefs of police of various cities had fallen victims of the revolutionists, who had frankly and openly vowed to take the life of the Tzar himself.

Was it any wonder, then, that the Emperor lived in bomb-proof rooms both in Petersburg and Tzarskoie-Selo, as well as at Gatchina; that he never slept in the same bed twice, that all food served to him was previously tasted, that he never gave audience without a loaded revolver lying upon the table before him, and that he surrounded himself by hordes of police-agents and spies? Surely none could envy him such a life of constant apprehension and daily terror; for twice in a month had bombs been thrown at his carriage, while five weeks before he had had both horses killed by an explosion in Moscow and only escaped death by a sheer miracle.

True, the revolutionists were unusually active at that moment, and the throne of Russia had become seriously menaced. Any other but a man of iron constitution and nerves of steel would surely have been driven to lunacy by the constant terror in which he was forced to exist. Yet, though he took ample precaution, he never betrayed the slightest anxiety, a fact which held everyone amazed. He was a true Russian, an autocrat of dogged courage, quick decision, always forceful and impelling, a faithful friend, but a bitter and revengeful enemy; a born ruler and a manly Emperor in every sense of the word.

"The Grand Duchess Natalia has been with the Emperor. Did she return with you this morning?" I inquired.

"Yes," drawled the equerry. "She's been admired everywhere, as usual, and half our staff are over head and ears in love with her. She's been flirting outrageously."

"Then half your staff are fools," I exclaimed bluntly.

"Ah, my dear Trewinnard, she is so sweet, so very charming, so exquisite, so entirely unlike the other girls at Court—so delightfully unconventional."

"A little too unconventional to suit some—if all I hear be true," I remarked with a smile.

"You know her, of course. She's an intimate friend of yours. I overheard her one day telling the Emperor what an excellent tennis player you were."

"Well, I don't fancy His Majesty interests himself very much in tennis," I laughed. "He has other, and far more important, matters to occupy his time—the affairs of his great nation."

"Natalia, or Tattie, as they call her in the Imperial circle, is his favourite niece. Nowadays she goes everywhere with him, and does quite a lot of his most private correspondence—that which he does not even trust to Calitzine."

"Then the Emperor is more friendly towards Her Imperial Highness than before—eh?" I asked, for truth to tell I was very anxious to satisfy myself upon this point.

"Yes. She has been forgiven for that little escapade in Moscow."

"What escapade?" I asked, feigning surprise.

"What escapade?" my friend echoed. "Why, you know well enough! I've heard it whispered that it was owing to your cleverness as a diplomat that the matter was so successfully hushed up—and an ugly affair it was, too. The suicide of her lover."

"That's a confounded lie!" I said quickly. "He did not commit suicide at all. At most, he left Russia with a broken heart, and that is not usually a fatal malady."

"Well, you needn't get angry about it, my dear fellow," complained my friend. "The affair is successfully hushed up, and I fancy she's got a lot to thank you for."

"Not at all," I declared. "I know that you fellows have coupled my name with hers, just because I've danced with her a few times at the Court balls, and I've been shooting at her father's castle away in Samara. But I assure you my reputation as the little Grand Duchess's intimate friend is entirely a mythical one." Captain Stoyanovitch only smiled incredulously, stretched out his long legs and shrugged his shoulders.

"Well," I went on, "has she been very terrified about all these reports of conspiracies?"

"Frightened out of her life, poor child! And who would not be?" he asked. "We didn't know from one hour to another that we might not all be blown into the air. Everywhere the railway was lined by Cossacks, of course. Such a demonstration is apt to lend an air of security, but, alas! there is no security with the very Ministry undermined by revolution, as it is."

I sighed. What he said was, alas! too true. Russia, at that moment, was in very evil case, and none knew it better than we, the impartial onlookers at the British Embassy.

The warm June sun fell across the rather faded carpet of that sombre old-fashioned room with its heavy furniture, which was my own sanctum, and as the smart captain of the Imperial Guard lolled back picturesquely in the big armchair I looked at him reflectively.

They were strange thoughts which flooded my brain at that moment—thoughts concerning that pretty, high-born young lady whom we had just been discussing, the girl to whom, he declared, His Majesty entrusted the greatest secrets of the throne.

Stoyanovitch was an extremely elegant and somewhat irresponsible person, and the fact that the Emperor had allowed the Grand Duchess Natalia to write his private letters did not strike me as the actual truth. The Tzar was far too cautious to entrust the secrets of a nation to a mere girl who was certainly known to be greatly addicted to the gentle pastime of flirtation.

Whatever the equerry told us, we at the Embassy usually added the proverbial grain of salt. Indeed, the diplomat at any post abroad learns to believe nothing which he hears, and only half he actually sees.

But the Emperor had sent me, by the mouth of that smart young officer, the word "Bathildis"—which was an ancient woman's Christian name—and to me it conveyed a secret message, an announcement which held me in surprise and apprehension.

What could have happened?

I dreaded to think.

Chapter Two
An Audience of the Emperor

"You understand, Trewinnard. There must be no scandal. What I have just revealed to you is in strictest confidence—an inviolable secret—a personal secret of my own."

"I understand Your Majesty's commands perfectly."

"There is already a lot of uncharitable chatter in the Court circle regarding the other matter, I hear. Has anything reached you at the Embassy?"

"Not a whisper, as far as I am aware. Indeed, Your Majesty's words have greatly surprised me. I did not believe the affair to be so very serious."

"Serious!" echoed the Emperor Alexander, speaking in English, his dark, deep-set eyes fixed upon me. "I tell you it is all too serious, now that I find myself completely isolated—oh! yes, Trewinnard, isolated—with scarce one single friend. God knows! I have done my best for the nation, but, alas! everyone's hand is raised against me." And his firm mouth hardened behind his full, dark beard, and he drew his hand wearily across his broad, white brow.

The room in the Winter Palace in which we sat was cosy and luxuriantly furnished, the two windows looking forth upon a grey, cheerless quadrangle whence came the tramp of soldiers at drill.

Where we sat we could hear the sharp words of command in Russian, and the clang of the rifle-butts striking the stones.

The room was essentially English in its aspect, with its rich china-blue Axminster carpet, and silk upholstery with curtains to match, while the panelling from floor to ceiling was enamelled dead white, against which the fine water-colour drawings of naval scenes stood out in vivid relief. Upon a buhl table was a great silver bowl filled with Marshal Niel roses—for His Majesty was passionately fond of flowers—and beside it, large framed panel photographs of the Tzarina and his children. And yet those dead white walls and the shape of those square windows struck a curious incongruous note, for if the actual truth be told, those walls were of steel, and that private cabinet of the Emperor had been constructed by the Admiralty Department with armour-plates which were bomb-proof.

That apartment in the west angle of the Palace quadrangle was well-known to me, for in it His Majesty had given me private audience many times. That long white door which had been so silently closed upon me by the Cossack sentry when I entered was, I knew, of armour-plate, four inches in thickness, while beside the windows were revolving shutters of chilled steel.

There, at that great littered roll-top writing-table, upon which was the reading-lamp with its shade of salmon-pink silk with the loaded revolver beside it, the Emperor worked, attending to affairs of State. And in his padded chair, leaning back easily as he spoke to me, was His Majesty himself, a broad-shouldered, handsome man just past middle-age, dressed in a suit of navy blue serge. He was a big-faced, big-limbed, big-handed man of colossal physique and marvellous intelligence. Though haunted by the terror of violent death, he was yet an autocrat to the finger-tips, whose bearing was ever that of a sovereign; yet his eyes had a calm, sympathetic, kindly look, and those who knew him intimately were well aware that he was not the monster of oppression which his traducers had made him out to be before the eyes of Europe.

True, with a stroke of that grey quill pen lying there upon his blotting-pad he had sent many a man and woman without trial to their unrecorded doom, either in the frozen wastes of Northern Siberia, to the terrible mines of Nerchinsk, to the horrors of the penal island of Sakhalin, or to those fearful subterranean *oubliettes* at Schusselburg, whence no prisoner has ever returned. But, as an autocrat, he dealt with his revolutionary enemies as they would deal with him. They conspired to kill him, and he retaliated by consigning them to a lingering death.

On the other hand, I myself knew how constant was his endeavour to ferret out abuses of administration, to alleviate the sufferings of the poor, to give the peasantry education and all the benefits of modern civilisation as we in England know them, and how desperate, alas! were his constant struggles with that unscrupulous camarilla which ever surrounded him, constantly preventing him from learning the truth concerning any particular matter.

Thus, though striving to do his best for his subjects and for his nation, yet, surrounded as he was by a corrupt Ministry and a more corrupt Court, this big, striking man in blue serge was, perhaps, next to the Sultan of Turkey, the best-hated man in all Europe.

My own position was a somewhat singular one. A few months after my appointment to Petersburg from Brussels I had been able to render His Majesty a slight personal service. In fact, I had, when out one evening with two other attachés of the German Embassy, learned by mere accident of a desperate plot which was to be put into execution on the following day. My informant was a dancer at the Opera, who had taken too much champagne at supper. I sought audience of the Emperor early next day, and was fortunately just in time to prevent him from passing a certain spot near the Michailovski Palace, where six men were stationed with bombs of picric acid, ready to hurl. For that service His Majesty had been graciously pleased to take me into his confidence—a confidence which, I hope, I never abused. From me he was always eager to ascertain what was really happening beyond that high wall of untruth which the camarilla had so cleverly built up and preserved, and more than once had he entrusted me with certain · secret missions.

I was not in uniform, as that audience was a private one; but as His Majesty, ruler of one hundred and thirty millions of people, passed me his finely-chased golden box full of cigarettes—and we both lit one, as was our habit—his brow clouded, and with a sigh he said:

"To tell the truth, Trewinnard, I am also very anxious indeed concerning the second matter—concerning the little rebel."

"I know that Your Majesty must be," I replied. "But, after all, Her Imperial Highness is a girl of exceptional beauty and highest spirits; and even if she indulges in—well, in a little harmless flirtation, she surely may be forgiven."

"Other girls may be forgiven, but not those of the blood-royal," he said in mild rebuke. "The Empress is quite as concerned about her as I am. Why, even upon this last journey of ours I found her more than once flirting with Stoyanovitch, my equerry. True, he's a good-looking young fellow, and of excellent family, yet she ought to know that such a thing is quite unwarrantable; she ought to know that to those of the blood-royal love is, alas! forbidden."

I was surprised at this. I had no idea that she and Ivan Stoyanovitch had become friends. He had never hinted at it.

"The fact is, Trewinnard," the Emperor went on, blowing a cloud of cigarette smoke from his lips, "if this continues I shall be reluctantly compelled to banish her to the Caucasus, or somewhere where she will be kept out of mischief."

"But permit me, Sire, to query whether flirting is really mischief," I exclaimed with a smile. "Every girl of her age—and she is hardly nineteen—fancies herself in love, mostly with men much older than herself."

"Our women, Trewinnard, are, alas! not like women of the people," was the Sovereign's calm reply, his deep, earnest eyes upon mine. "It is their misfortune that they are not. They can never enjoy the same freedom as those fortunate ones of the middle-class; they seldom are permitted to marry the man they love, and though they may live in palaces and move amid the gay society of Court, yet their ideas are warped from birth, and broken hearts, alas! beat beneath their diamonds."

"Yes, I suppose what Your Majesty says is, alas! too true. Ladies of the blood-royal are forbidden freedom, love and happiness. And when one of them happens to break the iron bonds of conventionality, then scandal quickly results; the Press overflows with it."

"In this case scandal would already have resulted had you not acted as promptly as you did," His Majesty said. "Where is that lad Geoffrey Hamborough now?" asked the autocrat suddenly.

"Living on his father's estate in Yorkshire," I replied. "I hope I have been able to put an end to that fatal folly; but with a girl of the Grand Duchess's type one can never be too certain."

"Ah! the mischievous little minx!" exclaimed the Emperor with a kindly smile. "I've watched, and seen how cunning she is—and how she has cleverly misled even me. Well, she must alter, Trewinnard, she must alter—or she must be sent away to the Caucasus."

"Where she would have her freedom, and probably flirt more outrageously than ever," I ventured to remark.

"You seem to regard her as hopeless," he said, looking sharply into my eyes as he leaned back in his chair.

"Not entirely hopeless, Sire, only as a most interesting character study."

"I have been speaking to her father this morning, and I have suggested sending her to Paris, or, perhaps, to London; there to live *incognito* under the guardianship of some responsible middle-aged person, until she can settle down. At present she flirts with every man she meets, and I am greatly concerned about her."

"Every man is ready to flirt with Her Imperial Highness—first, because of her position, and, secondly, because of her remarkable beauty," I assured him.

"You think her beautiful—eh, Trewinnard?"

"I merely echo the popular judgment," I replied. "It is said she is one of the most beautiful girls in all Russia."

"Ah!" he laughed. "Next we shall have her flirting with you, Trewinnard. You are a bachelor. Do beware of the little dark-eyed witch, I beg of you!"

"No fear of such *contretemps*, Sire," I assured him with a smile. "I am double her age, and, moreover, a confirmed bachelor. The Embassy is expensive, and I cannot afford the luxury of a wife—and especially an Imperial Grand Duchess."

"Who knows—eh, Trewinnard? Who knows?" exclaimed the Sovereign good-naturedly. "But let's return to the point. Am I to understand that you are ready and willing to execute this secret commission for me? You are well aware how highly I value the confidential services you have already rendered to me. But for you, remember, I should to-day have been a dead man."

"No, Sire," I protested. "Please do not speak of that. It was the intervention of Providence for your protection."

"Ah, yes!" he said in a low, fervent tone, his brows contracting. "I thank God constantly for sparing me for yet another day from the hands of my unscrupulous enemies, so that I may work for the good of the beloved nation over which I am called to rule."

There, in that room, wherein I had so often listened to his words of wisdom, I sat fully recognising that though an Emperor and an autocrat, he was, above all, a Man.

With all the heavy burden of affairs of State—and not even a road could be made anywhere in the Russian Empire, or a bridge built, or a gas-pipe laid, without his signature—with all the onus of the autocratic Sovereign-power upon his shoulders, and with that constant wariness which he was compelled to exercise against that cunning camarilla of Ministers, yet one of his chief concerns was with that pretty little madcap Natalia, daughter of his brother, the Grand Duke Nicholas.

He wished to suppress her superabundance of high spirits and stamp out her tomboy instincts.

"I am reading your thoughts, Trewinnard," the Emperor remarked at last, pressing his cigarette-end slowly into the silver ashtray to extinguish it. "My request has placed you in a rather awkward position—eh?"

"What Your Majesty has revealed to me this afternoon has utterly amazed me. I feel bewildered, for I see how dire must be the result if the truth were ever betrayed."

"It will never be. You are the only person who has suspicion of it besides myself."

"And I shall never speak—never!" I assured him gravely.

"I know that you are entirely loyal to me. I am Emperor, it is true, but I am, nevertheless, a man of my word, just as you are," he replied, his intelligent face dark and grave. "Yes. I thought you would realise the seriousness of the present situation, and I know that you alone I can trust. I have not even told the Empress."

"Why not?"

"For obvious reasons."

I was silent. I only then realised the motive of his hesitation.

"I admit that Your Majesty's request has placed me in a somewhat awkward position," I said at last, bending forward in my chair. "Truth to tell, I—well, I'm hardly hopeful of success, for the mission with which I am entrusted is so extremely difficult, and so—"

"I am fully aware of that," he interrupted. "Yet I feel confident that you, who have saved my life on one occasion, will not hesitate to undertake this service to the best of your ability. Use the utmost discretion, and you may get at the truth. I do not disguise from you the fact that upon certain contingencies, dependent on the success of your mission, depends the throne of Russia—the dynasty. Do you follow?" And he looked me straight in the face with those big, round brown eyes, an open, straight, honest look, as became a man who was fearless—an Emperor.

"I regret that I do not exactly understand," I ventured to exclaim, whereat he rose, tall, handsome and muscular, and strode to the window. The band of the Imperial Guard was playing below in the great paved quadrangle, as it always did each day at four o'clock when the Emperor was in residence. For a few seconds he stood peering forth critically at the long lines of soldiers drawn up across the square. Then the man whose word was law turned back to me with a sigh, saying:

"No, Trewinnard, I suppose you do not follow me. It is all a mystery to you, of course,"—and he paused—"as mysterious as the sudden disappearance of Madame de Rosen and her daughter Luba from Petersburg."

"Disappearance?" I echoed, amazed. "They are still in Petersburg. I dined with them only last night!"

"They are not now in Petersburg," replied the Emperor very quietly. "They left at nine o'clock this morning on a long journey—to Siberia."

My heart gave a great bound.

"To Siberia!" I gasped, staring at him. "Are they exiled? Who has done this?"

"I have done it," was his hard reply. "They are revolutionists—implicated in the attempt that was to be made upon me early this morning as I drove up the Nevski."

"Markoff has denounced them?"

"He has. See, here is a full list of names of the conspirators," and he took a slip of paper from his desk.

"And General Markoff told Your Majesty of my friendliness with Madame and her daughter?"

"Certainly."

"Markoff lied when he denounced them as revolutionists!" I cried angrily. "They were my friends, and I know them very intimately. Let me here declare, Sire, that no subject of Your Majesty was more loyal than those two ladies. Surely the *agent-provocateur* has been at work again."

"Unfortunately I am bound to believe the word of the head of my political police," he said rather briefly.

I knew, alas! how fierce and bitter was the Emperor's hatred of those who plotted against his life. A single word against man or woman was sufficient to cause them to be arrested and sent to the other side of Asia, never again to return.

"And where have the ladies been sent?" I inquired. The Emperor consulted a slip of paper, and then replied:

"To Parotovsk."

"The most far-distant and dreaded of all the Arctic penal settlements!" I cried. "It is cruel and unjust! It is death to send a woman there, where it is winter for nine months in the year, and where darkness reigns five months out of the twelve."

"I regret," replied the Emperor, with a slight gesture of the hand. "But they were conspirators."

"With all respect to Your Majesty, I beg to express an entirely different opinion. Markoff has long been Madame de Rosen's enemy."

His Majesty made a quick imperious gesture of impatience and said:

"Please do not let us discuss the matter further—at least, until you are in a position to prove your allegation."

"I will," I cried. "I know that your Majesty will never allow such injustice to be done to two innocent, delicate ladies."

"If injustice has really been done, then those responsible shall suffer. Discover the truth, and report to me later," he said.

"I will do my very utmost," was my reply.

"And at the same time, Trewinnard, I trust you will endeavour to carry out the confidential mission which I have entrusted to you," he said. "Recollect that I treat you, not as a foreign diplomat, but as a loyal and true personal friend of myself and my house. Ah!" he sighed again; "Heaven knows, I have but few trustworthy ones about me."

"I am profoundly honoured by Your Majesty's confidence," I assured him, bowing low. "I certainly shall respect it, and act exactly as you desire."

"The Court dislikes confidence being placed in any foreigner, even though he be an Englishman," the Emperor said in a changed voice; "therefore, remain discreet always, and disclaim that I have ever treated you other than with the formal courtesy which is expected by all diplomats."

"I quite understand," I said.

"You will see Natalia at the Court ball to-night, and you can speak to her diplomatically, if opportunity occurs. But recollect that she must know nothing of what I have said. I believe you know Hartwig, chief of the criminal detective force."

"Quite well," was my reply.

"Then I will give him orders. Use him as you wish, but tell him nothing."

"I shall remain silent."

"And you are entitled to leave of absence—eh? You can return to England without arousing suspicion?"

"Yes. I have eight weeks due to me."

"Excellent. I can do nothing more—except to thank you, Trewinnard, to thank you most sincerely for assisting me, and to await word from you. Sign it with 'Bathildis,' and I shall know." And the great burly, bearded man held out his big, strong hand—the iron hand—as sign that my audience was at an end.

I bowed low over it, and next moment the heavy white door of enamelled steel swung open and I backed out of the Imperial presence, the bearer of a secret as strange and grim as it has ever been the lot of any man to lock within his breast.

What the Emperor had revealed to me was undreamed of by that gay, reckless and intriguing circle which comprised the Russian Court— undreamed of by the chancelleries of Europe.

The merest whisper of it would, I knew, stagger the world. And yet he had, in sheer desperation, confided in me a most amazing truth. As I descended that broad, handsome flight of thickly-carpeted marble steps, where flunkeys in brilliant grey and purple livery bowed at every turn, and equerries and officials in smart uniforms came and went, my brain was awhirl at the magnitude of the affair, and the terrible scandal which must result if ever the secret were betrayed—the secret of a throne.

A thought flashed across my mind—the knowledge of my own personal peril. I had enemies—bitter enemies. My heart sank within me as I stepped into the great gilded hall, for I had given a promise which I much feared I would never be permitted to live and fulfil.

Chapter Three
Contains Certain Confidences

Six hours later, accompanied by Saunderson, our tall, thin Chargé d'Affaires, and the Embassy staff, all in our uniforms and decorations, I entered the huge white-and-gold ballroom of the Winter Palace, where the Russian Court, the representatives of exclusive Society, the bureaucracy of the Empire and the *corps diplomatique* had assembled.

The scene was perhaps the most brilliant and picturesque that could be witnessed anywhere in the world. Beneath the myriad lights of those huge cut-glass chandeliers, and reflected by the gigantic mirrors upon the walls, were hundreds of gold-laced uniforms of every shade and every style. Across the breasts of many of the men were gay-coloured scarves of the various orders, with diamond stars, while others wore around their necks parti-coloured ribbons with enamelled crosses at their throat, or rows of decorations across their breasts.

And to this phantasmagoria of colour, as all stood in little groups chattering and awaiting Their Majesties, was added that of the splendid long-trained dresses of the women, nearly all of whom wore their diamond tiaras, or diamond ornaments in their corsage.

It was indeed, a cosmopolitan gathering, half of Russians and half of the diplomatic set, and around me, as I bowed over the hand of a well-known Baroness, wife of the Minister of War, I heard animated chatter in half a dozen tongues. The Emperor had returned, and there would now be a month of gaiety before he retired for the summer to Gatchina. The spring season in Petersburg had been cut short—first by the indisposition of the Empress, and afterwards by reason of the Emperor's tour to the distant shore of the Caspian.

Therefore at this, the delayed Court ball, everybody who was anybody in Russia was present.

In one end of the huge Renaissance salon, with its wonderful painted ceiling and gilded cupids, was a great semicircular alcove, with a slightly raised daïs, whereon sat the Dowager-Empress, the Grand Duchesses and those of the blood-royal, with their attendant ladies, while the male members of the Court lounged behind.

The opposite end of the great ballroom led to another salon with parquet floor, decorated in similar style, and with many mirrors, and almost as large, while beyond was a somewhat smaller room, the whole effect being one of gorgeous grandeur and immensity.

I had paused to chat with a stout lady in cream, who wore a beautiful tiara. Princess Lovovski, wife of the Governor-General of Finland, and she had commenced to tell me the latest tit-bit of scandal concerning the wife of a certain War Office official, a matter which did not interest me in the least, when suddenly there came three loud taps—the taps of the Grand Chamberlain—announcing the entrance of His Majesty. As by enchantment a wide door in the side of the ballroom flew open, and the glittering throng, bejewelled and perfumed, flashing colours amid plumes, aigrettes and flowers, laughing and murmuring to the clink of gala swords and sabres, was struck to silence.

His Majesty passed—a tall, commanding figure in a white uniform covered with the stars, crosses and many-coloured ribbons of the various European orders. Beneath the thousand lights the bare shoulders of the beautiful women inclined profoundly.

Then again the loud chatter recommenced.

The Emperor's presence, tall, erect, muscular, was indeed a regal one. He looked every inch a ruler and an autocrat as he advanced to the alcove, where the whole Court had risen to receive him, and with a quick gesture he gave the signal for dancing to commence.

I retreated to the wall, being in no humour to dance, and stood gazing at him. He seemed, indeed, a different person to that deep-eyed, earnest man in dark-blue serge who had sat chatting with me so affably six hours ago. He was in that hour a man, but now the centre of that gay patrician throng, he was ruler, the autocrat who by a stroke of the grey quill could banish to the mines or the *oubliettes* any of those of his subjects who bowed before him—sweep them out of existence as completely as though the grave had claimed them; for every exile lost his identity and became a mere number; his estate was administered as though he were dead, and apportioned, with the usual forfeiture to the State, among his heirs. So that it was impossible for an exile to be traced.

I thought of Madame Marya de Rosen and of poor little Luba. Ah! I wondered how many delicate women and handsome, intelligent men who had danced over that polished floor were now dragging out their weary lives in those squalid, filthy Yakut yaurtas of Eastern Siberia. How many, alas! had, in innocence, fallen victims to that corrupt bureaucracy which always concealed the truth from His Majesty.

To the camarilla, a dozen or so men who were present there in brilliant uniforms and wearing the Cross of St. Andrew, with the pale-blue ribbon, the highest Order of the Empire, bestowed upon them for their "fidelity," that present reign of terror was solely due. It was to the interests of those men that the Emperor should be perpetually terrorised. Half those so-called conspiracies were the work of the Secret Police themselves and their *agents-provocateurs*; and hundreds of innocent persons were being spirited away without trial to the frozen wastes of Northern and Eastern Siberia, upon no other charge than the trivial one that they were "dangerous" persons!

Madame de Rosen and her pretty daughter had fallen victims of the bitter unscrupulousness of that short, stout, grey-moustached man, who at that moment was bowing so obsequiously before his Sovereign, the man who was one of the greatest powers in the Empire, General Serge Markoff, Chief of Secret Police.

The first dance was in progress. Pretty women, with their smart, good-looking cavaliers, were whirling about me to the slow, tuneful strains of one of the latest of Strauss's waltzes, when Colonel Mellini, the Italian military attaché, halted before me to chat. He had just returned from leave, and had much Embassy gossip to relate to me from the Eternal City, where I had served for two years.

"I hear," he remarked at last, "that another plot was discovered early this morning—a desperate one in the Nevski. Markoff really seems ubiquitous."

I looked into his dark eyes and smiled.

"Ah! I see, *caro mio*," he laughed. "Your thoughts are similar to mine—eh? These plots are a little too frequent to be genuine," and, lowering his voice to a whisper, he added: "I can't understand how His Majesty does not see through the transparency of it. They are terrorising him every day—every hour. A man of less robust physique or mental balance would surely be driven out of his mind."

"I agree with you entirely, my dear friend. But," I added, "this is not the place to discuss affairs of State. Ah, Madame!" and turning, I bent over the gloved hand of old Madame Neilidoff, one of the leaders of Society in Moscow, with whom I stood chatting for a long time, and who kindly invited me for a week out at her great country estate at Sukova in Tver.

Captain Stoyanovitch, gay with decorations, hurried past me on some errand for the Emperor, and gave me a nod as he went on, while young

Bertram Tucker, our third secretary, came up and began to chat with the yellow-toothed old lady, who was such a power in the Russian social circle.

I suppose it must have been nearly two o'clock, when, after wandering through the *salons*, greeting many men and women I knew, I suddenly heard a voice behind me exclaim in English:

"Hulloa, old Uncle Colin! Am I too small to be recognised?"

I turned quickly and confronted the pretty laughing girl of nineteen of whom I had been in search all the night—Her Imperial Highness the Grand Duchess Natalia Olga Nicolaievna.

Tall, slim, with a perfect figure, she was dressed in cream, a light simple gown which suited her youth and extreme beauty admirably. Across her dark, well-dressed hair she wore a narrow band of forget-me-nots; at her throat was a large single emerald of great value, suspended by a fine chain of platinum, a present from His Majesty, while on the edge of her low-cut corsage she wore a bow of pale-blue ribbon embroidered in silver with a Russian motto, and from it was suspended a medallion set with diamonds and bearing in the centre the enamelled figure of Saint Catherine—the exclusive Order of Saint Catherine bestowed upon the Grand Duchesses.

"How miserable you look, Uncle Colin!" exclaimed the dark-eyed girl before I could reply. "Whatever is the matter? Is the British Lion sick—or what?"

"I really must apologise to Your Imperial Highness," I said, bowing. "I was quite unaware that I looked miserable. I surely could never look miserable in your presence."

We both laughed, while standing erect and defiant, before me she held up a little ivory fan, threatening to chastise me with it.

"Well," I said, "and so you are safely back again in Petersburg, after all your travels! Why, it's surely eight weeks since we were at the ball at the Palace of your uncle, the Grand Duke Serge."

"Where you danced with me. Do you remember how we laughed? You said some nasty sarcastic things, so I punished you. I told Captain Stoyanovitch and some of the others that you had flirted with me and kissed me. So there!"

I looked at her in stern reproach.

"Ah!" I said. "So that is the source of all those rumours—eh? You're a very wicked girl," I added, "even though you are a Grand Duchess."

"Well, I suppose Grand Duchesses are in no way different to other girls—eh?" she pouted. "Sometimes I wish I were back again at school at Eastbourne. Ah! what grand times I used to have in those days—hockey and tennis and gym, and I was not compelled to perform all sorts of horrible, irksome etiquette, and be surrounded by this crowd of silly dressed-up apes. Why, Uncle Colin, these are not men—all these tight-uniformed popinjays at Court."

"Hush, my child!" I said. "Hush! You will be overheard."

"And I don't care if I am. Surely a girl can speak out what she thinks!"

"In England, yes, in certain circumstances, but in Russia—and especially at Court—never!"

"Oh, you are so horribly old-fashioned, Uncle Colin. When shall I bring you up-to-date?" cried the petted and spoiled young lady, whose two distinctions were that she was one of the most beautiful girls in all Russia, and the favourite niece of the Tzar Alexander. She had nicknamed me "Uncle," on account of my superior age, long ago.

"And you are utterly incorrigible," I said, trying to assume an angry look.

"Ah! You're going to lecture me!" she exclaimed with another pout. "I suppose I ought never to dance at all—eh? It's wicked in your eyes, isn't it? You are perhaps, one of those exemplary people that I heard so much of when in England—such an expressive name—the Kill-joys!"

"No, Your Highness," I protested. "I really don't think I'm a killjoy. If I were, I couldn't very well be a diplomat. I—"

"But all diplomats are trained liars," she asserted with abrupt frankness. "The Emperor told me so only the other day. He said they were men one should never trust."

"I admit that, without the lie *artistique*, diplomacy would really be non-existent," I said, with a laugh. "But is not the whole political world everywhere in Europe a world of vain promise, intrigue and shame?"

"Just as our social world seems to me," she admitted.

"Ah! Then you are beginning to realise the hollow unreality of the world about you—eh?" I said.

"Dear me!" she exclaimed, "you talk just like a bishop! I really don't know what has come to my dear old Uncle Colin. You must be ill, or something. You never used to be like this," she added, with a sigh and a well-feigned look of regret that was really most amusing, while at the same time she made eyes at me.

Truly, she was a most charming little madcap, this Imperial Grand Duchess—the most charming in all Europe, as the diplomatic circle had long ago agreed.

So she had taken revenge upon me for uttering words of wisdom by telling people that I had flirted with and kissed her! She herself was responsible for the chatter which had gone round, with many embellishments, concerning myself, and how deeply I was in love with her. I wondered if it had reached the Emperor's ears?

I felt annoyed, I here confess. And yet so sweet and irresponsible was she, so intelligent and quick at repartee, that next moment I had forgiven her.

And I frankly told her so.

"My dear Uncle Colin, it would have been all the same," she declared airily. "You shouldn't have lectured me. I assure you I have had enough of that at home. Ever since I came back from England everybody seems to have conspired to tell me that I'm the most terrible girl in Russia. Father holds up his hands; why, I really don't know."

"Because you are so extremely unconventional," I said. "A girl of the people can act just as she likes; but you are a Grand Duchess—and you can't."

"Bother my birth. That's my misfortune. I wish I were a shopgirl, or a typist, or something. Then I should be free!" she exclaimed impatiently. "As it is, I can't utter a word or move a little finger without the whole of Russia lifting up their hands in pious horror. I tell you, Uncle Colin," she added, her fine, big, dark eyes fixed upon me, "I'm sick of it all. It is simply unbearable. Ah! how I wish I were back at dear old Southdene College. I hate Russia and all her works!"

"Hush!" I cried again. "You really must not say that. Remember your position—the niece of His Majesty."

"I repeat it!" she cried in desperation, her well-formed little mouth set firmly. "And I don't care who hears me—even if it's Uncle Alexander himself!"

Chapter Four
Concerns Madame de Rosen

At Her Highness's side I had strolled through the smaller salon and along the several great corridors to the splendid winter garden, on the opposite side of the palace. It was one of the smaller courtyards which had been covered in with glass and filled with high palms and tropical flowers ablaze with bloom. There, in that northern latitude, Asiatic and African plants flourished and flowered, with little electric lights cunningly concealed amid the leaves.

Several other couples were seated there, away from the whirl and glitter of the Court; but taking no notice, we halted at two wicker chairs set invitingly in a corner. Into one of these she flung herself with a little sigh, and, bowing, I took the other.

I sat and watched her. Her beauty was, indeed, exquisite. She had the long, tender, fluent lines of body and limb, the round waist, the deep chest and small bust, the sturdy throat of those ancient virgins that the greatest sculptors of the world worshipped and wrought into imperishable stone. She was not very tall, though she appeared so. It was something in pose and movement that did it. A beautiful soul looked from Her Highness's beautiful eyes whenever she smiled upon me.

I found myself examining every line and turn and contour of the prettily-poised head. She was dark, with that lovely complexion like pure alabaster tinted with rose sometimes seen in Russian women. Her eyes, under the sweeping lashes, seemed capable of untold depths of tenderness. Hers was the perfect oval of a young face across whose innocent girlishness experience had written no line, passion cast no shadow.

"One thing I've heard to-day has greatly pained me," I said presently to my dainty little companion. "You'll forgive me for speaking quite frankly— won't you?"

"Certainly, Uncle Colin," she replied, opening her big eyes in surprise. "But I thought you had brought me here to flirt with me—not to talk seriously."

"I must talk seriously for a moment," I said apologetically. "It is in Your Highness's interests. Listen. I heard something to-day at which I know that you yourself will be greatly annoyed. I heard it whispered that Geoffrey Hamborough had killed himself because of you."

"Geoffrey dead!" she gasped, starting up and staring at me, her face blanched in an instant.

"No. He is not dead," I replied calmly, "for as soon as I heard the report I sent him a wire to Yorkshire and to the Travellers', in London. He replied from the club half an hour before I came here."

"But who could have spread such a report?" the girl asked. "It could only be done to cast opprobrium upon me—to show that because—because we parted—he had taken his life. It's really too cruel," she declared, and I saw hot tears welling in her beautiful eyes.

"I agree. But you must deny the report."

"Who told you?"

"I regret that I must not say. It was, however, a friend of yours."

"A man?"

I nodded in the affirmative.

"Ah!" she cried impatiently. "You diplomats are always so full of secrets. Really you must tell me. Uncle Colin."

"I can't," was my brief reply. "I only ask you to refute the untruth."

"I will—at once. Poor Geoffrey."

"Have you heard from him lately?" I asked.

"You're very inquisitive. I have not."

"I'm very glad of that," I answered her. "You know how greatly the affair annoyed the Emperor. You were awfully injudicious. It's a good job that I chanced to meet you both at the station in Moscow."

"Well," she laughed, "I was going to England with him, and we had arranged to be married at a registrar's office in London. Only you stopped us—you nasty old thing!"

"And you ought to be very glad that I recognised you just in the nick of time. Ten minutes later and you would have left Moscow. Think of the scandal—the elopement of a young Imperial Grand Duchess of Russia with an English commoner."

"Well, and isn't an English commoner as good, and perhaps better, than one of these uniformed and decorated Russian aristocrats? I am Russian," she added frankly, "but I have no love for the Muscovite man."

"It was a foolish escapade," I declared; "but it's all over now. The one consolation is that nobody knows the actual truth."

"Except His Majesty. I told him everything; how I had met Geoffrey in Hampshire when I went to stay with Lady Hexworthy; how we used to meet in secret, and all that," she said.

"Well now," I exclaimed, looking straight into her face, "I want to ask you a plain open question. I have a motive in doing so—one which I will explain to you after you have answered me honestly and truthfully. I—"

"At it again!" cried the pretty madcap. "You're really not yourself to-night, Uncle Colin. What is the matter with you?"

"Simply I want to know the truth—whether there is still any love between Geoffrey and yourself?"

"Ah! no," she sighed, pulling a grimace. "It's all over between us. It broke his heart, poor fellow, but some kind friend, at your Embassy, I think, wrote and told him about Paul Urusoff and—well, he wrote me a hasty letter. Then I replied, a couple of telegrams, and we agreed to be strangers for ever. And so ends the story. Like a novel, isn't it?" she laughed merrily.

My eyes were fixed upon her. I was wondering if she were really telling me the truth. As the Emperor had most justly said, she was an artful little minx where her love-affairs were concerned.

Colonel Polivanoff, the Grand Chamberlain of the Court, crossed the great palm-garden at that moment, and bowed to my pretty companion.

"But," she added, turning back to me, "people ought not to say that he's been foolish enough to do away with himself on my account. It only shows that I must have made some enemies of whom I'm quite unaware."

"Everyone has enemies," I answered her. "You are no exception. But, is it really true that Geoffrey is no longer in your thoughts?" I asked her very seriously.

"Truth and honour," she declared, with equal gravity.

"Then who is the fortunate young man at present—eh?"

"That's my own secret. Uncle Colin," she declared, drawing herself up. "I'll ask you the same question. Who is the lady you are in love with at the present moment?"

"Shall I tell you?"

"Yes. It would be interesting."

"I'm in love with you."

"Ah?" she cried, nodding her head and laughing. "I thought as much. You've brought me out here to flirt with me. I wonder if you'll kiss me— eh?" she asked mischievously.

"I will, if you tempt me too much," I said threateningly. "And then the report you've spread about will be the truth."

She laughed merrily and tapped my hand with her fan.

"I never can get the better of you, dear old uncle," she declared. "You always have the last word, and you're such a delightfully old-fashioned person. Now let's try and be serious." And she settled herself and, turning to me, added: "Why do you wish to know about Geoffrey Hamborough?"

"For several reasons," I said. "First, I think Your Highness knows me quite well enough to be aware that I am your very sincere friend."

"My best friend," she declared quickly; her manner changed in an instant from merry irresponsibility to deep earnestness. "That night on the railway platform at Moscow you saved me making a silly fool of myself. It was most generous of the Emperor to forgive me. I know how you pleaded for me. He told me so."

"I am your friend," I replied. "Now, as to the future. You tell me that you find all the Court etiquette irksome, and that you are antagonistic to this host of young men about you. You are, in brief, sorry that you are back in Russia. Is that so?"

"It is so exactly."

"And how about Prince Urusoff—eh?"

"I haven't seen him for fully three months, and I don't even know where he is. I believe he's with his regiment, the 21st Dragoons of White Russia, somewhere away in the Urals. I heard that the Emperor sent him there. But he certainly need not have done so. I found him only a foolish young boy."

Her Imperial Highness was a young lady of very keen intelligence. After several governesses at home, she had been sent to Paris, and afterwards to a college at Eastbourne—where she was known as Miss Natalia Gottorp, the latter being one of the family names of the Imperial Romanoffs—and there she had completed her education. From her childhood she had always had an English governess, Miss West, consequently, with a Russian's adaptability, she spoke English almost without a trace of accent. Though so full of fun and frolic, and so ready to carry on a violent flirtation, yet she was, on the other hand, very thoughtful and level-headed, with a keen sense of humour, and a nature extremely sympathetic with any person in distress, no matter whom they might be. Hers was a bright, pleasant nature, a smiling face, and ever-twinkling eye full of mischief and merriment.

"Well," I said, looking into her face, "I've been thinking about you a good deal since you've been away—and wondering."

"Wondering what?"

"Whether, as you have no love for Russia, you might not like to go back to England?" I said slowly.

"To England!" she cried in delight. "Ah! If I only could! I love England, and especially Eastbourne, with the sea and the promenade, the golf, and the concerts at the Devonshire Park, and all that. Ah! I only wish I could go."

"But if you went you'd fall in love with some young fellow, and then we should have another scandal at Court," I said.

"I wouldn't. Believe me, I wouldn't, really, Uncle Colin," she pleaded, looking up into my face with almost childish simplicity.

I shook my head dubiously.

"All I've told you is the real truth," she assured me. "I've only amused myself. Every girl likes men to make love to her. Why should I be so bitterly condemned?"

"Because you are not a commoner."

"That's just it. But if I went to England and lived again as Miss Natalia Gottorp, nobody would know who I am, and I could have a really splendid time. Here," she cried, "all the glitter and etiquette of Court life stifle me. I've been bored to death on the tour round the Empire, but couldn't you try and induce the Emperor to let me go back to England? Do, Uncle Colin, there's a dear. A word from the Emperor, and father would let me go in a moment. I wish poor mother were alive. She would soon let me go, I know."

"And what would you do in England if you went back?"

"Why, I'd have my old governess, Miss West—the one I had at Strelna—to live with me, and I'd be ever so happy. I'd take a house on the sea-front at Eastbourne, so as to be near the old college, and see the girls. Try what you can do with Uncle Alexander, won't you? there's a dear old uncle," she added, in her most persuasive tones.

"Well," I said, with some show of reluctance, "if I succeed, you will be responsible to me, remember. No flirtations."

"I promise," she said. "Here's my hand," and she put her tiny white-gloved hand into mine.

"And if I heard of any affectionate meetings I should put down my foot at once."

"Yes, that's agreed," she exclaimed, with enthusiasm. "At once."

"And I should, perhaps, want you to help me in England," I added slowly, looking into her pretty face the while.

"Help you, in what way?" she asked.

"At present, I hardly know. But if I wanted assistance might I count on you?"

"Count on me, Uncle Colin!" she echoed. "Why, of course, you can! Look at my indebtedness to you, and it will be increased if you can secure me permission to go back to England."

"Well," I said, "I'll do what I can. But you have told me no untruths to-night, not one—?" I asked very seriously. "If so, admit it."

"Not one. I swear I haven't."

"Very well," I said. "Then I'll do my best."

"Ah! you are a real dear!" cried the girl enthusiastically. "I almost feel as though I could hug and kiss you!"

"Better not," I laughed. "There are some people sitting over there, and they would talk—"

"Yes," she said slowly. "I suppose really one ought to be a bit careful, after all. When will you see the Emperor?"

"Perhaps to-morrow—if he gives me audience." Then I related to her the story of the attempt in the Nevski on the previous morning, and the intention of assassinating the Emperor as he drove from the Nicholas station to the Palace.

"Ah, yes!" she cried. "It is all too dreadful. For seven weeks we have lived in constant terror of explosions. I could not go through it again for all the world. Those days in that stuffy armoured train were simply awful. His Majesty only undertook the journey in order to defy those who declared that some terrible catastrophe would happen. The Empress knew nothing of the danger until we had started."

"And yet the only danger lay within half a mile of the Palace on your return," I said. "There have, I hear, been thirty-three arrested to-day, including my friends Madame de Rosen and Luba. You knew them."

"Marya de Rosen!" gasped the Grand Duchess, staring at me. "She is not under arrest?"

"Alas! she is already on her way, with her daughter, to Eastern Siberia."

"But that is impossible. She was no revolutionist. I knew them both very intimately."

"General Markoff was her enemy," I said in a whisper. "Ah, yes! I hate that man!" cried Her Highness. "He is a clever liar who has wormed himself completely into the Emperor's confidence, and now, in order to sustain a reputation as a discoverer of plots, he is compelled to first manufacture them. Hundreds of innocent men and women have been exiled by administrative order during the past twelve months for complicity in conspiracies which have never had any existence save in the wicked imagination of that brutal official. I know it—*I can prove it!*"

"Hush!" I said. "You may be overheard. You surely do not wish the man to become your enemy. Remember, he is all-powerful here—in Russia."

"I will speak the truth when the time comes," she said vehemently. "I will show the Emperor certain papers which have come into my own hands which will prove how His Majesty has been misled, tricked and terrorised by this Markoff, and certain of his bosom friends in the Cabinet."

"It is really most unwise to speak so loudly," I declared. "Somebody may overhear."

"Let them overhear!" cried the girl angrily. "I do not fear Markoff in the least. I will, before long, open the Emperor's eyes, never fear—and justice shall be done. These poor wretches shall not be sent to the dungeons beneath the lake at Schusselburg, or to the frozen wastes of Yakutsk, in order that Markoff shall remain in power. Ah! he little dreams how much I know!" she laughed harshly.

"It would hardly be wise of you to take any such action. You might fail—and—then—"

"I cannot fail to establish at least the innocence of Madame de Rosen and of Luba. The reason why they have been sent to Siberia is simple. Into Madame de Rosen's possession there recently came certain compromising letters concerning General Markoff. He discovered this, and hence her swift exile without trial. But, Uncle Colin," she added, "those letters are in my possession! Madame de Rosen gave them to me the night before I went south with the Emperor, because she feared they might be stolen by some police-spy. And I have kept them in a place of safety until such convenient time when I can place them before His Majesty. The latter will surely see that justice is done, and then the disgraceful career of this arch-enemy of Russian peace and liberty will be at an end."

"Hush!" I cried anxiously, for at that moment a tall man, in the bright green uniform of the Lithuanian Hussars, whose face I could not see, passed close by us, with a handsome middle-aged woman upon his arm. "Hush! Do, for heaven's sake, be careful, I beg of you!" I exclaimed. "Such intention should not even be whispered. These Palace walls have ears, for spies are everywhere!"

Chapter Five
The Man in Pince-Nez

Next day was Wednesday.

At half-past five in the afternoon I was seated in my room at the Embassy, busy copying out the last of my despatches which were to be sent that week by Foreign Office messenger to London.

The messenger himself, in the person of my friend Captain Hubert Taylor, a thin, long-limbed, dark-haired cosmopolitan, was stretched lazily in my chair smoking a cigarette, impatient for me to finish, so that the white canvas bag could be sealed and he could get away.

The homeward Nord express to Ostend was due to leave at six o'clock; therefore he had not much time to spare.

"Do hurry up, old man," he urged, glancing at his watch. "If it isn't important, keep it over until Wednesday week. Despatches are like wine, they improve with keeping."

"Shut up!" I exclaimed, for I saw I had a good deal yet to copy—the result of an important inquiry regarding affairs south of the Caspian, which was urgently required at Downing Street. Our Consul in Baku had been travelling for three months in order to supply the information.

"Well, if I miss the train I really don't mind, my dear Colin. I can do quite well with a few days' rest. I was down in Rome ten days ago; and, besides, I only got here the night before last."

"I do wish you'd be quiet, Taylor," I cried. "I can't write while you chatter."

So he lit a fresh cigarette and repossessed himself in patience until at last I had finished my work, stuck down the long envelope with the printed address, and placed it with thirty or forty other letters into the canvas bag; this I carefully sealed with wax with the Embassy seal.

"There you are!" I exclaimed at last. "You've plenty of time for the train—and to spare."

"I shouldn't have had if I hadn't hurried you up, my dear boy. Everyone seems asleep here. It shows your chief's away on leave. You should put in a day in Paris. They're active there. It would be an eye-opener for you."

"Paris isn't Petersburg," I laughed.

"And an attaché isn't a foreign service messenger," he declared. "Government pays you fellows to look ornamental, while we messengers have to travel in hot haste and live in those rocking sleeping-cars of the wagon-lits."

"Horribly hard work to spend one's days travelling from capital to capital," I said, well knowing that this remark to a foreign service messenger is as a red rag to a bull.

"Work, my dear fellow. You try it for a month and see," Taylor snapped.

"Well," I asked with a laugh, "any particular news in London?" for the messengers are bearers of all the diplomatic gossip from embassy to embassy.

"Oh, well—old Petheridge, in the Treaty Department, is retiring this month, and Jack Scrutton is going to be transferred from Rome to Lima. Some old fool in the Commons has, I hear, got wind of that bit of scandal in Madrid—you know the story, Councillor of Embassy and Spanish Countess—and threatens to put down a question concerning it. I hear there's a dickens of a row over it. The Chief is furious. Oh!—and I saw your Chief in the St. James's Club the day I left London. He'd just come from Windsor—been kissing hands, or something. Well," he added, "I suppose I may as well have some cigarettes before I go, even though you don't ask me. But they are always *pro bono*, I know. The Embassy at Petersburg is always noted for its hospitality and its cigarettes!" And he emptied the contents of my cigarette-box into the capacious case he took from his pocket.

"Here you are," I said, taking from my table another sealed despatch bearing a large blue cross upon it, showing that it was a confidential document in cipher upon affairs of State.

"Oh, hang!" he cried. "I didn't know you had one of those."

And then, unbuttoning his waistcoat, he fumbled about his waist, and at last placed it carefully in the narrow pocket of the belt he wore beneath his clothes, buttoning the flap over the pocket.

"Well," he said at last, putting on his overcoat, "so long, old man. I'll just have time. I wonder what old Ivanoff, in the restaurant-car, will have for dinner to-night? Borstch, of course, and caviare."

"You fellows have nothing else to think about but your food," I laughed.

"Food—yes, it's railway-food with a vengeance in this God-forgotten country. Lots to drink, but nothing decent to eat."

And taking the little canvas bag he shook my hand heartily and strode out.

I stood for some time gazing through the open window out upon the sunlit Neva across to the grim fortress on the opposite bank—the prison of many terrible tales.

My thoughts were running, just as they had run all day, upon that strange suspicion which the Emperor had confided to me. It seemed too remarkable, too strange, too amazing to be true.

And again before my vision there arose the faces of those two refined and innocent ladies, Madame de Rosen and her daughter, who had been so suddenly hurried away to a living tomb in that far-off Arctic region. I remembered what the little Grand Duchess had told me, and wondered whether her allegations were really true.

I was wondering if she would permit me to see those incriminating letters which Madame had given to her for safe-keeping, for at all costs I felt that, for the safety of the Emperor and the peace and prosperity of Russia, the country should be rid of General Serge Markoff.

And yet the difficulties were, I knew, insurmountable. His Majesty, hearing of these constant plots being discovered and ever listening to highly-coloured stories of the desperate attempts of revolutionists, naturally believed his personal safety to be due to this man whom he had appointed as head of the police of the Empire. To any word said against Serge Markoff he turned a deaf ear, and put it down to jealousy, or to some ingenious plot to withdraw from his person the constant vigilance which his beloved Markoff had established. More than once I had been bold enough to venture to hint that all those plots might not be genuine ones; but I had quickly understood that such suggestion was regarded by the Emperor as a slur cast upon his favourite official and personal friend.

The more I reflected, the more unwise seemed that sudden outburst of my pretty little companion in the winter garden on the night before. If anyone had overheard her threat, then no doubt it would reach the ears of that man who daily swept so many innocent persons into the prisons and *étapes* beyond the Urals. I knew, too well, of those lists of names which he placed before the Emperor, and to which he asked the Imperial signature, without even giving His Majesty an opportunity to glance at them.

Truly, those were dark days. Life in Russia at that moment was a most uncertain existence, for anyone incurring the displeasure of General

Markoff, or any of his friends, was as quickly and effectively removed as though death's sword had struck them.

Much perturbed, and not knowing how to act in face of what the Emperor had revealed to me, I was turning from the window back to my writing-table, when one of the English footmen entered with a card.

"Oh, show him up, Green. And bring some cigarettes," I said.

My visitor was Ivan Hartwig, the famous chief of the Russian Criminal Detective Service—an entirely distinct department from the Secret Police.

A few moments later he was ushered in by Green, and, bowing, took the hand I offered him.

A lean, bony-faced man, of average height, alert, clean-shaven, and aged about forty-five. His hair was slightly streaked with grey, and his eyes, small and shrewd, beamed behind a pair of round gold-rimmed pince-nez. I had never seen him in glasses before, but I only supposed that he had suddenly developed myopia for some specific purpose. As he smiled in greeting me, his narrow jaws widened, displaying an even row of white teeth, while the English he spoke was as perfect as my own. At that moment, in his glasses, his black morning-coat and grey trousers, he looked more like a grave family physician than a police officer whose career was world-famous.

And yet he was a man of striking appearance. His broad white forehead, his deep-set eyes so full of fire and expression, his high, protruding cheek-bones, and his narrowing chin were all characteristics of a man of remarkable power and intelligence. His, indeed, was a face that would arrest attention anywhere; hence the hundred and one disguises which he so constantly adopted.

"I have had private audience of His Majesty this afternoon, Mr Trewinnard," he said, as he took the chair I offered him. "He has sent me to you. You wish to see me."

"Yes," I said. "I need your assistance."

"So His Majesty has told me, but he explained nothing of the affair. He commanded me to place myself entirely at your disposal," replied the man, who, in himself, was a man of mystery.

His nationality was obscure to most people, yet we at the Embassy knew that he was in reality a British subject, and that Ivan Hartwig was merely the Russian equivalent of Evan Hardwicke.

I handed him the box of cigarettes which Green had replenished, and took one myself.

As he slowly lit his, I recollected what a strange career he had had. Graduating from Scotland Yard, where on account of his knowledge of German and Russian he had been mainly employed in the arrest of alien criminals in England, he had for several years served under Monsieur Goron, Préfet of Police of Paris, and after being attached to the Tzar on one of his visits to the French capital, had been personally invited by the Emperor to become head of the Criminal Investigation Department of Russia.

He was a quiet-spoken, alert, elusive, but very conscientious man, who had made a study of crime from a psychological standpoint, his many successes being no doubt due to his marvellously minute examination of motives and his methodical reasoning upon the most abstruse clues. There was nothing of the ordinary blunt official detective about him. He was a man of extreme refinement, an omnivorous reader and a diligent student of men. He was a passionate collector of coins, a bachelor, and an amateur player of the violin. I believe that he had never experienced what fear was, and certainly within my own knowledge, he had had a dozen narrow escapes from the vengeance of the Terrorists. Once a bomb was purposely exploded in a room into which he and his men went to arrest two students in Moscow, and not one present escaped death except Hartwig himself.

And as he now sat there before me, so quiet and attentive, blinking at me through those gold-rimmed pince-nez, none would certainly take him for the man whose hairbreadth escapes, constant disguises, exciting adventures and marvellous successes in the tracking of criminals all over Europe had so often amazed the readers of newspapers the world over.

"Well, Mr Hartwig," I said in a low voice, after I had risen and satisfied myself that Green had closed the door, "the matter is one of strictest confidence—a suspicion which I may at once tell you is the Emperor's own personal affair. To myself alone he has confided it, and I requested that you might be allowed to assist me in finding a solution of the problem."

"I'm much gratified," he said. "As an Englishman, you know, I believe, that I am ever ready to serve an Englishman, especially if I am serving the Emperor at the same time."

"The inquiry will take us far afield, I expect—first to England."

"To England!" he exclaimed. "For how long do you anticipate?"

"Who knows?" I asked. "I can only say that it will be a very difficult and perhaps a long inquiry."

"And how will the department proceed here?"

"Your next in command will be appointed in your place until your return. The Emperor arranged for this with me yesterday. Therefore, from to-morrow you will be free to place yourself at my service."

"I quite understand," he said. "And now, perhaps, you will in confidence explain exactly the situation, and the problem which is presented," and he settled himself in his chair in an attitude of attention.

"Ah! that, I regret, is unfortunately impossible. The Emperor has entrusted the affair to me, and to me alone. I must direct the inquiry, and you will, I fear, remain in ignorance—at least, for the present."

"In other words, you will direct and I must act blindly—eh?" he said in a rather dubious voice. "That's hardly satisfactory to me, Mr Trewinnard, is it?—hardly fair, I mean."

"I openly admit that such an attitude as I am compelled to adopt is not fair to you, Hartwig. But I feel sure you will respect the Emperor's confidence, and view the matter in its true light. The matter is a personal one of His Majesty's, and may not be divulged. He has asked me to tell you this frankly and plainly, and also that he relies upon you to assist him."

My words convinced the great detective, and he nodded at last in the affirmative.

"The problem I alone know," I went on. "His Majesty has compelled me to swear secrecy. Therefore I am forbidden to tell you. You understand?"

"But I am not forbidden to discover it for myself?" replied the keen, wary official.

"If you do, I cannot help it," was my reply.

"If I do," he said, "I promise you faithfully, Mr Trewinnard, that His Majesty's secret, whatever it is, shall never pass my lips."

Chapter Six Relates
a Sensation

Ten days had gone by. I had applied to Downing Street for leave of absence, and was awaiting permission.

One afternoon I had again been commanded to private audience at the Palace, and in uniform, had spent nearly two hours with the Emperor, listening to certain confidential instructions which he had given me—instructions for the fulfilment of a somewhat difficult task.

Twice during our chat I had referred to the case of my friends Madame and Mademoiselle de Rosen, hoping that he would extend to them the Imperial clemency, and by a stroke of that well-worn quill upon the big writing-table recall them from that long and weary journey upon which they had been sent.

But His Majesty, who was wearing the undress uniform of a general with a single cross at his throat, uttered an expression of regret that I had been friendly with them.

"In Russia, in these days, a foreigner should exercise the greatest caution in choosing his friends," he said. "Only the day before yesterday Markoff reported it was to those two women that the attempt in the Nevski was entirely due. The others, thirty or so, were merely tools of those clever women."

"Forgive me, Your Majesty, when I say that General Markoff lies," I replied boldly.

"Enough! Our opinions differ, Trewinnard," he snapped, with a shrug of his broad shoulders.

It was on the tip of my tongue to make a direct charge against his favourite official, but what was the use when I held no actual proof. Twice recently I had seen Natalia, but she refused to allow me sight of the letters, telling me that she intended herself to show up the General in her own way—and at her own time.

So the subject had dropped, for I saw that mention of it only aroused the Emperor's displeasure. And surely the other matter which we were discussing with closed doors was weighty enough.

At last His Majesty tossed his cigarette-end away, and, his jewelled cross glittering at his throat, rose with outstretched hand, as sign that my audience was at an end.

That eternal military band was playing in the grey courtyard below, and the Emperor had slammed-to the window impatiently to keep out the sound. He was in no mood for musical comedy that afternoon. Indeed, I knew that the military music often irritated him, but Court etiquette— those iron-bound, unwritten laws which even an Emperor cannot break— demanded it. Those same laws decreed that no Emperor of Russia may travel *incognito*, as do all other European sovereigns; that at dinner at the Winter Palace there must always be eight guests; and that the service of gold plate of Catherine the Great must always be used. At the Russian Court there are a thousand such laws, the breach of a single one being an unpardonable offence, even in the case of the autocratic ruler himself.

"Then you understand my wishes—eh, Trewinnard?" His Majesty said at last in English, gripping my hand warmly.

"Perfectly, Sire."

"I need not impress upon you the need for absolute and entire discretion. I trust you implicitly."

"I hope Your Majesty's trust will never be betrayed," I answered fervently, bowing over the strong outstretched hand.

And then, backing out of the door, I bowed and withdrew.

Through the long corridor with its soft red carpet I went, passing Calitzine, a short, dark man in funereal black, the Emperor's private secretary, to whom I passed the time of day.

Then, reaching the grand staircase with its wonderful marble and gold balustrades and great chandeliers of crystal, I descended to the huge hall, where the echoes were constantly aroused by hurrying footsteps of ministers, officials, chamberlains, courtiers and servants—all of them sycophants.

The two gigantic sentries at the foot of the stairs held their rifles at the salute as I passed between them, when of a sudden I caught sight of the Grand Duchess Natalia in a pretty summer gown of pale-blue, standing with a tall, full-bearded elderly man in the brilliant uniform of the 15th Regiment of Grenadiers of Tiflis, of which he was chief, and wearing many decorations. It was her father, the Grand Duke Nicholas.

"Why, here's old Uncle Colin!" cried my incorrigible little friend in pleased surprise. "Have you been up with the Emperor?"

I replied in the affirmative, and, bowing, greeted His Imperial Highness, her father, with whom I had long been on friendly terms.

"Where are you going?" asked the vivacious young lady quickly as she rebuttoned her long white glove, for they had, it seemed, been on a visit to the Empress.

"I have to go to the opening of the new wing of the Naval Hospital," I said. "And I haven't much time to spare."

"We are going there, too. I have to perform the opening ceremony in place of the Emperor," replied the Grand Duke. "So drive with us."

"That's it, Uncle Colin!" exclaimed his daughter. "Come out for an airing. It's a beautiful afternoon."

So we went forth into the great courtyard, where one of the Imperial state carriages, an open one, was in waiting, drawn by four fine, long-tailed Caucasian horses.

Behind it was a troop of mounted Cossacks to act as escort.

We entered, and the instant the bare-headed flunkeys had closed the door the horses started off, and we swung out of the handsome gateway into the wide Place, in the centre of which stood the grey column of Peter the Great.

Turning to the left we went past the Alexander Gardens, now parched and dusty with summer heat, and skirted the long façade of the War Office.

"I wonder what tales you've been telling the Emperor about me, Uncle Colin?" asked the impudent little lady, laughing as we drove along, I being seated opposite the Grand Duke and his daughter.

"About you?" I echoed with a smile. "Oh, nothing, I assure you—or, at least, nothing that was not nice."

"You're a dear, I know," declared the girl, her father laughing amusedly the while. "But you are so dreadfully proper. You're worse about etiquette than father is—and he's simply horrid. He won't ever let me go out shopping alone, and I'm surely old enough to do that!"

"You're quite old enough to get into mischief, Tattie," replied her father, speaking in French.

"I love mischief. That's the worst of it," and she pouted prettily.

"Yes, quite true—the worst of it, for me," declared His Imperial Highness. "I thought that when you went to school in England they would teach you manners."

"Ordinary manners are not Court manners," the girl argued, trying to rebutton one of her gloves which had come unfastened.

"Let me do it," I suggested, and quickly fastened it.

"Thank you," she laughed with mock dignity. "How charming it is to have such a polished diplomat as Mr Colin Trewinnard to do nice things for one. Now, isn't that a pretty speech? I suppose I ought to study smart things to say, and practise them on the dog—as father does sometimes."

"Really, Tattie, you forget yourself, my dear," exclaimed her father, with distinct disapproval.

"Well, that's nothing," declared my charming little companion. "Don't parsons practise preaching their sermons, and lawyers and statesmen practise their clever untruths? You can't expect a woman's mouth to be full of sugar-plums of speech, can you?"

My eyes met those of the Grand Duke, and we both burst out laughing at the girl's quaint philosophy.

"Why, even the Emperor has his speeches composed and written for him by silly old Calitzine," she went on. "And at Astrakhan the other day I composed a most telling and patriotic speech for His Majesty, which he delivered when addressing the officers of the Army of the Volga. I sat on my horse and listened. The old generals and colonels, and all the rest of them, applauded vociferously, and the men threw their caps in the air. I wonder if they would have done this had they known that I had written those well-turned patriotic sentences, I—a mere chit of a girl, as father sometimes tells me!"

"And the terror of the Imperial family," I ventured to add.

"Thank you for your compliment. Uncle Colin," she laughed. "I know father endorses your sentiments. I see it in his face."

"Oh, do try and be serious, Tattie," he urged. "See all those people! Salute them, and don't laugh so vulgarly." And he raised his white-gloved hand to his shining helmet in recognition of the shouts of welcome rising from those assembled along our route.

Whereat she bowed gracefully again with that slight and rather frigid smile which she had been taught to assume on public occasions.

"If I put up my sunshade they won't see me, and it will avoid such a lot of trouble," she exclaimed suddenly, and she put up her pretty parasol, which matched her gown and softened the light upon her pretty face.

"Oh, no, Uncle Colin!" she exclaimed suddenly, as we turned the corner into the Yosnesenskaya, a long, straight street where the throng, becoming greater, was kept back by lines of police in their grey coats, peaked caps and revolvers. "I know what you are thinking. But it isn't so. I'm not in the least afraid of spoiling my complexion."

"Then perhaps it is a pity you are not," I replied. "Complexions, like all shining things, tarnish quickly."

"Just like reputations, I suppose," she remarked, whereupon her father could not restrain another laugh.

Then again, at word in an undertone from the Grand Duke, both he and his daughter saluted the crowd, our horses galloping, as they always do in Russia, and our Cossack-escort clattering behind.

There were a good many people just at this point, for it was believed that the Emperor would pass on his way to perform the opening ceremony, and his loyal subjects were waiting to cheer him.

On every hand, the people, recognising the popular Grand Duke and his daughter, set up hurrahs, and while His Imperial Highness saluted, his pretty daughter, the most admired girl in Russia, bowed, and I, in accordance with etiquette, made no sign of acknowledgment.

As we came to the narrow bridge which spans the canal, the road was flanked on the left by the Alexander Market, and here was another huge crowd.

Loud shouts of welcome in Russian broke forth from those assembled, for the Grand Duke and his daughter were everywhere greeted most warmly.

But as we passed the market, the police keeping back the crowd, I saw a thin, middle-aged man in dark clothes lift his hand high above his head. Something came in our direction, yet before I had time to realise his action a blood-red flash blinded me, my ears were deafened by a terrific report, a hot, scorching breath swept across my face, and I felt myself hurled far into space amid the mass of falling débris.

It all occurred in a single instant, and I knew no more. I had a distinct feeling that some terrific explosion had knocked the breath clean out of my body. I recollect seeing the carriage rent into a thousand fragments just at the same instant that black unconsciousness fell upon me.

Chapter Seven
Tells Tragic Truths

When, with extreme difficulty, I slowly struggled back to a knowledge of things about me, I found myself, to my great surprise, in a narrow hospital-bed, with a holy *ikon* upon the whitewashed wall before me, and a Red Cross sister bending tenderly over me.

Beside her stood two Russian doctors regarding me very gravely, and at their side was Saunderson, our Councillor of Embassy.

"Well, how are you feeling now, Colin, old man?" the latter whispered cheerfully.

"I—I don't know. Where am I?" I asked. "What's happened?"

"My dear fellow, you can thank your lucky stirs that you've escaped from the bomb," he said.

"The bomb!" I gasped, and then in a flash all the horrors of that sudden explosion crowded upon me. "What happened?" I inquired, trying to raise myself, and finding my head entirely enveloped in surgical bandages. "What happened to the others?"

"The Grand Duke was, alas! killed, but his daughter fortunately escaped only with a scratch on her arm," was his reply. "The carriage was blown to atoms, the two horses and their driver and footman were killed, while three Cossacks of the escort were also killed and two injured."

"Then—then she—she is alive!" I managed to gasp, dazed at the tragic truth he had related to me.

"Yes—it was a desperate attempt. Fifteen arrests have been made up to the present."

And while he was speaking, Captain Stoyanovitch advanced to my bedside, and leaning over, asked in a low voice:

"How are you, Trewinnard? The Emperor has sent me to inquire."

"Tell His Majesty that I—I thank him. I'm getting round—I—I hope I'll soon be well. I—I—"

"That's right. Take great care of yourself, *mon cher*," he urged.

And then the doctors ordered my visitors away, and I sank among my pillows into a state of semi-consciousness.

How long I lay thus I do not know. I remember seeing soldiers come and go, and at length discovered that I was in the hospital attached to the artillery barracks on the road to Warsaw Station. Beside me always sat a grave-eyed nursing sister, silent and watchful, while ever and anon one or other of the doctors would approach, bend over me, and inquire of her my condition.

Saunderson came again some hours later. It was then night. And from him, now that I was completely conscious, I learnt how, after the explosion, the police had in the confusion shot down two men, afterwards proved to be innocent spectators, and made wholesale indiscriminate arrests. It was believed, however, that the man I had seen, the perpetrator of the dastardly act, had escaped scot-free.

Dozens of windows in the market-hall opposite where the outrage was committed had been smashed, and many people besides the killed and injured had been thrown down by the terrific force of the explosion.

"The poor Grand Duke Nicholas has, alas! been shattered out of recognition," he told me. "His body was taken at once to his palace, where it now lies, while you were brought here together with the Grand Duchess Natalia. But her wound being quite a slight one, was dressed, and she was driven at once to the Winter Palace, at the order of the Emperor. Poor child! I hear that she is utterly prostrated by the fearful sight which her father presented to her eyes."

I drew a long breath.

"I suppose I was struck on the head by some of the débris and knocked insensible—eh?" I asked.

"Yes, probably," he replied. "But the doctors say the wound is only a superficial one, and in a week's time you'll be quite right again. So cheer up, old chap. You'll get the long leave which you put in for the other day, and a bit more added to it, no doubt."

"But this state of things is terrible," I declared, shifting myself upon my side so that I could better look into his face. "Surely the revolutionists could have had no antagonism towards the Grand Duke Nicholas! He was most popular everywhere."

"My dear fellow, who can gauge the state of the Russian mind at this moment? Plots seem to be of daily occurrence."

"If you believe the reports of the Secret Police. But I, for one, don't," I declared frankly.

"No, no," he said reprovingly. "Don't excite yourself. Be thankful that you've escaped. You might have shared the same fate as those poor Cossacks."

"I know," I said. "I thank God that I was spared. But it will be in the London papers, no doubt. Reuter's man will send it; therefore, will you wire to my mother at once. You know her address—Hayford Manor, near Newquay, Cornwall. Wire in my name, and tell her that the affair is greatly exaggerated, and that I'm all right, will you?"

He promised.

I knew with what eagerness my aged mother always followed all my movements, for I made it a practice to write to her twice every week with a full report of my doings. I was as devoted to her as she was to me. And perhaps that accounted for the fact that I had never married. My father, the Honourable Colin Trewinnard, had been one of the largest landowners in Cornwall, and my family was probably one of the oldest in the county. But evil times had fallen upon the estate in the last years of my father's life; depreciation in the value of agricultural land, failing crops and foreign competition had ruined farming, and now the income was not one-half that it had been fifty years before. Yet it was sufficient to keep my mother and myself in comfort; and this, in addition to my pay from the Foreign Office, rendered me better off than a great many other men in our Service.

Through Stoyanovitch, on the following morning, I received a message from Natalia. He said:

"Her Highness, whom I saw in the Palace an hour ago, told me to say that she sent you her best wishes for a speedy recovery. She is greatly grieved over the death of her father, and, of course, the Court has gone into mourning for sixty days. She told me to tell you that as soon as you are able to return to the Embassy she wishes to see you on a very important matter."

"Tell her that I am equally anxious to see her, and that she has all my sympathy in her sad bereavement," I replied.

"Terrible, wasn't it?" the Imperial equerry exclaimed. "The poor girl looks white, haggard and entirely changed."

"No wonder—after such an awful experience."

"There were, I hear, twenty more arrests to-day. Markoff had audience with His Majesty at ten o'clock this morning, and eight of the prisoners of yesterday have been sent to Schusselburg."

"From which they will never emerge," I said, with a shudder at the thought of that living tomb as full of horrors as was the Bastille itself.

"Well, I don't see why they should, my dear friend," the Captain replied. "If I had had such an experience as yours, I shouldn't feel very lenient towards them—as you apparently do."

"I am not thinking of the culprit," I said. "He certainly deserves a death-sentence. It is the innocents who, here in Russia, suffer for the guilty, with whom I deeply sympathise. Every day unoffending men and women are arrested wholesale in this drastic, unrelenting sweeping away of prisoners to Siberia. I tell you that half of them are loyal, law-abiding subjects of the Tzar."

The elegant equerry-in-waiting only grinned and shrugged his shoulders. He was too good a Russian to adopt such an argument. As personal attendant upon His Majesty, he, of course, supported the Imperial autocracy.

"This accursed system of police-spies and *agents-provocateurs* manufactures criminals. Can a man wrongly arrested and sent to the mines remain a loyal subject?"

"The many have to suffer for the few. It is the same in all lands," was his reply. "But really the matter doesn't concern me, my dear Trewinnard."

"It will concern you one day when you are blown up as I have been," I exclaimed savagely.

Shortly afterwards he left, and for hours I lay thinking, my eyes upon that square gilt holy picture before me, the *ikon* placed before the eyes of every patient in the hospital. Nurses in grey and soldiers in white cotton tunics passed and repassed through the small ward of which I was the only occupant.

The pains in my head were excruciating. I felt as though my skull had been filled with boiling water. Sometimes my thoughts were perfectly normal, yet at others my mind seemed full of strange, almost ridiculous phantasies. My whole career, from the days when I had been a clerk in that sombre old-fashioned room at Downing Street, through my service at Madrid, Brussels, Berlin and Rome to Petersburg—all went before me, like a cinema-picture. I looked upon myself as others saw me—as a man never sees himself in normal circumstances—a mere struggling entity upon the tide of that sea of life called To-day.

We are so very apt to think ourselves indispensable to the world. Yet we have only to think again, and remember that the unknown to-morrow may bring, us death, and with it everlasting oblivion, as far as this world is concerned. Queen Victoria and Pope Leo XIII were the two greatest figures of our time; yet a month after their deaths people had to recall who they were, and what they had actually done to earn distinction.

These modern days of rush and hurry are forgetful, irresponsible days, when public opinion is manufactured by those who rule the halfpenny press, and when the worst and most baneful commodities may be foisted upon the public by means of efficient advertisement.

The cleverest swindler may by payment become a baronet of England, even a peer of the realm, providing he subscribes sufficient to Somebody's Newspaper Publicity Agency; and any blackguard with money or influence may become a Justice of the Peace and sentence his fellows to fourteen days' imprisonment.

But the reader will forgive me. Perhaps remarks such as these ill become a diplomat—one who is supposed to hold no personal opinions. Yet I assert that to-day there is no diplomat serving Great Britain in a foreign country who is not tired and disgusted with his country's antiquated methods and her transparent weaknesses.

The papers speak vigorously of Britain's power, but men in my service—those who know real international truths—smile at the defiant and well-balanced sentences of the modern journalist, whose blissful ignorance of the truth is ofttimes so pathetic. Yes, it is only the diplomat serving at a foreign Court who can view Great Britain from afar, and accurately gauge her position among modern nations.

For ten days I remained in that whitewashed ward, many of my friends visiting me, and Stoyanovitch coming daily with a pleasant message from His Majesty. Then one bright morning the doctors declared me to be fit enough to drive back to the Embassy.

An hour later, with my head still bandaged, I was seated in my own room, in my own big leather armchair, with the July sun streaming in from across the Neva.

Saunderson was sitting with me, describing the great pomp of the funeral of the Grand Duke Nicholas, and the service at the Isaac Church, at which the Tzar, the Court, and all the *corps diplomatique* had attended.

"By the way," he added, "a note came for you this morning," and he handed me a black-edged letter, bearing on the envelope the Imperial arms embossed in black.

I tore it open and found it to be a neatly-written little letter from the Grand Duchess Natalia, asking me to allow her to call and see me as soon as ever I returned to the Embassy.

"I must see you, Uncle Colin," she wrote. "It is most pressing. So do please let me come. Send me word, and I will come instantly. I cannot write anything here. *I must see you at once!*"

Chapter Eight
Describes a Mysterious Incident

Two days later, the ugly bandages having been removed from my head, Natalia was seated in the afternoon in my den.

Exquisitely neat in her dead black, with the long crape veil, she presented an altogether different appearance to the radiant girl who had sat before me on that fatal drive. Her sweet face was now pale and drawn, and by the dark rings about her eyes I saw how full of poignant grief her heart had lately been.

She had taken off her long, black gloves and settled herself cosily in my big armchair, her tiny patent-leather shoe, encasing a shapely silk-clad ankle, set forth beneath the hem of her black skirt.

"I was so terrified. Uncle Colin, that you were also dead!" the girl was saying in a low, sympathetic voice, after I had expressed my deepest regret regarding the unfortunate death of her father, to whom she had been so devoted.

"I suppose I had a very narrow escape," I said cheerfully. "You came out best of all."

"By an absolute miracle. The Emperor is furious. Twenty of those arrested have already been sent to Schusselburg," she said. "Only yesterday, he told me that he hoped you would be well enough in a day or two to go to the Palace. I was to tell you how extremely anxious he is to see you as soon as possible."

"I will obey the command at the earliest moment I am able," I replied. "But how horribly unfortunate all this is," I went on. "I fully expected that you would be in England by this time."

"As soon as you are ready, Uncle Colin, I can go. The Emperor has already told me that he has placed me under your guardianship. That you are to be my equerry. Isn't it fun?" she cried, her pretty face suddenly brightening with pleasure. "Fancy you! dear old uncle, being put in charge of me—your naughty niece!"

"His Majesty wished it," I said. "He thinks you will be better away from Court for a time. Therefore, I have promised to accept the responsibility. For one year you are to live *incognito* in England, and I have been appointed your equerry and guardian—and," I added very seriously, "I hope that my naughty niece will really behave herself, and do nothing which will cause me either annoyance or distress."

"I'll really try and be very good, Uncle Colin," declared the girl with mock demureness, and laughing mischievously. "Believe me, I will."

"It all remains with you," I said. "Remember I do not wish it to be necessary that I should furnish any unfavourable report to the Emperor. I want us to understand each other perfectly from the outset. Recollect one point always. Though you may be known in England as Miss Gottorp, yet remember that you are of the Imperial family of Russia, and niece of the Emperor. Hence, there must be no flirtations, no clandestine meetings or love-letters, and such-like, as in the case of young Hamborough."

"Please don't bring up that affair," urged the little madcap. "It is all dead, buried and forgotten long ago."

"Very well," I said, looking straight into her big, velvety eyes so full of expression. "But remember that your affection is absolutely forbidden except towards a man of your own birth and station."

"I know," she cried, with a quick impatience. "I'm unlike any other girl. I am forbidden to speak to a commoner."

"Not in England. Preserve your *incognito*, and nobody will know. At His Majesty's desire, I have obtained leave of absence from the service for twelve months, in order to become your guardian."

"Well, dear old Uncle Colin, you are the only person I would have chosen. Isn't that nice of me to say so?" she asked, with a tantalising smile.

"But I tell you I shall show you no leniency if you break any of the rules which must, of necessity, be laid down," I declared severely. "As soon as I find myself well enough, you will take Miss West, your old governess, and Davey, your English maid, to England, and I will come and render you assistance in settling down somewhere in comfort."

"At Eastbourne?" she cried in enthusiasm. "We'll go there. Do let us go there?"

"Probably at Brighton," I said quietly. "It would be gayer for you, and—well, I will be quite frank—I think there are one or two young men whom you know in Eastbourne. Hence it is not quite to your advantage to return there."

She pouted prettily in displeasure.

"Brighton is within an hour of London, as you know," I went on, extolling the praises of the place.

"Oh, yes, I know it. We often went over from Eastbourne, to concerts and things. There's an aquarium there, and a seaside railway, and lots of trippers. I remember the place perfectly. I love to see your English trippers. They are such fun, and they seem to enjoy themselves so much more than we ever do. I wonder how it is—they enjoy their freedom, I suppose, while we have no freedom."

"Well," I said cheerfully, "in a week or ten days I hope I shall be quite fit to travel, and then we will set out for England."

"Yes. Let us go. The Emperor leaves for Peterhof on Saturday. He will not return to Petersburg until the winter, and the Court moves to Tzarskoie-Selo on Monday."

"Then I will see His Majesty before Saturday," I said. "But, tell me, why did Your Highness write to me so urgently three days ago? You said you wished to see me at once."

The girl sprang from her chair, crossed to the door, and made certain it was closed.

Then, glancing around as though apprehensive of eavesdroppers, she said:

"I wanted to tell you, Uncle Colin, of something very, very curious which happened the other evening. About ten o'clock at night I was with Miss West in the blue boudoir—you know the room in our palace, you've been in it."

"I remember it perfectly," I said.

"Well, I went upstairs to Davey for my smelling-salts as Miss West felt faint, and as I passed along the corridor I saw, in the moonlight, in my own room a dark figure moving by the window. It was a man. I saw him searching the drawers of my little writing-table, examining the contents by means of an electric-torch. I made no sound, but out of curiosity, drew back and watched him. He was reading all my letters—searching for something which he apparently could not find. My first impulse was to ring and give the alarm, for though I could not see the individual's face, I knew he must be a thief. Still, I watched, perhaps rather amused at the methodical examination of my letters which he was making, all unconscious that he was being observed, until suddenly at a noise made by a servant approaching from the other end of the corridor, he started, flung back the letters into the drawer, and mounting to the open window, got out and disappeared. I shouted and rushed after him to the window, but he had gone. He must have dropped about twelve feet on to the roof of the ballroom and thus got away.

"Several servants rushed in, and the sentries were alarmed," she went on. "But when I told my story, it was apparent that I was not believed. The drawer in the writing-table had been reclosed, and as far as we could see all was in perfect order. So I believe they all put it down to my imagination."

"But you are quite certain that you saw the man there?" I said, much interested in her story.

"Quite. He was of middle height, dressed in dark clothes, and wore a cloth peaked cap, like men wear when golfing in England," she replied. "He was evidently in search of something I had in my writing-table, but he did not find it. Nevertheless, he read a quantity of my letters mostly from school-friends."

"And your love-letters?" I asked, with a smile.

"Well, if the fellow read any of them," she laughed, "I hope he was very much edified. One point is quite plain. He knew English, for my letters were nearly all in English."

"Some spy or other, I suppose."

"Without a doubt," she said, clasping her white hands before her and raising her wonderful eyes to mine. "And do you know, Uncle Colin, the affair has since troubled me very considerably. I wanted to see you and hear your opinion regarding it."

"My opinion is that your window ought not to have been left open."

"It had not been. The maid whose duty it is to close the windows on that floor one hour before sunset every day has been closely questioned, and declares that she closed and fastened it at seven o'clock."

"Servants are not always truthful," I remarked dubiously.

"But the intruder was there with some distinct purpose. Don't you think so?"

"Without a doubt. He was endeavouring to learn some secret which Your Highness possesses. Cannot you form any theory what it can be? Try and reflect."

"Secret!" she echoed, opening her eyes wide. "I have no secrets. Everybody tells me I am far too outspoken."

"Here, in Russia, everyone seems to hold secrets of some character or other, social or political, and spies are everywhere," I said. "Are you quite certain you have never before seen the intruder?"

"I could only catch the silhouette of his figure against the moonlight, yet, to tell the truth, it struck me at that moment that I had seen him somewhere before. But where, I could not recollect. He read each letter through, so he must have known English very well, or he could not have read so quickly."

"But did you not tell me in the winter garden of the Palace, on the night of the last Court ball, that Marya de Rosen had given you certain letters—letters which reflected upon General Markoff?" I asked.

She sat erect, staring at me open-mouthed in sudden recollection. "Why, I never thought of that!" she gasped. "Of course! It was for those letters the fellow must have been searching."

"I certainly think so—without the shadow of a doubt."

"Madame de Rosen feared lest they should be stolen from her, and she gave them over to me—three of them sealed up in an envelope," declared my dainty little companion. "She expressed apprehension lest a domiciliary visit be made to her house by the police, when the letters in question might be discovered and seized. So she asked me to hold them for her."

"And what did you do with them?"

"I hid them in a place where they will never be found," she said; "at a spot where nobody would even suspect. But somebody must be aware that she gave them to me for safe-keeping. How could they possibly know?"

"I think Your Highness was—well, just a little indiscreet on the night of the Court ball," I said. "Don't you recollect that you spoke aloud when other people were in the winter garden, and that I queried the judiciousness of it?"

"Ah! I remember now!" she exclaimed, her face suddenly pale and serious. "I recollect what I said. Somebody must have overheard me."

"And that somebody told Serge Markoff himself—the man who was poor Madame de Rosen's enemy, and who has sent both her and Luba to their graves far away in Eastern Siberia."

"Then you think that he is anxious to regain possession of those letters?"

"I think that is most probable, in face of your statement that you intend placing them before the Emperor. Of course, I do not know their nature, but I feel that they must reflect very seriously upon His Majesty's favourite official—the oppressor of Russia. You still have them in your possession?" I asked.

"Yes, Uncle Colin. I feared lest some spy might find them, so I went up to my old nursery on the top floor of the Palace—a room which has not been used for years. In it stands my old doll's house—a big, dusty affair as tall as myself. I opened it and placed the packet in the little wardrobe in one of the doll's bedrooms. It is still there. I saw it only yesterday."

"Be very careful that no spy watches you going to that disused room. You cannot exercise too much caution in this affair," I urged seriously.

"I am always cautious," she assured me. "I distrust more than one of our servants, for I believe some of them to be in Markoff's pay. All that we do at home is carried at once to the Emperor, while I am watched at every turn."

"True; only we foreign diplomats are exempt from this pestilential surveillance and the clever plots of the horde of *agents-provocateurs* controlled by the all-powerful Markoff."

"But what shall I do, Uncle Colin?" asked the girl, her white hands clasped in her lap.

"If you think it wise to place the letter before the Emperor, I should certainly lose no time in doing so," I replied. "It may soon be too late. Spies will leave no hole or corner in your father's palace unexamined."

"You think there really is urgency?" she asked.

I looked my charming companion straight in the face and replied:

"I do. If you value your life, then I would urge you at once to get rid of the packet which poor Madame de Rosen entrusted to you."

"But I cannot place it before the Emperor just at present," the girl exclaimed. "I promised secrecy to Marya de Rosen."

"Then you knew something of the subject to which those letters refer—eh?"

"I know something of it."

"Why not pass them on to me? They will be quite secure here in the Embassy safe. Russian spies dire not enter here—upon this bit of British soil."

"A good idea," she said quickly. "I will. I'll go home and bring them back to you."

And in a few minutes she rose and with a merry laugh left me to descend to her carriage, which was waiting out upon the quay.

I stood looking out of the window as she drove away. I was thinking—thinking seriously over the Emperor's strange apprehension.

Two visitors followed her, the French naval attaché, and afterwards old Madame Neilidoff, the Society leader of Moscow, who called to congratulate me upon my escape, and to invite me to spend my convalescence at her country estate at Sukova. With the stout, ugly old lady, who spake French with a dreadfully nasal intonation and possessed a distinct moustache, I chatted for nearly an hour, as we sipped our tea with lemon, when almost as soon as she had taken her departure the door was flung open unceremoniously and the Grand Duchess Natalia burst in, her beautiful face blanched to the lips.

"Uncle Colin! Something horrible has happened; Those letters have gone!" she gasped in a hoarse whisper, staring at me.

"Gone!" I echoed, starting to my feet in dismay.

"Yes. *They've been stolen—stolen!*"

Chapter Nine
The Little Grand Duchess

In the golden September sunset, the long, wide promenade stretching beside the blue sea from Brighton towards the fashionable suburb of Hove was agog with visitors.

A cloudless sky, a glassy sea flecked by the white sails of pleasure yachts, and ashore a crowd of well-dressed promenaders, the majority of whom were Londoners who, stifled in the dusty streets, were now seeking the fresh sea air of the Channel.

I had dressed leisurely for dinner in the Hotel Métropole, where I had taken up my abode, and about seven o'clock descended the steps, and, crossing the King's Road to the asphalted promenade, set out to walk westward towards Hove.

Many things had happened since that well-remembered afternoon in July when Natalia had discovered the clever theft of Madame de Rosen's letters, and I had, an hour later, ill though I was, sent to His Majesty that single word "Bathildis" and was granted immediate audience.

When I told him the facts he appeared interested, paced the room, and then snapped his fingers with a careless gesture. The little madcap had certainly annoyed him greatly, and though feigning indifference, he nevertheless appeared perplexed.

Natalia was called at once and questioned closely; she was the soul of honour and would reveal nothing of the secret. Afterwards I returned to the Embassy and summoned Hartwig, to inform him of the Grand Duchess's loss. The renowned police official had since made diligent inquiry; indeed, the whole complicated machinery of the Russian criminal police had been put into motion, but all to no avail.

The theft was still an entire mystery.

As I approached the Lawns at Hove, those wide, grassy promenades beside the sea, I saw that many people were still lingering, enjoying the warm sunset, although the fashionable hour when women exercise their pet dogs, and idle men lounge and watch the crowd, had passed and the band had finished its performance.

My mind was filled by many serious apprehensions, as turning suddenly from the Lawns, I recrossed the road and entered Brunswick Square, that wide quadrangle of big, old-fashioned houses around a large railed-in garden filled with high oaks and beeches.

Before a drab, newly-painted house with a basement and art-green blinds, I halted, ascended the steps and rang.

A white-whiskered old manservant in funereal black bowed as I entered, and, casting off my overcoat, I followed the old fellow past a man who was seated demurely in the hall, to whom I nodded, and up thickly-carpeted stairs to the big white-enamelled drawing-room, where Natalia sprang up from a couch of daffodil silk and came forward to meet me with glad welcome and outstretched hand.

"Well, Uncle Colin!" she cried, "wherever have you been? I called for you at the 'Métropole' the day before yesterday, and your superb hall-porter told me that you were in London!"

"Yes. I had to go up there on some urgent business," I said. "I only returned to-day at five o'clock and received your kind invitation to dine," and then, turning, I greeted Miss West, the rather thin, elderly woman who for years had acted as English governess to Her Imperial Highness—or Miss Gottorp, as she was now known at Hove. Miss West had been governess in the Emperor's family for six years before she had entered the service of the Grand Duchess Nicholas, so life at Court, with all its stiff etiquette, had perhaps imparted to her a slightly unnatural hauteur.

Natalia looked inexpressibly sweet in an evening gown of fine black spotted net, the transparency of which about the chest heightened the almost alabaster whiteness of her skin. She wore a black aigrette in her hair, but no jewellery save a single diamond bangle upon her wrist, an ornament which she always wore.

"Sit down and tell me all the news," she urged, throwing herself into an armchair and patting a cushion near by as indication where I should sit.

"There is no news," I said. "This morning I was at the Embassy, and they were naturally filled with curiosity regarding you—a curiosity which I did not satisfy."

"Young Isvolski is there, isn't he?" she asked. "He used to be attached to my poor father's suite."

"Yes," I replied. "He's third secretary. He wanted to know whether you had police protection, and I told him they had sent you another agent from Petersburg. I suppose it is that melancholy man I've just seen sitting in the hall?"

"Yes. Isn't it horrid? He sits there all day long and never moves," Miss West exclaimed. "It is as though the bailiffs are in the house."

"Bailiffs?" repeated the girl. "What are they?" I explained to her, whereupon she laughed heartily. "Hartwig is due in Brighton to-night or to-morrow morning," I said. "I have received a telegram from him, despatched from Berlin early yesterday morning. But," I added, "I trust that you are finding benefit from the change."

"I am," she assured me. "I love this place. I feel so free and so happy here. Miss West and I go for walks and drives every day, and though a lot of people stare at me very hard, I don't think they know who I am. I hope not."

"They admire your Highness's good looks," I ventured to remark. But she made a quick gesture of impatience, and declared that I only intended sarcasm.

"I suppose Miss West, that all the men turn to look at Her Highness?" I said. "Englishmen at the seaside during the summer are always impressionable, so they must be forgiven."

"You are quite right, Mr Trewinnard. It is really something dreadful. Only to-day a young man—quite a respectable young fellow, who was probably a clerk in the City—followed us the whole length of the promenade to the West Pier and kept looking into her Highness's face."

"He was really a very nice-looking boy," the girl declared mischievously. "If I'd been alone he would have spoken to me. And, oh, I'd have had such ripping fun."

"No doubt you would," I said. "But you know the rule. You are never upon any pretext to go out alone. Besides, you are always under the observation of a police-agent. You would scarcely care to do any love-making before him, would you?"

"Why not? Those persons are not men—they're only machines," she declared. "The Emperor told me that long ago."

"Well, take my advice," I urged with a laugh, "and don't attempt it."

"Oh, of course, Uncle Colin; you're simply dreadful. You're a perfect Saint Anthony. It's too jolly bad," she declared.

"Yes. Perhaps I might be a Saint Anthony where you are concerned. Still, you must not become a temptress," I laughed, when at that moment, old Igor, the butler, entered to announce that dinner was served.

So we descended the stairs to the big dining-room, where the table at which she took the head was prettily decorated with Marshal Neil roses, and, a merry trio, we ate our meal amid much good-humoured banter and general laughter.

As she sat beneath the pink-shaded electric lamp suspended over the table, I thought I had never seen her looking so inexpressibly charming. Little wonder, indeed, that young City men down for a fortnight's leisure at the seaside, the annual relaxation from their weary work-a-day world of office and suburban railway, looked upon her in admiration and followed her in order to feast their eyes upon her marvellous beauty. What would they have thought, had they but known that the girl so quietly and well-dressed in black was of the bluest blood of Europe, a daughter of the Imperial Romanoffs.

That big, old-fashioned house which I had arranged for her six weeks ago belonged to the widow of a brewery baronet, a man who had made a great fortune out of mild dinner-ale. The somewhat beefy lady—once a domestic servant—had gone on a voyage around the world and had been pleased to let it furnished for a year. With her consent I had had the whole place repainted and decorated, had caused new carpets to be provided, and in some instances the rooms had been refurnished in modern style, while four of the servants, including Igor, the butler, and Davey, Her Highness's maid, had been brought from her father's palace beside the Neva.

For a girl not yet nineteen it was, indeed, quite a unique establishment. Miss West acting as chaperone, companion and housekeeper.

Seated at the head of the table, the little Grand Duchess did the honours as, indeed, she had so often done them at the great table in that magnificent salon in Petersburg, for being the only child, it had very often fallen to her lot to help her father to entertain, her mother having died a month after her birth.

Dinner over, the ladies rose and left, while I sat to smoke my cigarette alone. Outside in the hall the undersized, insignificant little man in black sat upon a chair reading the evening paper, and as old Igor poured out my glass of port I asked him in French how he liked England.

"Ah! m'sieur," he exclaimed in his thin, squeaky voice. "Truly it is most beautiful. We are all so well here—so much better than in Petersburg. Years ago I went to London with my poor master, the Grand Duke. We stayed at Claridge's. M'sieur knows the place—eh?"

"Of course," I said. "But tell me, Igor, since you've been in Brighton—over a month now—have you ever met, or seen, anybody you know? I mean anyone you have seen before in Petersburg?"

I was anxious to learn whether young Hamborough, Paul Urusoff, or any of the rest, had been in the vicinity.

The old fellow reflected a few moments. Then he replied:

"Of course I saw M'sieur Hartwig three weeks ago. Also His Excellency the Ambassador when he came down from London to pay his respects to Her Imperial Highness."

"Nobody else?" I asked, looking seriously into his grey old face, my wine-glass poised in my hand.

"Ah, yes! One evening, three or four days ago, I was walking along King's Road, towards Ship Street, when I passed a tall, thin, clean-shaven man in brown, whose face was quite familiar. I know that I've seen him many times in Petersburg, but I cannot recall who or what he is. He looked inquisitively at me for a moment, and apparently recognising me, passed on and then hurriedly crossed the road."

"Was he a gentleman?" I asked with curiosity.

"He was dressed like one, M'sieur. He had on a dark grey Homburg hat and a fashionable dark brown suit."

"You only saw him on that one occasion?"

"Only that once. When I returned home I told Dmitri, the police-agent, and described him. You don't anticipate that he is here with any evil purpose, I suppose?" he added quickly.

"I can't tell, Igor. I don't know him. But if I were you I would not mention it to her Highness. She's only a girl, remember, and her nerves have been greatly shaken by that terrible tragedy."

"Rely upon me. I shall say no word, M'sieur," he promised.

Then I rose and ascended to the drawing-room, where Natalia was seated alone.

"Miss West will be here in a few minutes," she said. "Tell me, Uncle Colin, what have you been doing while you've been away—eh?"

"I had some business in London, and afterwards went on a flying visit to see my mother down in Cornwall," I said.

"Ah! How is she? I hope you told her to come and see me. I would be so very delighted if she will come and stay a week or so."

"I gave her Your Highness's kind message, and she is writing to thank you. She'll be most delighted to visit you," I said.

"Nothing has been discovered regarding Madame de Rosen's letters, I suppose?" she asked with a sigh, her face suddenly grown grave.

"Hartwig arrives to-night, or to-morrow," I replied. "We shall then know what has transpired. From his Majesty he received explicit instructions to spare no effort to solve the mystery of the theft."

"I know. He told me so when he was here three weeks ago. He has made every effort. Of all the police administration I consider Hartwig the most honest and straightforward."

"Yes," I agreed. "He is alert always, marvellously astute, and, above all, though he has had such an extraordinary career, he is an Englishman."

"So I have lately heard," replied my pretty companion. "I know he will do his best on my behalf, because I feel that I have lost the one piece of evidence which might have restored poor Marya de Rosen and her daughter to liberty."

"You have lost the letters, it is true," I said, looking into her splendid eyes. "You have lost them because it was plainly in the interests of General Markoff, the Tzar's favourite, that they should be lost. Madame de Rosen herself feared lest they should be stolen, and yet a few days later she and Luba were spirited away to the Unknown. Search was, no doubt, made at her house for that incriminating correspondence. It could not be found; but, alas! you let out the secret when sitting out with me at the Court ball. Somebody must have overheard. Your father's palace was searched very thoroughly, and the packet at last found."

"The Emperor appeared to be most concerned about it before I left Russia. When I last saw him at Tzarskoie-Selo he seemed very pale, agitated and upset."

"Yes," I said. Then, very slowly, for I confess I was much perturbed, knowing how we were at that moment hemmed in by our enemies, I added: "This theft conveyed more to His Majesty than at present appears to your Highness. It is a startling coup of those opposed to the monarchy—the confirmation of a suspicion which the Emperor believed to be his—and his alone."

"A suspicion!" she exclaimed. "What suspicion? Tell me."

Next moment Miss West, thin-faced and rather angular, entered the room, and we dropped our confidences. Then, at my invitation, my dainty little hostess went to the piano, and running her white fingers over the keys, commenced to sing in her clear, well-trained contralto "L'Heure Exquise" of Paul Verlaine:

> La lune blanche
>   Luit dans les bois;
> De chaque branche
>   Part une voix
> Sous la ramée...
>   O bien-aimée.

Chapter Ten
Reveals Two Facts

When I entered my bedroom at the Hotel Métropole it wanted half an hour to midnight. But scarce had I closed the door when a waiter tapped at it and handed me a card.

"Show the gentleman up," I said in eager anticipation, and a few minutes later there entered a tall, thin, clean-shaven, rather aristocratic-looking man in a dark brown suit—the same person whom old Igor had evidently recognised walking along King's Road.

"Well, Tack? So you are here with your report—eh?" I asked.

"Yes, sir," was his reply, as I seated myself on the edge of the bed, and he took a chair near the dressing-table and settled himself to talk.

Edward Tack was a man of many adventures. After a good many years at Scotland Yard, where he rose to be the chief of the Extradition Department on account of his knowledge of languages, he had been engaged by the Foreign Office as a member of our Secret Service abroad, mostly in Germany and Russia. During the past two years he had, as a blind to the police, carried on a small insurance agency business in Petersburg; but the information he gathered from time to time and sent to the Embassy was of the greatest assistance to us in our diplomatic dealings with Russia and the Powers.

He never came to the Embassy himself, nor did he ever hold any direct communication with any of the staff. He acted as our eyes and ears, exercising the utmost caution in transmitting to us the knowledge of men and matters which he so cleverly gained. He worked with the greatest secrecy, for though he had lived in Petersburg two whole years, he had never once been suspected by that unscrupulous spy-department controlled by General Markoff.

"I've been in Brighton several days," my visitor said. "The hotel porter told me here that you were away, so I went to the 'Old Ship!' and waited for you."

"Well—what have you discovered?" I inquired, handing him my cigarette-case. "Anything of interest?"

"Nothing very much, I regret to say," was his reply. "I've worked for a whole month, often night and day, but Markoff's men are wary—very wary birds, sir, as you know."

"Have you discovered the real perpetrator of that bomb outrage?"

"I believe so. He escaped."

"No doubt he did."

"There have been in all over forty persons arrested," my visitor said. "About two dozen have been immured in Schusselburg, in those cells under the waters of Lake Ladoga. The rest have been sent by administrative process to the mines."

"And all of them innocent?"

"Every one of them."

"It's outrageous!" I cried. "To think that such things can happen every day in a country whose priests teach Christianity."

"Remove a certain dozen or so of Russia's statesmen and corrupt officials, put a stop to the exile system, and give every criminal or suspect a fair trial, and the country would become peaceful to-morrow," declared the secret agent. "I have already reported to the Embassy the actual truth concerning the present unrest."

"I know. And we have sent it on to Downing Street, together with the names of those who form the camarilla. The Emperor is, alas! merely their catspaw. They are the real rulers of Russia—they rule it by a Reign of Terror."

"Exactly, sir," replied the man Tack. "I've always contended that. In the present case the outrage is not a mystery to the Secret Police."

"You think they know all about it—eh?" I asked quickly.

"Well, sir. I will put to you certain facts which I have discovered. About two years ago a certain Danilo Danilovitch, an intelligent shoemaker in Kazan, and a member of the revolutionary group in that city, turned police-spy, and gave evidence of a *coup* which had been prepared to poison the Emperor at a banquet given there after the military manoeuvres last year. As a result, there were over a hundred arrests, and as reprisal the chief of police of Kazan was a week later shot while riding through one of the principal streets. Next I know of Danilovitch is that he was transferred to Petersburg, where, though in the pay of the police, he was known to the Party of the People's Will as an ardent and daring reformer, and foremost in his fiery condemnation of the monarchy. He made many inflammatory speeches at the secret revolutionary meetings in various parts of the city, and was hailed as a strong and intrepid leader. Yet frequently the police made raids upon these meeting-places and arrested all found there. After each attempted outrage they seemed to be provided with lists of everyone who had had the slightest connection with the affair, and hence they experienced no difficulty in securing them and packing them off to Siberia. The police were all-ubiquitous, the Emperor was greatly pleased, and General Markoff was given the highest decorations, promotion and an appointment with rich emoluments.

"But one day, about four months ago," Tack went on, "a remarkable but unreported tragedy occurred. Danilovitch, whose wife had long ago been arrested and died on her way to Siberia, fell in love with a pretty young tailoress named Marie Garine, who was a very active member of the revolutionary party, her father and mother having been sent to the mines of Nerchinsk, though entirely innocent. Hence she naturally hated the Secret Police and all their detestable works. More than once she had remarked to her lover the extraordinary fact that the police were being secretly forewarned of every attempt which he suggested, for Danilovitch had by this time become one of the chief leaders of the subterranean revolution, and instigator of all sorts of desperate plots against the Emperor and members of the Imperial Family. One evening, however, she went to his rooms and found him out. Some old shoes were upon a shelf ready for mending, for he still, as a subterfuge, practised his old trade. Among the shoes was a pair of her own. She took them down, but she mistook another pair for hers, and from one of them there fell to her feet a yellow card—the card of identity issued to members of the Secret Police! She took it up. There was no mistake, for her lover's photograph was pasted upon it. Her lover was a police-spy!"

"Well, what happened?" I asked, much interested in the facts.

"The girl, in a frenzy of madness and anger, was about to rush out to betray the man to her fellow-conspirators, when Danilovitch suddenly entered. She had, at that moment, his yellow card in her hand. In an instant he knew the truth and realised his own peril. She intended to betray him. It meant her life or his! Not a dozen words passed between the pair, for the man, taking up his shoemaker's knife, plunged it deliberately into the girl's heart, snatched the card from her dying grasp, and strode out, locking the door behind him. Then he went straight to the private bureau of General Markoff and told him what he had done. Needless to relate, the police inquiry was a very perfunctory one. It was a love tragedy, they said, and as Danilo Danilovitch was missing, they soon dropped the inquiry. They did not, of course, wish to arrest the assassin, for he was far too useful a person to them."

"Then you know the fellow?"

"I have met him often. At first I had no idea of his connection with the revolutionists. It is only quite recently through a woman who is in the pay of the Secret Police, and whose son has been treated badly, that I learned the truth. And she also told me one very curious fact. She was present in the crowd when the bomb was thrown at the Grand Duke Nicholas's carriage, and she declares that Danilo Danilovitch—who has not been seen in Petersburg since the tragic death of Marie Garine—was there also."

"Then he may have thrown the bomb?" I said, amazed.

"Who knows?"

"But I saw a man with his arm uplifted," I exclaimed. "He looked respectable, of middle-age, with a grey beard and wore dark clothes."

"That does not tally with Danilovitch's description," he replied. "But, of course, the assassin must have been disguised if he had dared to return to Petersburg."

"But I suppose his fellow-conspirators still entertain no suspicion that he is a police-spy?"

"None whatever. The poor girl lost her life through her untoward discovery. The police themselves knew the truth, but on action being withdrawn, the fellow was perfectly free to continue his nefarious profession of *agent-provocateur*, for the great risk of which he had evidently been well paid."

"But does not Hartwig know all this?" I asked quickly, much surprised.

"Probably not. General Markoff keeps his own secrets well. Hartwig, being head of the criminal police, would not be informed."

"But he might find out, just as you have found out," I suggested.

"He might. But my success, sir, was due to the merest chance, remember," Tack said. "Hartwig's work lies in the detection of crime, and not in the frustration of political plots. Markoff knows what an astute official he is, and would therefore strive to keep him apart from his catspaw Danilovitch."

"Then, in your opinion, many of these so-called plots against the Emperor are actually the work of the Kazan shoemaker, who arranges the plot, calls the conspirators together and directs the arrangements."

"Yes. His brother is a chemist in Moscow and it is he who manufactures picric acid, nitro-glycerine and other explosives for the use of the unfortunate conspirators. Between them, and advised by Markoff, they form a plot, the more desperate the better; and a dozen or so silly enthusiasts, ignorant of their leaders' true calling, swear solemnly to carry it out. They are secretly provided with the means, and their leader has in some cases actually secured facilities from the very police themselves for the *coup* to be made. Then, when all is quite ready, the astute Danilovitch hands over to his employer, Markoff, a full list of the names of those who have been cleverly enticed into the plot. At night a sudden raid is made. All who are there, or who are even in the vicinity are arrested, and next morning His Excellency presents his report to the Emperor, with Danilovitch's list ready for the Imperial signature which consigns those arrested to a living grave on the Arctic wastes, or in the mines of Eastern Siberia."

"And so progresses holy Russia of to-day—eh, Tack?" I remarked with a sigh.

The secret agent of British diplomacy, shrugging his shoulders and with a grin, said:

"The scoundrels are terrorising the Emperor and the whole Imperial family. The killing of the Grand Duke Nicholas was evidence of that, and you, too, sir, had a very narrow escape."

"Do you suspect that, if the story of the woman who recognised Danilovitch be true, it was actually he himself who threw the bomb?"

"At present I can offer no opinion," he answered. "The woman might, of course, have been mistaken, and, again, I doubt whether Danilovitch would dare to show himself so quickly in Petersburg. To do so would be to defy the police in the eyes of his fellow-conspirators, and that might have aroused their suspicion. But, sir," Tack added, "I feel certain of two facts— absolutely certain."

"And what are they?" I inquired eagerly, for his information was always reliable.

"Well, the first is that the outrage was committed with the full connivance and knowledge of the police, and secondly, that it was not the Grand Duke whom they sought to kill, but his daughter, the Grand Duchess Natalia, and you yourself!"

"Why do you think that?" I asked.

"Because it was known that the young lady held letters given her by Madame de Rosen, and intended to hand them over to the Emperor. There was but one way to prevent her," he went on very slowly, "to kill her! And," he added, "be very careful yourself in the near future, Mr Trewinnard. Another attempt of an entirely different nature may be made."

"You mean that Her Highness is still in grave danger—even here—eh?" I exclaimed, looking straight at the clean-shaven man seated before me.

"I mean, sir, that Her Highness may be aware of the contents of these letters handed to her by the lady who is now exiled. If so, then she is a source of constant danger to General Markoff's interests. And you are fully well aware of the manner in which His Excellency usually treats his enemies. Only by a miracle was your life saved a few weeks ago. Therefore," he added, "I beg of you, sir, to beware. There may be pitfalls and dangers—even here, in Brighton!"

"Do you only suspect something, Tack," I demanded very seriously, "or do you actually know?"

He paused for a few seconds, then, his deep-set eyes fixed upon mine, he replied.

"I do not suspect, sir, I *know*."

Chapter Eleven
His Excellency General Markoff

What Tack had told me naturally increased my apprehension. I informed the two agents of Russian police who in turn guarded the house in Brunswick Square.

A whole month went by, bright, delightful autumn days beside the sea, when I often strolled with my charming little companion across the Lawns at Hove, or sat upon the pier at Brighton listening to the band.

Sometimes I would dine with her and Miss West, or at others they would take tea with me in that overheated winter garden of the "Métropole"— where half of the Hebrew portion of the City of London assembles on Sunday afternoons—or they would dine with me in the big restaurant. So frequently was she in and out of the hotel that "Miss Gottorp" soon became known to all the servants, and by sight to most of the visitors on account of the neatness of her mourning and the attractiveness of her pale beauty.

Tack had returned to Petersburg to resume his agency business, and Hartwig's whereabouts was unknown.

The last-named had been in Brighton three weeks before, but as he had nothing to report he had disappeared as suddenly as he had come. He was ubiquitous—a man of a hundred disguises, and as many subterfuges. He never seemed to sleep, and his journeys backwards and forwards across the face of Europe were amazingly swift and ever-constant.

I was seated at tea with Her Highness and Miss West in the winter garden—that place of palms and bird-cages at the back of the "Métropole"— when a waiter handed me a telegram which I found was from the secretary of the Russian Embassy, at Chesham House, in London, asking me to call there at the earliest possible moment.

What, I wondered, had occurred?

I said nothing to Natalia, but, recollecting that there was an express just after six o'clock which would land me at Victoria at half-past seven, I cut short her visit and duly arrived in London, unaware of the reason why I was so suddenly summoned.

I crossed the big, walled-in courtyard of the Embassy, and entering the great sombre hall, where an agent of Secret Police was idling as usual, the flunkey in green livery showed me along to the secretary's room, a big, gloomy, smoke-blackened apartment on the ground floor. The huge house was dark, sombre and ponderous, a house of grim, mysterious shadows, where officials and servants flitted up and down the great, wide staircase which led to His Excellency's room.

"His Excellency left for Paris to-day," the footman informed me, opening the door of the secretary's room, and telling me that he would send word at once of my arrival.

It was the usual cold and austere embassy room—differing but little from my own den in Petersburg. Count Kourloff, the secretary, was an old friend of mine. He had been secretary in Rome when I had been stationed there, and I had also known him in Vienna—a clever and intelligent diplomat, but a bureaucrat like all Russians.

The evening was a warm, oppressive one, and the windows being open, admitted the lively strains of a street piano, played somewhere in the vicinity.

Suddenly the door opened, and instead of the Count, whom I had expected, a stout, broad-shouldered, elderly man in black frock-coat and grey trousers entered, and saluted me gaily in French with the words:

"Ah, my dear Trewinnard! How are you, my friend—eh? How are you? And how is Her Imperial Highness—eh?"

I started as I recognised him.

It was none other than Serge Markoff.

"I am very well, General," I replied coldly. "I am awaiting Count Kourloff."

"He's out. It was I who telegraphed to you. I want to have a chat with you now that you have entered the service of Russia, my dear friend. Pray be seated."

"Pardon me," I replied, annoyed, "I have not entered the service of Russia, only the private service of her Sovereign, the Emperor."

"The same thing! The same thing!" he declared fussily, stroking his long, grey moustache, and fixing his cunning steel-blue eyes upon mine.

"I think not," I said. "But we need not discuss that point."

"*Bien*! I suppose Her Highness is perfectly comfortable and happy in her *incognito* at Brighton—eh? The Emperor was speaking of her to me only the other day."

"His Majesty receives my report each week," I said briefly.

"I know," replied the brutal remorseless man who was responsible for the great injustice and suffering of thousands of innocent ones throughout the Russian Empire. "I know. But I have asked you to London because I wish to speak to you in strictest confidence. I am here, M'sieur Trewinnard, because of a certain discovery we have recently made—the discovery of a very desperate and ingenious plot!"

"Another plot!" I echoed; "here, in London!"

"It is formed in London, but the *coup* is to be made at Brighton," he replied slowly and seriously, "a plot against Her Imperial Highness!"

I looked the man straight in the face, and then burst out laughing.

"You certainly do not appear to have any regard for the personal safety of your charge," he exclaimed angrily. "I have warned you. Therefore, take every precaution."

I paused for a few seconds, then I said:

"Forgive me for laughing. General Markoff. But it is really too humorous—all this transparency."

"What transparency?"

"The transparency of your attempt to terrify me," I said. "I know that the attempt made against the young lady and myself failed—and that His Imperial Highness the Grand Duke was unfortunately killed. But I do not think there will be any second attempt."

"You don't think so!" he cried quickly. "Why don't you think so?"

"For the simple reason that Danilo Danilovitch—the man who is a police-spy and at the same time responsible for plots—is just now a little too well watched."

The man's grey face dropped when I uttered the name of his catspaw. My statement, I saw, held him confounded and confused.

"I—I do not understand you," he managed to exclaim. "What do you mean?"

"Well, you surely know Danilovitch?" I said. "He is your most trusted and useful *agent-provocateur*. He is at this moment in England. I can take you now to where he is in hiding, if you wish," I added, with a smile of triumph.

"Danilovitch," he repeated, as though trying to recall the name.

"Yes," I said defiantly, standing with my hands in my trousers pockets and leaning against the table placed in the centre of the room. "Danilovitch—the shoemaker of Kazan and murderer of Marie Garine, the poor little tailoress in Petersburg."

His face dropped. He saw that I was aware of the man's identity.

"He is now staying with a compatriot in Blurton Road, Lower Clapton," I went on.

"I don't see why this person should interest me," he interrupted.

"But he is a conspirator. General Markoff; and I am giving you some valuable information," I said, with sarcasm.

"You are not a police officer. What can you know?"

"I know several facts which, when placed before the Revolutionary Committee—as they probably are by this time—will make matters exceedingly unpleasant for Danilo Danilovitch, and also for certain of those who have been employing him," was my quiet response.

"If this man is a dangerous revolutionist, as you allege, he cannot be arrested while in England," remarked the General, his thick grey eyebrows contracting slightly, a sign of apprehension. "This country of yours gives asylum to all the most desperate characters, and half the revolutionary plots in Europe are arranged in London."

"I do not dispute that," I said. "But I was discussing the highly interesting career of this Danilo Danilovitch. If there is any attempt upon Her Imperial Highness the Grand Duchess Natalia, as you fear, it will be by that individual. General. Therefore I would advise your department to keep close observation upon him. He is lodging at Number 30B, Blurton Road. And," I added, "if you should require any further particulars concerning him, I daresay I shall be in a position to furnish them."

"Why do you suspect him?"

"Because of information which has reached me—information which shows that it was his hand which launched the fatal bomb which killed the Grand Duke Nicholas. His Imperial Highness was actually killed by an agent of Secret Police! When that fact reaches the Emperor's ears there will, I expect, be searching inquiry."

"Have you actual proof of this?" he asked in a thick, hoarse voice, his cheeks paler than before.

"Yes. Or at least my informant has. The traitor was recognised among the crowd; he was seen to throw the bomb."

General Markoff remained silent. He saw himself checkmated. His secret was out. He had intended to raise a false scare of a probable attempt at Brighton in order to terrify me, but, to his amazement, I had shown myself conversant with his methods and aware of the truth concerning the mysterious outrage in which the Grand Duke Nicholas had lost his life.

From his demeanour and the keen cunning look in his steely eyes I gathered that he was all eagerness to know the exact extent of my knowledge concerning Danilo Danilovitch.

Therefore, after some further conversation, I said boldly:

"I expect that, ere this, the Central Committee of the People's Will has learned the truth regarding their betrayer—this man to whose initiative more than half of the recent plots have been due—and how he was in the habit of furnishing your department with the lists of suspects and those chosen to carry out the outrage. But, of course, General," I added, with a bitter smile, "you would probably not know of this manufacture of plots by one in the pay of the Police Department."

"Of course not," the unscrupulous official assured me. "I surely cannot be held responsible for the action of underlings. I only act upon reports presented to me."

I smiled again.

"And yet you warn me of an outrage which is to be attempted with your connivance by this fellow Danilovitch—the very man who killed the Grand Duke—eh?"

"With my connivance!" he cried fiercely. "What do you insinuate?"

"I mean this, General Markoff," I said boldly; "that the yellow card of identity found in Danilovitch's rooms by the girl to whom he was engaged bore your signature. That card is, I believe, already in the hands of the Revolutionary Committee!"

"I have all their names. I shall telegraph to-night ordering their immediate arrest," he cried, white with anger.

"But that will not save your *agent-provocateur*—the assassin of poor Marie Garine—from his fate. The arm of the revolutionist is a very long one, remember."

"But the arm of the Chief of Secret Police is longer—and stronger," he declared in a low, hard tone.

"The Emperor, when he learns the truth, will dispense full justice," I said very quietly. "His eyes will, ere long, be opened to the base frauds practised upon him, and the many false plots which have cost hundreds of innocent persons their lives or their liberty."

"You speak as though you were censor of the police," he exclaimed with a quick, angry look.

"I speak, General Markoff, as the friend of Russia and of her Sovereign the Emperor," I replied. "You warn me of a plot to assassinate the Grand Duchess Natalia. Well, I tell you frankly and openly I don't believe it. But if it be true, then I, in return, warn you that if any attempt be made by any of your dastardly hirelings, I will myself go to the Emperor and place before him proofs of the interesting career of Danilo Danilovitch. Your Excellency may be all-powerful as Chief of Secret Police," I added; "but as surely as the sun will rise to-morrow, justice will one day be done in Russia!"

And then I turned upon my heel and passed out of the room, leaving him biting his nether lip in silence at my open defiance.

Chapter Twelve
Watchers in the Night

After Her Highness and Miss West had dined with me at the "Métropole" at Brighton on the following evening, the trusted old companion complained of headache and drove home, leaving us alone together.

Therefore we strolled forth into the moonlit night and, crossing the road, walked out along the pier. There were many persons in the hall of the hotel, but though a good many heads were turned to see "Miss Gottorp" pass in her pretty *décolleté* gown of black, trimmed with narrow silver, over which was a black satin evening cloak, probably not one noticed the undersized, insignificant, but rather well-dressed man who rose from one of the easy chairs where he had been smoking to follow us out.

Who, indeed, of that crowd would have guessed that the pretty girl by whose side I walked was an Imperial Princess, or that the man who went out so aimlessly was Oleg Lobko, the trusty agent of the Russian Criminal Police charged by the Emperor with her personal protection?

With the man following at a respectable distance, we strolled side by side upon the pier, looking back upon the fairy-like scene, the long lines of light along King's Road, and the calm sea shimmering beneath the clear moon. There were many people enjoying the cool, refreshing breezes, as there always are upon an autumn night.

A comedy was in progress in the theatre at the pierhead, and it being the *entr'acte*, many were promenading—mostly visitors taking their late vacation by the sea.

My charming little companion had been bright and cheerful all the evening, but had more than once, by clever questions, endeavoured to learn what had taken me to the Embassy on the previous night. I, however, did not deem it exactly advisable to alarm her unduly, either by telling her of my defiance of General Markoff, of my discovery of Danilo Danilovitch, or of the attempt to terrify me by the declaration that another plot was in progress.

Truth to tell, Tack, before his return to Petersburg, had run Danilovitch to earth in Lower Clapton, and two private detectives, engaged by me, were keeping the closest surveillance upon him.

Twice had we circled the theatre at the pierhead, and had twice strolled amid the seated audience around the bandstand where military music was being played in the moonlight, when we passed two young men in Homburg hats, wearing overcoats over their evening clothes. One of them, a tall, slim, dark-haired, good-looking, athletic young fellow, of perhaps twenty-two, raised his hat and smiled at my companion.

She nodded him a merry acknowledgment. Then, as we passed on, I exclaimed quickly:

"Hulloa! Is that some new friend—eh?"

"Oh, it's really all right, Uncle Colin," she assured me. "I've done nothing dreadful, now. You needn't start lecturing me, you know, or be horrified at all."

"I'm not lecturing," I laughed. "I'm only consumed by curiosity. That's all."

"Ah! You're like all men," she declared. "And suppose I refuse to satisfy your curiosity—eh?"

"You won't do that, I think," was my reply, as we halted upon one of the long benches which ran on either side of the pier. "Remember, I am responsible to the Emperor for you, and I'm entitled to know who your friend is."

"He's an awfully nice boy," was all she replied.

"He looks so. But who is he?"

"Somebody—well, somebody I knew at Eastbourne."

"And you've met him here? How long ago?"

"Oh! nearly a month."

"And so it is he whom you've met several times of late—eh?" I said. "Let's see—according to the report furnished to me, you were out for half an hour on the sea-front on Tuesday night; five minutes on Wednesday night;

not at all on Thursday night, and one whole hour on Friday night—eh? And with a young man whose name is unknown."

"Oh, I'll tell you his name. He's Dick Drury."

"And who, pray, is this Mr Richard Drury?"

"A friend of mine, I tell you. The man with him is his friend—Lance Ingram, a doctor."

"And what is this Mr Drury's profession?"

"He does nothing, I suppose," she laughed. "I can't well imagine Dick doing much."

"Except flirting—eh?" I said with a smile.

"That's a matter of opinion," she replied, as we again rose and circled the bandstand, for I was anxious to get another look at the pair.

On the evenings I had referred to, it appeared that Her Highness, after dinner, had twisted a shawl over her head, and ran down to the sea-front—a distance of a hundred yards or so—to get a breath of air, as she had explained to Miss West. But on each occasion the watchful police-agent had seen her meet by appointment this same young man. Therefore some flirtation was certainly in progress—and flirtation had been most distinctly forbidden.

My efforts were rewarded, for a few minutes later the two young men repassed us, and this time young Drury did not raise his hat. He only smiled at her in recognition.

"Where are they staying?" I asked.

"Oh you are so horribly inquisitive, Uncle Colin," she said. "Well, if you really must know, they're staying at the 'Royal York.'"

"How came you to know this young fellow at Eastbourne?" I asked. "I thought you were kept in strictest seclusion from the outside world. At least, you've always led me to believe that," I said.

She laughed heartily.

"Well, dear old uncle, surely you don't think that any school could exactly keep a girl a prisoner. We used to get out sometimes alone for an hour of an evening—by judicious bribery. I've had many a pleasant hour's walk up the road towards Beachy Head. And, moreover, I wasn't alone, either. Dick was usually with me."

"Really, this is too dreadful!" I exclaimed in pious horror. "Suppose anyone had known who you really were!"

"Well, I suppose even if they had the heavens wouldn't have fallen," she laughed.

"Ah!" I said, "you are really incorrigible. Here you are flirting with an unsuspected lover."

"And why shouldn't I?" she asked in protest. "Dick is better than some chance acquaintance."

"If you are only amusing yourself," I said. "But if you love him, then it would be a serious matter."

"Oh, horribly serious, I know," she said impatiently. "If I were a typist, or a shopgirl, or a waitress, or any girl who worked for her living, I should be doing quite the correct thing; but for me—born of the great Imperial Family—to merely look at a boy is quite unpardonable."

I was silent for a few moments. The little madcap whom the Emperor had placed in my charge, because her presence at Court was a menace to the Imperial family, was surely unconventional and utterly incorrigible.

"I fear Your Highness does not fully appreciate the heavy responsibilities of Imperial birth," I said in a tone of dissatisfaction.

"Oh, bother! My birth be hanged!" she exclaimed, with more force than politeness. "In these days it really counts for nothing. I was reading it all in a German book last week. Every class seems to have its own social laws, and what is forbidden to me is quite good form with my dressmaker. Isn't it absurdly funny?"

"You must study your position."

"Why should I, if I strictly preserve my *incognito*? That I do this, even you, Uncle Colin, will admit!"

"Are you quite certain that this Mr Drury is unaware who you really are?" I asked.

"Quite. He believes me to be Miss Natalia Gottorp, my father German, my mother English, and I was born in Germany. That is the story—does it suit?"

"I trust you will take great care not to reveal your true identity," I said.

"I have promised you, haven't I?"

"You promised me that you would not flirt, and yet here you are, having clandestine meetings with this young man every evening!"

"Oh, that's very different. I can't help it if I meet an old friend accidentally, can I?" she protested with a pretty pout.

At that moment we were strolling along the western side of the pierhead, where it was comparatively ill-lit, on one side being the theatre, while on the other the sea. The photographer's and other shops were closed at that late hour, and the light being dim at that spot, several flirting couples were passing up and down arm in arm.

Suddenly, as we turned the corner behind the theatre, we came face to face with a dark-featured, middle-aged man, with deeply-furrowed brow, narrowly set eyes and small black moustache. He wore a dark suit and a hard felt hat, and had something of the appearance of a middle-class paterfamilias out for his annual vacation.

He glanced quickly in our direction, and, I thought, started, as though recognising one or other of us.

Then next moment he was lost in the darkness.

"Do you know that man?" asked my companion suddenly.

"No. Why?"

"I don't know," she answered. "I fancy I've seen him somewhere or other before. He looked like a Russian."

That was just my own thought at that moment, and I wondered if Oleg, who was lurking near, had noticed him.

"Yes," I said. "But I don't recollect ever having seen him before. I wonder who he is? Let's turn back."

We did so, but though we hastened our steps, we did not find him. He had, it seemed, already left the pier. Apparently he believed that he had been recognised.

Once again we repassed Drury and his friend just as the theatre disgorged its crowd of homeward-bound pleasure-seekers.

We were walking in the same direction, Oleg following at a respectable distance, and I was enabled to obtain a good look at him, for, as though in wonder as to whom I could be, he turned several times to eye me, with some little indignation, I thought.

I judged him to be about twenty-five, over six feet in height, athletic and wiry, with handsome, clear-cut, clean-shaven features and a pair of sharp, dark, alert eyes, which told of an active outdoor life. His face was a refined one, his gait easy and swinging, and both in dress and manner he betrayed the gentleman.

Truth to tell, though I did not admit it to Natalia, I became very favourably impressed by him. By his exterior he seemed to be a well-set-up, sportsmanlike young fellow, who might, perhaps, belong to one of the Sussex county families.

His friend the doctor was of quite a different type, a short, fair-haired man in gold-rimmed spectacles, whose face was somewhat unattractive, though it bore an expression of studiousness and professional knowledge. He certainly had the appearance of a doctor.

But before I went farther I resolved to make searching inquiry unto the antecedents of this mysterious Dick Drury.

The walk in the moonlight along the broad promenade towards Hove was delightful. I begged Her Highness to drive, but she preferred to walk; the autumn night was so perfect, she said.

As we strolled along, she suddenly exclaimed:

"I can't help recalling that man we saw on the pier. I remember now! I met him about a week ago, when I was shopping in Western Road, and he followed me for quite a distance. He was then much better dressed."

"You believe, then, he is a Russian?" I asked quickly.

"I feel certain he is."

"But you were not alone—Oleg was out with you, I suppose?"

"Oh, yes," she laughed. "He never leaves me. I only wish he would sometimes. I hate to be spied upon like this. Either Dmitri or Oleg is always with me."

"It is highly necessary," I declared. "Recollect the fate of your poor father."

"But why should the revolutionists wish to harm me—a girl?" she asked. "My own idea is that they're not half as black as they're painted."

I did not reveal to her the serious facts which I had recently learnt.

"Did you make any mention to Oleg of the man following you?"

"No, it never occurred to me. But there, I suppose, he only followed me, just as other men seem sometimes to follow me—to look into my face."

"You are used to admiration," I said, "and therefore take no notice of it. Pretty women so soon become blasé."

"Oh! So you denounce me as blasé—eh, Uncle Colin?" she cried, just as we arrived before the door in Brunswick Square. "That is the latest! I really don't think it fair to criticise me so constantly," and she pouted.

Then she gave me her little gloved hand, and I bent over it as I wished her good-night.

I wished to question Oleg regarding the man we had seen, but I could not do so before her.

I turned back along the promenade, and was walking leisurely towards the "Métropole," when suddenly from out of the shadow of one of the glass-partitioned shelters the dark figure of a man emerged, and I heard my name pronounced.

It was the ubiquitous Hartwig, wearing his gold pince-nez. As was his habit, he sprang from nowhere. I had clapped my hand instinctively upon my revolver, but withdrew it instantly.

"Good evening, Mr Trewinnard," he said. "I've met you here as I don't want to be seen at the 'Métropole' to-night. I have travelled straight through from Petersburg here. I landed at Dover this afternoon, went up to Victoria, and down here. I arrived at eight o'clock, but learning that Her Highness was dining with you, I waited until you left her. It is perhaps as well that I am here," he added.

"Why?" I asked.

"Because I've been on the pier with you to-night," was the reply of the chief of the detective department of Russia, "and I have seen how closely you have been watched by a person whom even Oleg Lobko, usually so well-informed, does not suspect—a person who is extremely dangerous. I do not wish to alarm you, Mr Trewinnard," he added in a low voice, "but I heard in Petersburg that something is intended here in Brighton, and the Emperor sent me post-haste to you."

"Who is this person who has been watching us?" I asked eagerly. "I noticed him."

"Oleg doesn't know him, but I do. I have had certain suspicions, and only five days ago I made a discovery in Petersburg—an amazing discovery— which confirmed my apprehensions. The man who has been watching you with distinctly evil intent is a most notorious and evasive character named Danilo Danilovitch."

"Danilovitch!" I cried. "I know him, but I did not recognise him to-night. His appearance has so changed."

"Yes, it has. But I have been watching him all the evening. He returned by the midnight train to London."

"I can tell you where he is in hiding," I said.

"You can!" he cried. "Excellent! Then we will both go and pay him a surprise call to-morrow. There is danger—a grave and imminent danger—for both Her Highness and yourself; therefore it must be removed. There is peril in the present situation—a distinct peril which I had never suspected. A disaster may happen at any moment if we are not wary and watchful. And there's another important point, Mr Trewinnard," added the great detective; "do you happen to know a tall, thin, sharp-featured young man called Richard Drury?"

Chapter Thirteen
The Catspaw

Just as the dusk had deepened into grey on the following evening I alighted from a tram in the Lower Clapton Road, and, accompanied by Hartwig, we turned up a long thoroughfare of uniform houses, called Powerscroft Road, until we reached Blurton Road, where, nearly opposite the Mission House, we found the house of which we were in search.

Hartwig had altered his appearance wonderfully, and looked more like a Devonshire farmer up in London on holiday than the shrewd, astute head of the Sûreté of the Russian Empire. As for myself, I had assumed a very old suit and wore a shabby hat.

The drab, dismal house, which we passed casually in order to inspect, was dingy and forbidding, with curtains that were faded with smoke and dirt, holland blinds once yellow, but the ends of which were now dark and stained, and windows which had not been cleaned for years, while the front door was faded and blistered and some of the tops of the iron railings in front had been broken off. The steps leading to the front door had not been hearthstoned as were those of its neighbour, while in the area were bits of wastepaper, straw, and the flotsam and jetsam of the noisy, overcrowded street.

Unkempt children were romping or playing hopscotch on the pavement, while some were skipping and others playing football in the centre of the road—all pupils of the great County Council Schools in the vicinity.

At both the basement window and that of the room above—the front parlour—were short blinds of dirty muslin, so that to see within while passing was impossible. In that particular it differed in no way from some of its neighbours; for in those parts front parlours are often turned into bedrooms, and a separate family occupies every floor. Only one fact was apparent—that it was the dirtiest and most neglected house in the whole of that working-class road, bordering upon the Hackney Marsh.

To me that district was as unfamiliar as were the wilds of the Sahara. Indeed, to the average Londoner Lower Clapton is a mere legendary district, the existence of which is only recorded by the name written upon tramcars and omnibuses.

Together we strolled to the bottom of Blurton Road, to where Glyn Road crosses it at right angles, and then we stopped to discuss our plans.

"I shall ascend the steps, knock, and ask for Danilovitch," the great detective said. "The probability is that the door will be unceremoniously slammed in my face. But you will be behind me. I shall place my foot in the door to prevent premature closing, and at first sign of resistance you, being behind me, will help me to force the door, and so enter. At word from me don't hesitate—use all your might. I intend to give whoever lives there a sudden and sharp surprise."

"But if they are refugees, they are desperate. What then?"

"I expect they are," he laughed. "This is no doubt the hornets' nest. Therefore it behoves us to be wary, and have our wits well about us. You're not afraid, Mr Trewinnard?"

"Not at all," I said. "Where you dare go, there I will follow."

"Good. Let's make the attempt then," he said, and together we strolled leisurely back until we came to the flight of unclean front steps, whereupon both of us turned and, ascending, Hartwig gave a sharp postman's knock at the door.

An old, grey-whiskered, ill-dressed man, palpably a Polish Jew, opened the door, whereupon Hartwig asked in Russian:

"Is our leader Danilo Danilovitch here?"

The man looked from him to me inquiringly.

"Tell him that Ivan Arapoff, from Petersburg, wishes to speak with him."

"I do not know, Gospodin, whether he is at home," replied the man with politeness. "But I will see, if you will wait," and he attempted to close the door in our faces.

Hartwig, however, was prepared for such manoeuvre, for he had placed his foot in the door, so that it could not be closed. The Polish Jew was instantly on the alert and shouted some sharp word of warning, evidently a preconcerted signal, to those within, whereat Hartwig and myself made a sudden combined effort and next second were standing within the narrow evil-smelling little hall.

I saw the dark figures of several men and women against the stairs, and heard whispered words of alarm in Russian. But Hartwig lost no time, for he shouted boldly:

"I wish to see Danilo Danilovitch. Let him come forward. If he does not do so, then it is at his own peril."

"If you are police officers you cannot touch us here in England!" shouted a young woman with dark, tousled hair, a revolutionist of the female-student type.

"We are here from Petersburg as friends, but you apparently treat us as enemies," said Hartwig.

"If you are traitors you will, neither of you, leave this house alive," cried a thick-set man, advancing towards me threateningly. "So you shall see Danilovitch—and he shall decide."

I heard somebody bolting the front door heavily to prevent our escape, while a voice from somewhere above, in the gloom of the stairs, shouted:

"Comrades, they are police-spies!"

A young, black-haired Jewess of a type seen everywhere in Poland, thin-featured and handsome, with a grey shawl over her shoulders, emerged from a door and peered into my face. There seemed fully fifteen persons in that dingy house, all instantly alarmed at our arrival. Here was, no doubt, the London centre of revolutionary activity directed against the Russian Imperial family and Danilo Danilovitch was in hiding there. It was fortunate, indeed, that the ever-vigilant Tack had succeeded in running him to earth.

I had told Hartwig of the allegation which Tack had made against Danilovitch, that, though in the service of the Secret Police, he had arranged certain attempts against members of the Imperial family, and how he had deliberately killed his sweetheart, Marie Garine. But Hartwig, being chief of the Sûreté, had no connection with the political department, and was, therefore, unaware of any agent of Secret Police known as Danilovitch.

"I remember quite well the case of Marie Garine," he added. "I thoroughly investigated it and found that she had, no doubt, been killed by her lover. But I put it down to jealousy, and as the culprit had left Russia I closed the inquiry."

"Then you could arrest him, even now," I said.

"Not without considerable delay. Besides, in Petersburg they are against applying for extradition in England. The newspapers always hint at the horrors of Siberia in store for the person arrested. And," he added, "I agree that it is quite useless to unnecessarily wound the susceptibilities of my own countrymen, the English." It was those words he had spoken as we had come along Blurton Road.

Our position at that moment was not a very pleasant one, surrounded as we were by a crowd of desperate refugees. If any one of them recognised Ivan Hartwig, then I knew full well that we should never leave the house alive. Men who were conspiring to kill His Majesty the Emperor would not hesitate to kill a police officer and an intruder in order to preserve their secret, "Where is my good friend Danilovitch?" demanded Hartwig, in Russian. "Why does he not come forward?"

"He has not been well, and is in bed," somebody replied. "He is coming in a moment. He lives on the top floor."

"Well, I'm in a hurry, comrades," exclaimed the great detective with a show of impatience. "Do not keep me waiting. I am bearer of a message to you all—an important message from our great and beloved Chief, the saviour of Russia, whose real identity is a secret to all, but whom we know as 'The One'!"

"The One!" echoed two of the men in Russian. "A message from him! What is it? Tell us," they cried eagerly.

"No. The message from our Chief is to our comrade Danilovitch. He will afterwards inform you," was Hartwig's response.

"Who is it there who wants me?" cried an impatient voice in Russian over the banisters.

"I have a message for Danilo Danilovitch," my friend shouted back.

"Then come upstairs," he replied. "Come—both of you."

And we followed a dark figure up to a back room on the second floor—a shabby bed and sitting-room combined.

He struck a match, lit the gas and pulled down the blind. Then as he faced us, a middle-aged man with deeply-furrowed countenance and hair tinged with grey, I at once recognised him—though he no longer wore the small black moustache—as the man I had met on Brighton Pier on the previous night.

"Well," he asked roughly in Russian, "what do you want with me?"

I was gratified that he had not recognised Ivan Hartwig. For a moment he looked inquiringly at me, and no doubt recognised me as the Grand Duchess's companion of the previous night.

His hair was unkempt, his neck was thick, and his unshaven face was broad and coarse. He had the heavy features of a Russian of the lower class, yet his prominent, cunning eyes and high, deeply-furrowed forehead betokened great intelligence. Though of the working-class, yet in his eyes there burned a bright magnetic fire, and one could well imagine how by his inflammatory speeches he led that crowd of ignorant aliens into a belief that by killing His Imperial Majesty they could free Russia of the autocratic yoke. Those men and women, specimens of whom were living in that house at Clapton, never sought to aim at the root of the evil which had gripped the Empire, that brutal camarilla who ruled Russia, but in the madness of their blood-lust and ignorance that they were being betrayed by their leader, and their lives made catspaws by the camarilla itself, they plotted and conspired, and were proud to believe themselves martyrs to what they foolishly termed The Cause!

The face of the traitor before us was full of craft and cunning, the countenance of a shrewd and clever man who, it struck me, was haunted hourly by the dread of betrayal and an ignominious end. Even though he might have been a shoemaker, yet from his perfect self-control, and the manner in which he greeted us, I saw that he was no ordinary man. Indeed, few men could have done—would have dared to do—what he had done, if all Tack had related were true. His personal appearance, his unkempt hair, his limp collar and loosely-tied cravat of black and greasy silk, and his rough suit of shabby dark tweed, his whole ensemble, indeed, was that of the political agitator, the revolutionary firebrand.

"I am here, Danilo Danilovitch," Hartwig said at last very seriously, looking straight at him, "in order to speak to you quite frankly, to put to you several questions."

The man started, and I saw apprehension by the slight movement in the corners of his mouth.

"For what reason?" he snapped quickly. "I thought you were here with a message from our Chief in Russia?"

"I am here with a message, it is true," said the renowned chief of the Russian Sûreté. "You had, I think, better lock that door, and also make quite certain that nobody in this house overhears what I am about to say," he added very slowly and meaningly.

"Why?" inquired the other with some show of defiance.

"If you do not want these comrades of yours to know all your private business, it will be best to lock that door and take care that nobody is listening outside. If they are—well, it will be you, Danilo Danilovitch, who will suffer, not myself," said Hartwig very coolly, his eyes fixed upon the *agent-provocateur*. "I urge you to take precautions of secrecy," he added. "I urge you—for your own sake!"

"For my own sake!" cried the other. "What do you mean?"

Hartwig paused for a few seconds, and then, in a lower voice, said:

"I mean this, Danilo Danilovitch. If a single word of what I am about to say is overheard by anyone in this house you will not go forth again alive. We have been threatened by your comrades down below. But upon you yourself will fall the punishment which is meted out by your comrades to all traitors—*death*!" The man's face changed in an instant. He stood open-mouthed, staring aghast at Hartwig, haggard-eyed and pale to the lips.

Chapter Fourteen
Such is the Law

"Now," Hartwig said, assuming a firm, determined attitude, "I hope you entirely understand me. I am well aware of the despicable double game you are playing, therefore if you refuse me the information I seek I shall go downstairs and tell them how you are employed by His Excellency General Markoff."

The traitor's face was ashen grey. He was, I could see, in wonder at the identity of his visitor. Of course he knew me, but apparently my companion was quite unknown to him. It was always one of Hartwig's greatest precautions to remain unknown to any except perhaps a dozen or so of the detective police immediately under his direction. From the Secret or Political Police he was always careful to hide his identity, knowing well that by so doing he would gain a free hand in his operations in the detection of serious crime. At his own house, a neat, modest little bachelor abode just outside Petersburg, in the Kulikovo quarter, he was known as Herr Otto Schenk, a German teacher of languages, who, possessing a small income, devoted his leisure to his garden and his poultry. None, not even the agents of Secret Police in the Kulikovo district, who reported upon him regularly each month, even suspected that he was the renowned head of the Sûreté.

Standing there presenting such a bucolic appearance, so typically English, and yet speaking Russian perfectly, he caused Danilovitch much curiosity and apprehension.

Suddenly he asked of the spy:

"You were at Brighton last night? With what motive? Tell me."

The man hesitated a moment and replied:

"I went there to visit a friend—a compatriot."

"Yes. Quite true," exclaimed the great police official, leaning against the end of the narrow iron bedstead. "You went to Brighton with an evil purpose. Shall I tell you why? Because you were sent there by your employer General Markoff—sent there as a paid assassin!"

The fellow started.

"What do you mean?" he gasped.

"Just this. That you followed a certain lady who accompanied this gentleman here—followed and watched them for two hours." And then, fixing his big, expressive eyes upon the man he was interrogating, he added: "You followed them because your intention was to carry out the plot conceived by your master—the plot to kill them both!"

"It's a lie!" cried the traitor. "There is no plot."

"Listen," exclaimed Hartwig, in a low, firm voice. "It is your intention to commit an outrage, and having done so, you will denounce to the police certain persons living in this house. Arrests will follow, if any return to Russia, the General will be congratulated by the Emperor upon his astuteness in laying hands so quickly upon the conspirators, and half-a-dozen innocent persons will be sentenced to long terms of imprisonment, if they dare ever go back to their own country. You see," he laughed, "that I am fully aware of the remarkably ingenious programme in progress."

The man's face was pale as death. He saw that his secret was out.

"And now," Hartwig went on: "when I tell these people who live below—your comrades and fellow-workers in the revolutionary cause—what will they say—eh? Well, Danilo Danilovitch, I shall, when I've finished with you, leave you to their tender mercies. You remember, perhaps, the fate of Boutakoff, the informer at Kieff, how he was attached to a baulk of timber and placed upon a circular saw, how Raspopoff died of slow starvation in the hands of those whom he had betrayed at Moscow, and how Mirski, in Odessa, was horribly tortured and killed by the three brothers of the unfortunate girl he had given into the hands of the police. No," he laughed, "your friends show neither leniency nor humanity towards those who betray them."

"But you will not do this!" gasped the man, his eyes dilated by fear, now that he had been brought to bay.

"I have explained my intention," replied Hartwig slowly and firmly.

"But you will not!" he cried. "I—I implore you to spare me! You appear to know everything."

"Yes," was the reply. "I know how, by your perfidious actions, dozens, nay hundreds, of innocent persons have been sent into exile. To the revolutionists throughout the whole of Russia there is one great leader known as 'The One'—the leader whose identity is unknown, but whose word is law among a hundred thousand conspirators. You are that man! Your mandates are obeyed to the letter, but you keep your identity profoundly secret. These poor misguided fools who follow you believe that the secrecy as to the identity of their fearless leader whom they only know as 'The Wonder Worker,' or generally 'The One,' is due to a fear of arrest. Ah! Danilo Danilovitch," he laughed, "you who lead them so cleverly are a strong man, and a clever man. You hold the fate of all revolutionary Russia in your hand. You form plots, you get your poor, ill-read puppets to carry them out, and afterwards you send them to Siberia in batches of hundreds. A clever game this game of terrorism. But I tell you frankly it is at an end now. What will these comrades of yours say when they are made aware that 'The One'—the man believed by so many to be sent providentially to sweep away the dynasty and kill the enemies of freedom—is identical with Danilo Danilovitch, the bootmaker of Kazan and police-spy. Rather a blow to the revolutionary organisation—eh?"

"And a blow for you," I added, addressing the unkempt-looking fellow for the first time. Though I confess that I did not recognise him as the man who threw the bomb in Petersburg, I added: "It was you who committed the dastardly outrage upon the Grand Duke Nicholas, and for which many innocent persons are now immured in those terrible cells below the water at Schusselburg—you who intend that His Imperial Highness's daughter and myself shall die!" I cried.

He made no reply. He saw that we were in possession of all the facts concerning his disgraceful past. I could see how intensely agitated he had become, and though he was striving to conceal his fear, yet his thin, sinewy hands were visibly trembling.

"You admit, by your silence, that you were author of that brutal outrage!" exclaimed Hartwig quickly. "In it, my friend here narrowly escaped with his life. Now, answer me this question," he demanded imperiously. "With what motive did you launch that bomb at the Grand Duke's carriage?"

"With the same motive that every attempt is made," was his bold reply.

"You lie!" Hartwig said bluntly. "That plot was not yours. Confess it."

"No plot is mine. The various revolutionary circles form plots, and I, as the unknown head, approve of them. But," asked the spy suddenly, "who are you that you should question me thus?"

"I have already given you my name," he said. "Ivan Arapoff, of Petersburg."

"Then, Mr Arapoff, I think we may change the topic of conversation," said the man, suddenly quite calm and collected. I detected that, though an unprincipled scoundrel and without either conscience or remorse, his was yet a strong and impelling personality—a man who, among the enthusiastic students and the younger generation of Russia, which form the bulk of the revolutionists, would no doubt be listened to and obeyed as a leader.

"Good. If you wish me to leave you, I will do so. I will go and have a little chat with your interesting and enlightened friends downstairs," exclaimed Hartwig with a triumphant laugh. Then, turning to me, he added: "Come, Mr Trewinnard, let's go."

"No!" gasped the spy. "No, stop! I—I want to fully understand what your intentions are—now that you know the truth concerning the identity of 'The One' and other recent matters."

"Intentions!" echoed the great detective. "I have none. I have merely forewarned you of what you must expect—the fate of the informer, unless—"

"Unless what?" he cried.

"Unless you confess the object of the outrage upon the Grand Duke."

"I tell you I do not know."

"But the plot was your own. None of your comrades knew of it."

"It was not my own."

"You carried it out?"

"And if I admit anything you will hand me over to the police—eh?"

"Surely you know that is impossible in England. You cannot be arrested here for a political crime," Hartwig said.

"I saw you throw the bomb," I added. "You were dressed differently, but I now recognise you. Come, admit it."

"I admit nothing," he answered sullenly. "You are both of you entirely welcome to your opinions."

"Forty persons are now in prison for your crime," I said. "Have you no remorse—no pity?"

"I have nothing to say."

"But you shall speak," I cried angrily. "Once I nearly lost my life because of the outrage you committed, and last night you followed me in Brighton with the distinct purpose of killing both Her Highness and myself. But you were frustrated—or perhaps you feared arrest. But I tell you plainly, if ever I catch you in our vicinity again I shall hand you over to the nearest policeman. And at the police-court the truth concerning 'The One' will quickly be revealed and seized upon by the halfpenny press."

"We need not wait for that, Mr Trewinnard," remarked Hartwig. "We can deal with him this evening—once and for all. When we leave here we shall leave with the knowledge that 'The One' no longer exists and the revolutionary party—Terrorists, as they are pleased to call themselves on account of the false bogy which the Secret Police have raised in Russia—will take their own steps towards punishing the man to whom they owe all the great disasters which have befallen their schemes during the past couple of years. Truly, the vengeance of the Terrorist against his betrayer is a terrible vengeance indeed."

As he spoke the creak of a footstep was heard on the landing outside the locked door.

I raised my finger to command silence, whereupon the man known throughout all revolutionary Russia as "The One" crossed the room swiftly, and unlocking the door, looked out. But he found no one.

Yet I feel certain that someone had been lurking there. That slow creak of the bare boards showed that the pressure of a foot had been released. Yet whoever had been listening had escaped swiftly down the stairs, now dark and unlighted. Danilovitch reentered the bedroom, his face white as a sheet.

"Somebody has overheard!" he gasped in a low, hoarse voice. "They know the truth!"

"Yes," responded my companion in a hard, distinct tone. "They know the truth because of your own failure to be frank with us. I warned you. But you have not heeded."

"Your words were overheard," he whispered. "They no doubt suspected you to be officers of police who had found me here in my hiding-place, and were, therefore, listening. I was a fool!" he cried, throwing his hands above his head. "I was an accursed fool!"

His lips were grey, his dark eyes seemed to be starting from his head.

Well did he know the terrible fate which awaited him as a betrayer and informer.

"Why did you throw that bomb?" I cried. "Why did you last night follow the Grand Duchess Natalia with such evil intent? Tell me," I urged.

"No!" cried "The One," springing at me fiercely. "I will tell you nothing—nothing!" he shrieked. "You have betrayed me—you have cast me into the hands of my enemies. But, by Heaven! you shall neither of you leave this place alive," he shrieked. "My comrades shall deal with you as you justly deserve. I will see that you are not allowed to speak. Neither of you shall utter a single word against me!"

Then with a harsh, triumphant laugh he called loudly for help to those below.

In an instant Hartwig and I both realised that the tables had been suddenly and unexpectedly turned upon us, and that we were now placed in most deadly and imminent peril. The object of the informer was to close our mouths at once, for only by so doing could he save himself from that terrible fate which must assuredly befall him.

It was his own life—or ours!

Chapter Fifteen
A Statement by the Informer

Quick as lightning, Hartwig drew a big Browning revolver and thrust it into the informer's face, exclaiming firmly:

"Another word and it will be your last!"

The fellow started back, unprepared for such defiance. He made a movement to cross the room, where no doubt he had his own weapon concealed, but the police officer was too quick for him and barred his passage.

"Look here!" he said firmly. "This is a matter to be settled between us, without any interference by your friends here. At word from me they would instantly turn upon you as an enemy. Think! Reflect well—before it is too late!" And he held the revolver steadily a foot from the man's hard, pale face.

Danilovitch hesitated. He controlled the so-called Terrorist movement with amazing ingenuity, playing three *rôles* simultaneously. He was "The One," the mysterious but all-powerful head of the organisation; the ardent worker in the cause known as "the shoemaker of Kazan"; and the base, unscrupulous informer, who manufactured plots, and afterwards consigned to prison all those men and women who became implicated in them.

"If I withdraw my cry of alarm will you promise secrecy?" he asked in a low, cringing tone.

From the landing outside came sounds of footsteps and fierce demands in Russian from those he had summoned to his assistance. Two of us against twenty desperate characters as they were, would, I well knew, stand but a poor chance. If he made any allegation against us, we should be caught like rats in a trap, and killed, as all police-spies are killed when denounced. The arm of the Russian revolution is indeed a long one—longer than that of the Secret Police itself.

"What has happened, Danilo?" demanded a man's rough voice. "Who are those strangers? Let us in!"

"Speak!" commanded Hartwig. "Reassure them, and let them go away. I have still much to say to you in private."

His arm with the revolver was upraised, his eyes unwavering. The informer saw determination in his gaze. A further word of alarm, and a bullet would pass through his brain.

For a few seconds he stood in sullen silence.

"All right!" he shouted to them at last. "It is nothing, comrades. I was mistaken. Leave us in peace."

We heard a murmuring of discontent outside, and then the footsteps commenced to descend the steep uncarpeted stairs. As they did so, Hartwig dropped his weapon, saying:

"Now let us sit down and talk. I have several questions I wish to put to you. If you answer frankly, then I promise that I will not betray you to your comrades."

"What do you mean by 'frankly'?"

"I mean that you must tell me the exact truth."

The man's face grew dark; his brows contracted; he bit his finger-nails.

"What was the motive of the attempt you made upon the Grand Duke Nicholas and his daughter, and the gentleman here, Mr Trewinnard?"

"I don't know," he replied.

"But you yourself committed the outrage?"

"At the orders of others."

"Whose orders?"

He did not reply. He was standing against the small, cheap chest of drawers, his drawn face full in the light of the hissing gas-jet.

"Come," said Hartwig firmly. "I wish to know this."

"I cannot tell you."

"Then I will tell you," the detective said in a hard voice. "It was at the orders of your master, General Markoff—the man who, finding that you were a revolutionist, is using you as his tool for the manufacture of bogus plots against the Emperor."

Danilovitch shrugged his shoulders, but uttered no word.

"And you went again to Brighton last night at his orders. You—"

"I went to Brighton, I admit. But not at the General's orders," he interrupted quickly.

"Why did you go? Why did you follow Her Imperial Highness and Mr Trewinnard?"

"I followed them because I had an object in so doing."

"A sinister object?"

"No. There you are mistaken. My object was not a sinister one. It was to watch and endeavour to make clear a certain point which is a mystery to me."

"A point concerning what?"

"Concerning Her Imperial Highness," was his reply.

"How does Her Highness concern you?" I asked. "You tried to kill her once. Therefore your intentions must be evil."

"I deny that," he protested quickly. "I tell you that I went to Brighton without thought of any evil intent, and without the orders, or even knowledge, of General Markoff."

"But he is Her Highness's enemy."

"Yes, Excellency—and yours also."

"Tell me all that you know," I urged, adopting a more conciliatory tone. "It is outrageous that this oppressor of Russia should conspire to kill an innocent member of the Imperial Family."

"I know nothing of the circumstances. Excellency," he said, feigning entire ignorance.

"But he gave you orders to throw that bomb," I said. "What were your exact orders?"

"I am not likely to betray my employer," he laughed. "If you do not answer these questions, then I shall carry out my threat of exposure," Hartwig said in a hard, determined voice.

"Well," said the informer hesitatingly, "my orders were not to throw the bomb unless the Grand Duchess Natalia was in the carriage."

"Then the plot was to kill her—but unfortunately her father fell the victim of the dastardly outrage!" I cried.

"Yes," the man replied. "It was to kill her—and you, Excellency."

"But why?"

He shrugged his shoulders, and exhibited his palms in a gesture of complete ignorance.

"And your present intention is to effect in Brighton what you failed to do in Petersburg—eh?"

"I have no orders, and it certainly is not my intention," responded the man, whom I remembered at that moment had deliberately killed the girl Garine in order to preserve his secret.

I turned from him in loathing and disgust.

"But you tell me that General Markoff intends that we both shall come to an untimely end," I said a few moments later.

"He does, Excellency, and the ingenuity of the plot against you both is certainly one which betrays his devilish cunning," was the fellow's reply. "I have, I assure you, no love for a man who holds my life in the hollow of his hand, and whose word I am compelled to obey on pain of exposure and death."

"You mean Markoff," I exclaimed. "Tell me something of this plot against me—so that I may be on my guard," I urged.

"I know nothing concerning it. For that very reason I went to Brighton yesterday, to try and discover something," he said.

"And what did you discover?"

"A very remarkable fact. At present it is only suspicion. I have yet to substantiate it."

"Cannot you tell me your suspicion?"

"Not until I have had an opportunity of proving it," was his quiet reply. "But I assure you that the observation I kept upon Her Imperial Highness and yourself was with no evil intent."

I smiled incredulously. It was hard indeed to believe a man of his subtle and unscrupulous character. All that Tack had told me crowded through my brain. As the catspaw of Markoff, it was not likely that he would tell me the truth.

Hartwig was leaning easily against the wooden mantelshelf, watching us keenly. Of a sudden an idea occurred to me, and addressing the informer, I said:

"I believe you are acquainted with my friend Madame de Rosen and her daughter. Tell me what you know concerning them."

"They were arrested and exiled to Siberia for the attempt in the Nevski on the return of the Emperor from the south," he said promptly.

Hartwig interrupted, saying gravely:

"And that attempt, Danilo Danilovitch, was conceived by you—conceived in order to strike terror into the Emperor's heart. You formed the plot and handed over the list of the conspirators to your employer, Markoff—you, the person known to the Party of the People's Will as 'The One.'"

"I knew of the plot," he admitted. "And though I gave certain names to the police, I certainly did not include the names of Madame de Rosen or of Mademoiselle."

"Why was she arrested?"

He was silent for a few moments.

"Because her presence in Petersburg was dangerous to the General," he said at last sullenly.

"You know this—eh? You are certain of it—you have evidence, I mean?" asked Hartwig.

"You ask me for the truth," the informer said, "and I tell you. I was extremely sorry for Madame and the young lady, for I knew them when I carried on my trade as bootmaker. An hour after their arrest, at about four o'clock in the morning, the General ordered me to go and search their house for certain letters which he described to me—letters which he was extremely anxious to obtain. I went alone, as he did not wish to alarm the neighbourhood by a domiciliary visit of the police. I searched the house for nearly nine hours, but failed to discover them. While still engaged in the investigation I was recalled to the house where it is my habit to meet the General in secret, when he told me that by a false promise of release he had extracted from Madame a statement that the letters were no longer in her possession, and that Her Imperial Highness the Grand Duchess Natalia held them in safe-keeping. Madame, perfectly innocent as she was of any connection with the conspirators, expected to be released after telling the truth; but the General said that he had only laughed in her face and ordered her and her daughter to be sent off with the next convoy of prisoners—who were leaving for Siberia that same night. By this time the ladies are, I expect, already in the great forwarding-prison at Tomsk."

"And the letters?" I demanded, my blood boiling at hearing his story.

"I was ordered to search for them." Danilovitch replied. "The General gave me instructions how to enter the palace of the Grand Duke Nicholas and there to investigate the apartments of the Grand Duchess Natalia. I refused at first, knowing that if I were detected as an intruder I should be shot at sight by the sentries. But he insisted," the man added. "He told me that if I persisted in my refusal he would expose me as a spy. So I was compelled to make the attempt, well knowing that discovery meant certain death. The sentries have orders to shoot any intruder in the Grand Ducal palace. On four occasions I went there at imminent risk, and on the fourth I was successful. I found the letters concealed in a room which had once been used as Her Highness's nursery."

"And what did you do with them?"

"I met the General at our usual meeting-place and handed them to him. He was at first delighted. But a moment later, finding that the seal of the envelope in which were the letters had been broken, he charged me with reading them. I denied it, and—"

"Then you did not read them? You do not know what they contained, or who they were from?"

"They were from General Markoff himself. I looked at the signatures, but, alas! I had no time to read them. I drove straight to the meeting-place, where the General was awaiting me."

"They were from the General!" I echoed. "To whom?"

"They bore his signature—one a long letter, closely written," was the informer's reply. "Seeing that the seal had been broken, the General flew into a sudden rage and declared that the Grand Duchess Natalia had learned what they contained. The words he used to me were: 'The girl must be silenced—silenced at once, Danilovitch. And you must silence her. She knows the truth!'"

"Well?" I asked.

"Well," he said, his mouth drawn and hard, "under compulsion and more threats of exposure, I launched the bomb, which, alas! killed her father, while the young lady escaped unhurt."

"Then he still intends that Her Highness shall die? His warning the other day was no idle attempt to terrorise me?"

"No, Excellency. Take every precaution. The General means mischief, for he is in hourly fear lest Her Highness should expose certain facts contained in those fateful letters which have already cost two ladies their liberty and a Grand Duke and several Cossacks their lives."

"Is this the actual truth?" asked Hartwig in a changed voice, looking the informer full in the face.

"Yes," he answered solemnly. "I have told you the truth; therefore I believe your solemn word that you will make no exposure to the Party."

"If you will disassociate yourself from these dastardly actions," he said.

"Ah!" sighed the other in despair, "that is impossible. The General holds me always to the compact I made with him. But I beg of you to be warned," he added. "Her Highness is daily in gravest peril!"

Chapter Sixteen
Incognita!

Shortly after eleven o'clock that same evening I was strolling with Hartwig up and down the deserted platform at Victoria Station, my intention being to take the eleven-fifty p.m. train back to Brighton.

For a full hour we had pressed the informer to explain the real reason of his visit to Brighton on the previous day. But beyond assuring us that it was not with any evil intent—which I confess we could scarcely believe—he declined to reveal anything.

He only repeated his warning that Natalia was in grave personal danger, and entreated me to be careful. The refugees in that house, all of them Russians, seemed filled with intense curiosity regarding us, and especially so, perhaps, because of Hartwig's declaration that he was bearer of a message from that mysterious leader who was believed to live somewhere in Moscow, and was known throughout the Russian Empire as "The One."

No doubt after our departure Danilovitch had told them of some secret message he had received from the mysterious head of the organisation, who was none other than himself.

But his confession had held both of us practically silent ever since we had left that dingy house in Lower Clapton.

"Markoff believes that Her Highness is aware of the contents of those letters," Hartwig said as we strolled together in the great, well-lit station. Few people were about just at that hour, for the suburban theatre-goers had not yet arrived. "For that reason it is intended that her mouth shall be closed."

"But this is murder!" I cried in hot indignation. "I will go straight to the Emperor, and tell him."

"And what benefit would that be? His Majesty would declare it to be an effort by some of the General's enemies to disgrace him," my companion said. "Such damning statements have been made before, but, alas! no heed has been taken of them!"

"But His Majesty shall hear—and he shall take notice! I will demand in inquiry into the arrest and exile of Madame de Rosen."

"I thought you told me that you had already mentioned her name to His Majesty," Hartwig said quietly.

I had forgotten. Yes. His words recalled to me my effort on her behalf, and the futility of my appeal. I sighed, and bit my lip. The two innocent ladies were on their way to that far-off dreaded penal settlement of Yakutsk. From the time which had elapsed since their arrest I calculated that they were already in Siberia, trudging that long, never-ending post road—that wide, deeply-rutted track which runs across those boundless plains between Tobolsk and Tomsk—on the first stage of their terrible journey of over six thousand miles on foot.

A sudden suggestion flashed across my mind. Should I follow, overtake them and hear the truth from Marya de Rosen's lips?

Yet before doing so I should be compelled to apply for a passport and permits at the Ministry of the Interior at Petersburg. If I did this, Markoff would at once suspect my intention, for travellers do not go to Siberia for pleasure. And if he suspected my intention a way would quickly be found by which, when I arrived at my destination, neither of the ladies would be alive. In Siberia, where there is neither law nor inquiry, it was, I knew, very easy to close the lips of any person whose existence might be prejudicial to the authorities. A word from General Markoff, and an accident would certainly occur.

No. I realised that to relax my vigilance over the safety of Natalia at that moment would be most injudicious. Besides, was not Natalia herself aware of the contents of the letters? If not, why had her enemies made the firm determination that she should meet with a sudden and mysterious end?

I mentioned to my companion my inclination to travel across Siberia in search of the exiles; but he only shook his head gravely, saying:

"You are, no doubt, under very close observation. Even if you went, you might, by so doing, place yourself in grave personal peril. Remember, Markoff is desperate. The contents of those letters, whatever they may be, are evidently so damning that he cannot afford exposure. The pains he took to secure them, and to send Madame de Rosen into exile, plainly show this. No," he added, "the most judicious plan is to remain here, near Her Highness, and watch Markoff's operations."

"If Her Highness would only reveal to me the secret of those letters, then we should be in a position to defy Markoff and reveal him before the Emperor in his true light," I said.

"She has refused—eh?"

"Yes. I have questioned her a dozen times, but always with the same result," was my answer.

"But will she refuse, if she knows that her father's tragic end was due to the wild desire of Markoff to close her lips?"

"Yes. I have already pointed that out to her. Her reply is that what she learnt was in confidence. It is her friend's secret, and she cannot betray it. She is the very soul of honour. Her word is her bond."

"You will tell her now of Danilovitch's confession; how the letters were stolen and handed back to the General by the man whom he holds so completely in his power?" Hartwig said.

"I shall. But I fear it will make no difference. She is, of course, eager to expose the General to the Emperor and effect his downfall. She is fully aware of his corrupt and brutal maladministration of the department of Political Police, of the bogus plots, and the wholesale deportment of thousands of innocent persons. But it seems that she gave a pledge of secrecy to poor madame, and that pledge she refuses to break at any cost. 'It is Marya's secret,' she told me, 'not mine.'"

As we were speaking, a tall, straight, good-looking young man in crush-hat and black overcoat over his dinner-clothes had strolled along the platform awaiting the train.

My eyes caught his features as he went, when suddenly I recognised in the young man Richard Drury, whom Her Highness had told me she had known in her school-days at Eastbourne. I glanced after him and watched his figure retreating leisurely as he smoked a cigarette until he came beneath a lamp where he halted. Then, producing an evening paper, he commenced to while away the time by reading. He was evidently returning to Brighton by my train.

Apparently the young fellow had not recognised me as Miss Gottorp's companion of the previous night, therefore standing near, I had an opportunity of examining him well. He was certainly a typical specimen of the keen, clean-shaven young Englishman, a man who showed good-breeding, and whose easy air was that of the gentleman.

Yet I confess that what Her Highness had revealed to me both alarmed and annoyed me. Madcap that she was, I knew not what folly she might commit. Nevertheless, after all, so long as she preserved her *incognito* no great harm would be done. It was hard upon her to deny her the least suspicion of flirtation, especially with one whom she had known in the days before she had put up her hair and put on her ankle-frocks.

Hartwig and I were undecided what our next move should be, and we were discussing it. One fact was plain, that in view of the assertion of Danilovitch, I would now be compelled to keep constant watch over the skittish young lady whom the Emperor had given into my charge. My idea of following and overtaking Madame de Rosen in Siberia was out of all question.

"Are you remaining long in London?" I asked the police official, just as I was about to step into the train.

"Who knows?" he laughed. "I am at the 'Savoy.' The Embassy is unaware I am in England. But I move quickly, as you know. Perhaps to-morrow I may have to return to Petersburg. *Au revoir*."

And I wished him adieu, and got into an empty first-class compartment just as the train was moving from the platform.

I sat in the corner of the carriage full of grave and apprehensive thoughts.

That strange suspicion which the Emperor had revealed to me on the afternoon before the last Court ball recurred to me. I held my breath as a sudden idea flashed across my brain. Had it any connection with this foul but cunningly-conceived plot to kill an innocent girl whose only offence was that she was in possession of certain information which, if revealed, would, I presumed, cause the downfall of that camarilla surrounding the Emperor?

The thought held me in wonder.

Ah! if only the Emperor would listen to the truth—if only he would view Markoff and his friends in their true character! But I knew, alas! that such development of the situation was impossible. Russia, and with her the Imperial Court, was being terrorised by these desperate attempts to assassinate the Emperor. Hence His Majesty relied upon Markoff for the safety of the dynasty. He looked upon him as a marvel of astuteness and cunning, as indeed he was. But, alas! the burly, grave-eyed man who led a life haunted by the hourly fear of death—an existence in armoured rooms and armoured trains, and surrounded by guards whom he even grew to suspect—was in ignorance that the greater part of the evidence of conspiracies, incriminating correspondence and secret proclamations put before him had been actually manufactured by Markoff himself!

At last, after an hour, the express ran slowly into the Brighton terminus, and as it did so, I caught sight of a figure waiting upon the platform, which caused me to quickly draw back. The figure was that of a young girl neatly dressed in black with a small black hat, and though she wore a veil of spotted net I recognised her at once as Natalia! She was smiling and waving her tiny black-gloved hand to someone. In an instant I knew the truth. She was there, even though it were past one o'clock in the morning, to meet her lover, Richard Drury.

I saw him spring out, raise his hat and shake her hand warmly, and then, taking care not to be seen, I followed them out as they walked side by side down the hill in the direction of King's Road.

This action of hers showed her recklessness and lack of discretion. Apparently she had walked all the way from Hove in order to meet him, and as they strolled together along the dark, deserted road he was evidently explaining something to her, while she listened very attentively.

Surely it was unsafe for her to go forth like that! I was surprised that Miss West allowed it. But, in all probability that worthy lady was in bed, and asleep, all unconscious of her charge's escapade.

I had not followed very far before I became aware of a footstep behind me, and, turning, I saw a small, insignificant-looking man in dark clothes, who came quickly up to me. It was one of the police-agents employed at the house in Brunswick Square.

"Well, Dmitri!" I exclaimed in a low voice in French. "So you are looking after your young mistress—eh?" I asked, with a laugh, pausing to speak with him in order to allow the lovers to get further off.

"Yes, m'sieur," replied the man in a tone of distinct annoyance.

"This is hardly wise of Her Highness," I said. "This is not the hour to go out for a stroll."

"No, m'sieur," replied the shrewd agent of police, who had been for years employed at the palace of the late Grand Duke Nicholas in Petersburg. "I tell you I do not think it either safe or proper. These constant meetings must result in scandal."

"Who is that young man?" I asked quickly. "You have made inquiry, no doubt?"

"Yes, m'sieur, I have. But I can learn very little. He seems to be a complete mystery—an adventurer, perhaps," declared the suspicious police-agent in a low, hard voice; adding: "The fact is, that man who calls himself Richard Drury is, I feel sure, no fit companion for Her Imperial Highness."

"Why not?" I demanded in eager surprise.

"Because he is not," was the man's enigmatical reply. "I do hope m'sieur will warn Her Imperial Highness of the danger," he said reflectively, looking in the direction of the retreating figures.

"Danger!" I echoed. "What danger?"

"There is a grave danger," he asserted firmly. "I have watched, as is my duty, and I know. Her Highness endeavours all she can to evade my vigilance, for naturally it is not pleasant to be watched while carrying on a flirtation. But she does not know what I have discovered concerning this stranger with whom she appears to have fallen so deeply in love. They must be parted, m'sieur—parted at once, before it is too late."

"But what have you discovered?" I asked.

"One astounding and most startling fact," was his slow, deliberate reply; "a fact which demands their immediate separation."

Chapter Seventeen
Her Highness is Outspoken

"Now, Uncle Colin! It's really too horrid of you to spy upon me like that! I had no idea you were behind us! I knew old Dmitri was there—he watches me just as a cat watches a mouse. But I never thought you would be so nasty and mean!" And the girl in her fresh white gown stood at the window of the drawing-room drumming impatiently upon the pane with the tips of her long, white fingers, for it was raining outside.

"My dear Natalia," I said paternally, standing upon the white goat-skin hearthrug, and looking across at her; "I did not watch you intentionally. I travelled by the same train as your friend, and I saw you meet him. Really," I laughed, "you looked a most interesting pair as you walked together down Queen's Road. I left you at the corner of Western Road and went on to the 'Métropole.'"

"Oh! you actually did have the decency to do that!" she exclaimed, turning to me her pretty face clouded by displeasure. "Well, I say quite frankly that I think it was absolutely horrid of you. Surely I may meet a friend without being spied upon at every turn!" she added resentfully.

"Dmitri only does his duty, remember," I ventured to remark.

"Oh, Dmitri's a perfect plague. He shadows me everywhere. His crafty face irritates me whenever I see it."

"This constant surveillance is only for your own protection," I said. "Recollect that you are a member of the Imperial family, and that already six of your uncles and cousins, as well as your poor father, have met with violent deaths at the hands of the revolutionists."

"I know. But it is perfectly absurd ever to dream that they want to kill me—a girl whose only object is to live quietly and enjoy her life."

"And her flirtations," I added, striving to make her laugh.

I was successful, for a smile came to her pretty, pouting lips, and she said:

"Well, Uncle Colin, other girls may flirt and have men friends. Therefore I can't see why it is so actually sinful for me to do the same."

"But think for a moment of your position!"

"Position!" she echoed. "I'm only plain Miss Natalia Gottorp here. Why should I study my family?"

"Ah!" I sighed. "I know how wayward you are. No amount of argument will, I fear, ever convince you of your error."

"Oh, yes," she sighed, in imitation of the sadness of my tone, saying: "I know what a source of trouble and deep anxiety the wicked, wayward child is to you." Then, next moment, she burst out into a merry, mischievous laugh, adding:

"It's really too bad of me to tease you, poor old Uncle Colin, isn't it? But there, you're not really old. I looked you up in 'Who's Who' only yesterday. You're only thirty-two next Thursday week. And if you are a very good boy I'll give you a nice little present. Shall I work you a pair of slippers—eh?" she asked, with sarcasm, "or a winter waistcoat?"

"Thanks. I hate girls' needlework," I replied frankly, amused at her sudden change of demeanour.

"Very well. You shall have a new cigarette-case, a solid gold one, with our grand Imperial arms engraved on it and underneath the words 'From Tattie.' How will that do—eh?" she laughed.

"Ah! now you're only trying to tease me," I said. "I wonder if you tease Mr Drury like that?"

"Oh! Dick knows me. He doesn't mind it in the least," she declared, looking at me with those wonderful eyes that were so much admired everywhere. "Have a cigarette," and she handed me a box of Petroffs, and taking one herself, lit it, and then threw herself negligently into an armchair, lazily displaying a pair of neat silk stockinged ankles and patent-leather shoes.

"I certainly think that Mr Dick is a very lucky young fellow," I said, "though I tell you openly that I entirely disapprove of these constant meetings. Remember your promise to me before we left Petersburg."

"Well, I've been a very wayward child—even an incorrigible child, I suppose—and I've broken my promise. That's all," she said, blowing a cloud of smoke from her red lips. Like all Russian ladies, she enjoyed a cigarette.

"I certainly think you ought to have kept your word," I said.

"But Dick, I tell you, is an old friend. I couldn't cut him, could I?"

"You need not have cut him," I said. "But I consider it unnecessary to steal out of the house after Miss West has gone to bed, and meet him at the station at one o'clock in the morning."

"Then upon that point we'll agree to differ. I'm old enough to be my own mistress, and if you continue to lecture me, I shall be very annoyed with you."

"My dear Natalia, I do not blame you in the least for falling in love. How can I?" I said in a changed tone, for I knew that the young lady so petted and spoiled by her earlier training must be treated with greatest caution and tact. "Why, shall I confess a truth?" I asked, looking her straight in the face.

"Yes, do," she said.

"Well, if I were ten years younger I should most certainly fall in love with you myself," I laughed.

"Don't be so silly, Uncle Colin!" she exclaimed. "But would that be so very terrible? Why, you're not an old man yet," she added, her cheeks having flushed slightly at my words.

"Now you're blushing," I said.

"I'm not!" she cried stoutly. "You're simply horrid this morning," she declared vehemently, turning away from me.

"Is it horrid of me to pay you a compliment?" I asked. "I merely expressed a devout wish that I were standing in Drury's shoes. Every man likes to be kissed by a pretty girl, whether she be a shopgirl or a Grand Duchess."

"Oh, yes. You are quite right there. Most men make fools of themselves over women."

"Especially when their beauty is so world-famed as that of the Grand Duchess Natalia!"

"Now, there you are again!" she cried. "I do wish you'd change the topic of conversation. You're horrid, I say."

And she gave a quick gesture of impatience, blew a great cloud of smoke from her lips and put down her half-consumed cigarette upon the little silver ashtray.

"Oh, my!" she exclaimed at last. "What a funny lover you would make, Uncle Colin! You fancy yourself as old as Methuselah, and your hidebound ideas of etiquette, your straitlaced morality, and your respect of *les convenances* are those in vogue when your revered Queen Victoria ascended the throne of Great Britain. You're not living with the times, my dear uncle. You're an old-fashioned diplomat. To-day the world is very different to that in which your father was born."

"I quite agree. And I regret that it is so," I replied. "These are surely very lax and degenerating days, when girls may go out unchaperoned, and the meeting of a man in the early hours of the morning passes unremarked."

"It unfortunately hasn't passed unremarked," she said, with a pretty pout. "You take jolly good care to rub it in every moment! It really isn't fair," she declared. "I'm very fond of you, Uncle Colin, but you are really a little too old-fashioned."

"You are comparing me with young Drury, I suppose?"

"Oh, Dick isn't a bit old-fashioned, I assure you," she declared. "He's been at Oxford. He doesn't dream and let the world go by. But, Uncle Colin," she went on, "I wonder that you, a diplomat, are so stiff and proper. I suppose it's the approved British diplomatic training. I'm only a girl, and therefore am not supposed to know any of the tremendous secrets of diplomacy. But it always strikes me that, for the most part, you diplomats are exceptionally dull folk. In our Court circle we always declare them to be inflated with a sense of their own importance, and fifty years behind the times."

I laughed outright. Her view was certainly a common-sense one. The whole training of British diplomacy is to continue the traditions of Pitt and Beaconsfield. Diplomacy does not, alas! admit a new and modern *régime* affecting the world; it ignores modern thought, modern conditions and modern methods. "Up-to-date" is an expression unknown in the diplomat's vocabulary. The Foreign Office instil the lazy, do-nothing policy of the past, the traditions of Palmerston, Clarendon and Dudley are still the traditions of to-day in every British Embassy throughout the world; and, unfortunately for Britain, the lesson has yet to be learned by our diplomacy that to be strong is to be acute and subtle, and to be dictatorial is to be entirely up-to-date. The German diplomacy is that of keen progress and anticipation; that of Turkey craft and cunning; of France, tact, with exquisite politeness. But Britain pursues her heavy, blundering "John Bull" programme, which, though effective in the days of Beaconsfield, now only results in the nation's isolation and derision, certain of her ambassadors to the Powers being familiarly known at the Courts to which they are accredited as "The Man with the Gun."

"What you say is, in a sense, quite true," I admitted. "But I'm so sorry if I'm really very dull. I don't mean to be."

"Oh! You'll improve under my tuition—and Dick's—no doubt," she exclaimed reassuringly.

Her Highness was nothing if not outspoken.

"The fact is, Uncle Colin," she went on seriously, "you're far too old-fashioned for your age. You are not old, but your ideas are so horribly antiquated. Girls of to-day are allowed a freedom which our grandmothers would have held as perfectly sinful. Girls have become independent. A young fellow takes a girl out to dinner and to the theatre, and even to supper nowadays, and nobody holds up their hands in pious horror—only you! It isn't fair," she declared.

"Girls of the people are allowed a great deal of latitude, I admit. And as far as I can see, the world is none the worse for it," I said. "But what other girls may do, you, an Imperial Highness, unfortunately may not."

"That's just where we don't agree," she said in a tone meant to be impertinent, her straight nose slightly raised as she spoke. "I intend to do as other girls do—at least, while I'm plain Miss Gottorp. They call me the 'Little Alien'—so Miss West heard me called the other day."

"No," I said very firmly, looking straight at her as she lolled easily in her chair, her chin resting on her white palm as she gazed at me from beneath her long, dark lashes. "You really must respect the *convenances*. If you take a stroll with young Drury, do so at least in the daylight."

"And with Dmitri watching me all the time from across the road. Not quite," she said. "I like the Esplanade when it is quiet and everybody is in bed. It is so pleasant on these warm nights to sit upon a seat and enjoy the moonlight on the sea. Sounds like an extract from a novel, doesn't it?" and she laughed merrily.

"I fear you are becoming romantic," I said. "Every girl becomes so at one period of her life."

"Do you think so?" she asked, smiling. "Myself, I don't fancy I have any romance in me. The Romanoffs are not a romantic lot as a rule. They are usually too mercenary. I love nice things."

"Because you are cultured and possess good taste. That is exactly what leads to romance."

"I have the good taste to choose Dick as a friend, I suppose you mean?" she asked, with an intention to irritate me.

"Ah, I did not exactly say that."

"But you meant it, nevertheless. You know you did, Uncle Colin."

I did not reply for a few moments. I was recalling what Dmitri had told me—that strange allegation of his that this young man, Richard Drury, was an enigma, an adventurer. He had told me that he was no fit companion for her, and yet when pressed he apparently could give no plain reason. He had been unable to discover much concerning the young fellow—probably because of his failure it seemed he had become convinced that the object of his inquiry was an adventurer.

Suddenly rising, I stood before her, and placing my hand upon her shoulder, said:

"I came here this morning to speak to you very seriously, Natalia. Can you really be serious for once?"

"I'm always serious," she replied. "Well—another lecture?"

"No, not a lecture, you incorrigible little flirt. I want to ask you a plain question. Please answer me, for a great deal—a very great deal—depends upon it. Are you aware of what was contained in those letters which Madame de Rosen gave you for safe-keeping?"

"I have long ago assured you that I am. Why do you ask again?"

"Because there is one point which I wish to clear up," I said. "I thought you told me that they were in a sealed envelope?"

"So they were. But when I heard of Marya's exile, and that Luba had been sent with her, I broke open the seal and investigated the contents."

"And what did you find?"

"Ah! That is my business, Uncle Colin. I have already told you that I absolutely refuse to betray the secrets of my poor dear friend. You surely ought not to ask me. You have no right to press me to commit such a breach of trust."

"I ask you because so much depends upon the extent of your knowledge," I said. "I have already solved the secret of the disappearance of the letters from the place where you hid them in the palace."

"Then you know who stole them!" she gasped, starting to her feet. "Tell me. Who was the thief?"

"A man whom you do not know. He has confessed to me. He was not a willing thief, but a wretched assassin, whom General Markoff holds as his catspaw, and compels to perform his dirty work."

"Then the General has secured them! My suspicions are confirmed!" she gasped, all the colour dying from her beautiful face.

"He has. The theft was committed under compulsion, and at imminent risk to the thief, who most certainly would have been shot by the sentries, if discovered. The letters were handed by him back to General Markoff."

My words held her dumbfounded for a few seconds. She did not speak. Then she said in a hard, changed tone:

"Ah! Markoff has destroyed them! The proof no longer exists, therefore I am powerless! How I wish I were permitted to speak—to reveal the truth!"

Her teeth were set, her face was white and hard, and the fingers of both hands had clenched themselves into the palms.

"But you know the truth!" I cried. "Will you not speak? Will you never reveal it? It is surely your duty to do so," I urged.

But she only shook her head sadly, saying:

"I cannot betray her confidence."

"Remember," I said, "by exposing this secret which Markoff has been at such infinite pains to keep, you can perhaps obtain the release of poor Marya and her daughter! Is it not your plain duty?" I urged in a low, earnest voice.

But she only again shook her head resolutely.

"No, I cannot expose the secrets of my lost friend. It was her secret which I swore to her I would never reveal," she responded in a harsh, strained voice. "Markoff has secured the proofs and destroyed them. I suspected it from the first. That brute is my bitterest enemy, as he is also Marya's. But, alas! he is all-powerful! He has played a clever double game—and he has won—*he has won!*"

Chapter Eighteen Shows Hartwig's Anxiety

Her Highness's firm refusal to reveal to me the contents of those letters, the knowledge of which had caused Madame de Rosen and her daughter to be sent to Siberia, while the Grand Duke Nicholas, her father, hid lost his life, disappointed me.

For a full hour I remained there, trying by all means in my power to persuade her to assist me in the overthrow of the fêted Chief of Secret Police.

She would have done so, she declared, were it not for the fact that she had given her solemn word of honour to Marya de Rosen not to divulge anything she knew concerning the contents of those mysterious letters. That compact she held sacred. She had given her faithful promise to her friend.

I pointed out to her the determination she had expressed to me in Petersburg that she intended to reveal to the Emperor his favourite in his true light, and thus avenge the lives of thousands of innocent persons who had died on their way to exile or in the foetid, overcrowded prisons of Moscow, and Tomsk, and the vermin-infested *étapes* of the Great Post Road.

But in reply she sighed deeply, and, looking straight before her in desperation, declared that she had now no proof; and even if she had, she had not the permission of Marya de Rosen to make the exposure. "It is her secret—her own personal secret," she said. "I vowed not to reveal it."

Then for the first time I indicated her own peril. Hitherto I had not wished to alarm her. But I now showed her how it would be to the advantage of the General, cunning, daring and unscrupulous as he was, that some untoward incident should occur by which her life would be sacrificed in his desperate attempt to conceal the truth.

In silence she listened to me, her beautiful face pale and graver than I had ever before seen it. At last she realised the peril.

"Ah!" she sighed, and then, as though speaking to herself, said: "If only I could obtain Marya's consent to speak—to tell the Emperor the truth! But that is now quite impossible. No letter could ever reach her, and, indeed, we have no idea where she is. She is, alas! as dead to the world as though she were in her grave!" she added sadly.

I reflected for a moment.

"If it were not that I feared lest misfortune might befall you during my absence, Highness, I would at once follow and overtake her."

"Oh, but the long journey to Siberia! Why, it would take you at least six months! That is quite impossible."

"Not impossible, Highness," I responded very gravely. "I am prepared to undertake the journey for your sake—and hers—for the sake of the Emperor."

"Ah! I know, Uncle Colin, how good you always are to me, but I couldn't ask you to undertake a winter journey such as that, in search of poor Marya."

"If I go, will you, on your part, promise me solemnly not to go out on these night escapades? Indeed, it is not judicious of you to walk out at all, unless one or other of the police-agents is in close attendance upon you. One never knows, in these present circumstances, what may happen," I said. "And as soon as Markoff knows that I have set out for Siberia, he will guess the reason, and endeavour to bring disaster upon both of us, as well as upon the exile herself."

For some minutes she did not reply. Then she said: "You must not go. It is too dangerous for you—far too dangerous. I will not allow it."

"If you refuse to reveal Marya's secret, then I shall go," was my quiet response. "I shall ask the Emperor to send you Hartwig, to be near you. He will watch over your safety until my return."

"Ah! his alertness is simply marvellous," she declared. "Did you read in the London papers last week how cleverly he ran to earth the three men who robbed the Volga Kama Bank in Moscow of a quarter of a million roubles?"

"Yes. I read the account of it. He was twice shot at by the men before they were arrested. But he seems always to lead a charmed life. While he is at your side, I shall certainly entertain no fear."

"Then you have really decided to go?" she said, looking at me with brows slightly knit. "I cannot tell—I cannot—what I read in those letters after giving my word of honour to Marya."

"I have decided," I said briefly.

"I do not like the thought of your going. Something dreadful may happen to you."

"I shall be wary—never fear," I assured her with a laugh. "I intend to secure the release of Madame and Luba—to set right an unjust and outrageous wrong. I admire your firm devotion to your friend, but I will bring back to you, I hope, her written permission to speak and reveal the truth."

Five minutes later I rose, and we descended to the hall, where patient Dmitri was idling over his French newspaper.

Then the weather being fine again, we passed out together into the autumn sunshine of the Lawns, at that hour of the morning agog with well-dressed promenaders and hundreds of pet dogs. And a few moments later we came face to face with Richard Drury, to whom she introduced me as "Mr Colin Trewinnard, my uncle, Mr Drury." We bowed mutually, and then all three of us strolled on together, though he seemed a little ill at ease in my presence.

I had made a firm resolution. In order to learn the secret of those letters and to place Her Highness, who so honourably refused to break her word, in a position to expose the unscrupulous official who was the real Oppressor of Russia, I intended to set out on that long journey in search of the exile, now, alas! unknown by name, but only by number.

Drury struck me as a rather good fellow, and no doubt a gentleman. We halted together, and, when near the pier, he raised his hat and left us.

Before leaving Brighton I had yet much to do. I was not altogether satisfied concerning the young man, my object being to try and learn for myself something more tangible regarding him.

"Well," she asked, when he had gone, "what is your verdict, Uncle Colin?"

"Favourable," I replied, whereat she smiled in gratification.

An hour later I succeeded in obtaining a short confidential chat with the hall-porter of the Royal York Hotel, whom I found quite ready to assist me. As I had suspected, Dmitri had failed and formed utterly wrong conclusions, because of his lack of fluent English. It is always extremely difficult for a foreigner to obtain confidential information in England.

The hall-porter, however, told me that their visitor was well-known to them, and had frequently stayed there for several months at a time. He had, he believed, formerly lived with his invalid mother at Eastbourne. But the lady had died, and he had then gone to live in bachelor chambers in London. From the bureau of the hotel he obtained the address, scribbled on a bit of paper—an address in Albemarle Street, Piccadilly, to which letters were sometimes re-directed.

"And he has a friend—a doctor—hasn't he?" I asked the man.

"Oh, yes, sir. You mean Doctor Ingram. He was down here with him the other day."

Having obtained all the information I could, I telegraphed to Hartwig at the Savoy Hotel, asking him to make inquiries at Albemarle Street and then to come to Brighton immediately, for I dared not leave until I could place my little madcap charge in safe hands. I knew not into what mischief she might get so soon as my back was turned.

That afternoon we strolled together across the Lawns, and presently sat down to listen to the military band.

She looked extremely neat in her dead-black gown, which, by its cut and material, bore the unmistakable *cachet* of the Rue de la Paix, and as we passed up and down I saw many a head turned in her direction in admiration of her remarkable beauty. Little did that crowd of seaside idlers dream that this extremely pretty girl in black who was so much of a mystery to everybody was a member of the great Imperial House of Russia. She was believed to be Miss Gottorp, whose father had been German and her mother English, both of whom were recently dead.

Seeing her so often walking with me, everyone, of course, put me down as the lucky man to whom she was engaged to be married, and I have little doubt that many a young man envied me. How strange is the world!

When in a tantalising mood she often referred to that popular belief, and that afternoon, while we rested upon two of the green chairs set apart from the others on the Lawn, she said:

"I'm quite sure that everybody in Hove is convinced that I am to be Mrs Trewinnard;" and then, referring to her English maid, she added: "Davey has heard it half a dozen times already."

I laughed merrily, saying:

"Well, that's only to be expected, I suppose. But what about Drury—eh?"

"They don't see very much of Dick. We only meet at night," she laughed, poking the grass with her sunshade.

"And that you really must not do in future," I said firmly.

"Then I can go about with him in the daytime—eh?" she asked, looking up imploringly into my face.

"My dear child," I said, "though I do not approve of it, yet how can I debar you from any little flirtation, even though the Emperor would, I know, be extremely angry if it came to his ears?"

"But it won't. I'm sure it won't, Uncle Colin, through you. You are such a funny old dear."

"Well," I said reluctantly, "for my own part I would much prefer that you invited your gentleman friend to the house, where Miss West could at least play propriety. But only now and then—for recollect one fact always, that you and he can never marry, however fond you may be of each other. It is that one single fact which causes me pain."

Her hard gaze was fixed upon the broad expanse of blue sea before her. I saw how grave she had suddenly become, and that in her great dark eyes stood unshed tears.

Her chest heaved slowly and fell. She was filled with emotion which she bravely repressed.

"Yes," she managed to murmur in a low whisper.

"It is too cruel. Because—"

"Because what?" I asked, in a sympathetic voice, bending towards her.

"Ah, don't ask me, Uncle Colin!" she said bitterly, her welling eyes still fixed blankly upon the sea. "It is cruel because—because I love Dick," she whispered in open confession.

"My little friend," I said, "I sympathise with you very deeply. It is, I admit, a very bitter truth which I have been compelled to point out. For that very reason I have been so much against your friendship with young men. Drury is in ignorance of your true identity. He believes you to be plain Miss Gottorp. But when I tell him the truth—"

"Ah, no!" she cried. "You will not tell him—you won't—will you? Promise me," she urged. "I must, I know, one day find a way of breaking the bond of love which exists between us. When—when—that—time—comes—then we must part. But he must never know that I have deceived him—he must never know that the reason we cannot be more than mere friends is on account of my Imperial birth. No," she added bitterly, "even though I love Dick so dearly and he loves me devotedly, I shall be compelled to do something purposely in order that his love for me may die." Then, sighing deeply, my dainty little companion implored: "You will therefore promise me, Uncle Colin, that you will never—never, under any circumstances, breathe a word to him of who I really am?"

I took her trembling hand for a second and gave her my promise.

I confess I felt the deepest sympathy for her, and told her so frankly and openly as I sat there taking leave of her, for that very evening I intended to leave Brighton and catch the night mail from Charing Cross direct for Moscow.

She said but little, but when we had returned to Brunswick Square and I stood with her at the window of the big drawing-room, she was unable to control her emotions further and burst into a flood of bitter tears.

In tenderness I placed my hand upon her shoulder, endeavouring to console her. Alas! I fear my words were stilted and very unconvincing. What could I say, when all the world over royal birth is a bar to love and happiness, and marriages in Imperial and Royal circles are, for the most part, loveless, unholy unions. The Grand Duchess or the royal Princess loves just as ardently and devotedly as does the free and flirting work-girl or the tea-and-tennis girl of the middle-classes. Alas! however, the heart of the Highness is not her own, but at the disposal of the family council, which discusses her marriage as a purely business proposition, and sells her, too frequently, to the highest bidder.

The poor girl, crushed by the hopeless bitterness of the situation, declared with a sob:

"To be born in the purple, as the outside world calls it, is, alas! to be born to unhappiness."

I remained there a full half-hour, until she grew calm again. Never in all the years I had known her—ever since she was a girl—had I seen her give way to such a paroxysm of despair. Usually she was so bright, buoyant and light-hearted. But that afternoon she had utterly broken down and been overcome by blank despair.

"You are young, Natalia," I said, with deep sympathy. "Enjoy your life to-day, and do not endeavour to meet the troubles of the future. As long as you remain here and are known as Miss Gottorp, so long may your friendship with young Drury be maintained. Live for the present—do not anticipate the future."

I said this because I knew that Time is the greatest healer of broken hearts.

But she only shook her head very sadly, without replying.

The black marble clock on the mantelshelf chimed six, and I recollected that Hartwig had wired that he would meet me at the "Métropole" at that hour. My train was due to leave for London at seven. I had already bidden Miss West adieu. So I took Natalia's hand, and pressing it warmly, wished her farewell, promising to regularly report by telegraph my progress across Siberia, as far as possible.

She struggled to her feet with an effort, and looking full into my face said in a voice choked by emotion:

"Good-bye, Uncle Colin, I am sorry I cannot betray Marya's secret. You are doing this in order to save two innocent women from the horrors of a living tomb in the Siberian snows—to demand that justice shall be done. Go. And may God in His great mercy take you under His protection."

What I replied I can scarcely tell. My heart was too full for words. All I know is that a few moments later I turned out of the great wide square, where the rooks were cawing in the high trees, and hurried along the wide promenade, where the red sun was setting behind me in the sea.

Hartwig I found at the "Métropole" awaiting me. He related how he had called at the flat in Albemarle street, and, by a judicious tip to the young valet he found there, had learnt that Mr Richard Drury was the son of old Sir Richard Drury, knight, the great ship-builder of Greenock, who had built a number of cruisers for the Navy. He was a self-made man, who commenced life as a fitter's labourer in a ship-builder's yard up at Craigandoran on the Clyde—a bluff, hearty man whose generosity was well-known throughout the kingdom.

"Young Richard, it seems," Hartwig went on, "after leaving Oxford became a director of the company, and though apparently leading a life of leisure, yet he takes quite an active part in the direction of the London office of the firm in Westminster."

He expressed the strongest disapproval when I told him of my intention to leave for Siberia and instructed him to remain there and to take the Grand Duchess under his protection until he received definite orders from the Emperor.

"I certainly don't like the idea of your going to Siberia alone, Mr Trewinnard," he declared. "Markoff will know the instant you start, and I fear that—well, that something may happen."

"It is just as likely to happen here in Brighton, Hartwig, as in Russia," I replied.

"Well," he said, shrugging his shoulders, "all I advise is that you exercise the very greatest care. Why not take my assistant, Petrakoff? I will give him secret orders to join you at the frontier at Ekaterinburg—and nobody will know. It will be best for you to have company on that long sledge journey."

"If I want him I will telegraph to you from Petersburg," was my reply.

"You will want him," he said, "depend upon it. If you go alone to Siberia, Mr Trewinnard," he added very earnestly, "then depend upon it you will go to your grave!"

Chapter Nineteen
Orders in Cipher

"And pray, Trewinnard, why are you so extremely desirous of following this woman into exile and speaking with her?" inquired the Emperor in French, as I sat with him, a week later, in a small, dismal, tapestried room in the old Castle of Berezov, the Imperial hunting-box on the edge of the Pinsk Marshes, in the Government of Minsk.

Dressed in a rough shooting-suit of drab Scotch tweed, he sat upon the edge of the table smoking a cigarette after a hard day after wild boar.

I had driven since dawn from the wayside station of Olevsk, three hundred miles south of Moscow, where I had arrived tired and famished from my long night and day journey of a week from Brighton.

On arrival in Moscow I had learnt that His Majesty was hunting at Berezov, and a telegram prefixed by the word "Bathildis," had at once been replied to by a command to audience. Hence I was there, and had placed my appeal before him.

He was much puzzled. In his eyes Madame de Rosen was a dangerous revolutionist who had conspired to kill him, therefore he regarded with entire disfavour my petition to be allowed to see her. There was annoyance written upon his strong features, and by the expression in his eyes I saw that he was entirely averse to granting my request.

"I am anxious, Sire, to see her upon a purely private matter. She was a personal friend," I replied.

"So you told me some time ago, I recollect," he remarked, twisting his cigarette between his fingers. "But Markoff has reported that both she and her daughter are highly dangerous to the security of the State. He was speaking of them only the other day."

I bit my lip fiercely.

"Perhaps he may be misinformed," I said coldly. "As far as I am aware—and I know both the lady and her daughter Luba intimately—they are most loyal subjects of Your Majesty."

"Tut," he laughed. "The evidence put before me was that they actually financed the attempt in the Nevski. I had a narrow escape, Trewinnard—a very narrow one," he added. "And if you were in my place how would you, I wonder, treat those scoundrels who attempted to kill you—eh?"

"I have no knowledge of the true facts, Sire," I replied. "All I petition Your Majesty is that I may be granted an Imperial permit for the post-horses, and a personal order from yourself to see and speak with the prisoners."

He shrugged his shoulders, and thrust his hands deeply in his breeches pockets.

"You do not tell me the reason you wish to see her," he said with a frown of displeasure.

"Upon a purely private matter," I said. "To ask her a question concerning a very dear friend. I beg that Your Majesty will not refuse me this request," I added, deeply in earnest.

"It is a long journey, Trewinnard. I believe she has been sent beyond Yakutsk," he remarked. "But, tell me, were you a very intimate friend of this woman? What do you actually know of her?"

"All I know of her," I replied, "is that she is suffering a great wrong, Your Majesty. She is in possession of certain information which closely concerns a friend. Hence my determination to try, if possible, to amend matters."

"What—you yourself desire to make amends—eh?"

"Not exactly that, Sire," I replied. "I wish to learn the truth concerning—well, concerning a purely private matter. I think that Your Majesty is convinced of my loyalty."

"Of course I am, Trewinnard," was his quick reply. "You have rendered me many important personal services, not the least being your kindness in looking after the welfare of that harebrained little flirt Tattie. By the way, how is she? As much a tomboy as ever, I suppose?" And his big, strong face relaxed into a humorous smile at thought of the girl who, at her own request, had been banished from Court.

"She is greatly improving," I assured him, with a laugh. "She and Miss West are quite comfortable, and I believe enjoying themselves immensely. Her Highness loves England."

"And so do I," he sighed. "I only wish I could go to London oftener. It is to be regretted that my recent visits there have not exactly found favour with the Council of Ministers." Then, after a long pause, he said: "Well, I suppose I must not refuse this request of yours, Trewinnard. But I fear you will find your winter journey an extremely uncomfortable one. When you are back, come direct to me. I would like to hear the result of your observations. Let me see? Besides the permit to use the post-horses, you will require an order to speak with the prisoner, Marya de Rosen, alone, and an order to the Governor of Tomsk, who has the register which will show to which settlement she has been deported."

My heart leaped within me, for at first I had feared refusal.

"As Your Majesty pleases," was my reply, and I added my warmest thanks.

"I'll write them out now," he said; and, turning, he seated himself at the little escritoire in the corner of the small, old-world room and commenced to scribble those Imperial decrees which no one within the Russian Empire would dare to disobey.

While he did so I stood gazing out of the small, deep-set double windows across a flat dismal landscape, brown with the tints of autumn—the wide and weedy moat which surrounded the castle, the stretch of grazing-land and then a belt of dense forest on the skyline—the Imperial game preserves.

That silent old room, dull, faded and sombre, was just the same as it had been when Catherine the Great had fêted her favourite Potemkin, the man who for years ruled Russia and who fought so valiantly against the Turks. There, in that very room, the Treaty of Jassy, which gave Russia the littoral between the Bug and the Dniester, had been signed by Catherine in 1792, and again in that room the Tzar Alexander the First had received the news of Napoleon's retreat from Moscow.

At that small buhl table whereat the Emperor was now writing out my permits the Tzar Nicholas had signed the decree taking away the Polish constitution, and, years later, he had written the final orders to his ill-fated army fighting against the British in the Crimea.

Somewhere in the stone corridor outside could be heard the measured tramp of the sentry, but that, and the rapid scratching of the Emperor's pen, were the only sounds which broke the quiet.

At last he rose and handed me three sheets of foolscap bearing the Imperial arms—the orders which I sought.

I took them with thanks, but after a moment's hesitation I ventured to add:

"I wonder if I might request of Your Majesty a further favour?"

"Well," he asked with a smile, "what is it?"

"That my journey to Siberia should be kept a secret from the police?"

"Eh—what?" he asked quickly, looking at me strangely. "You do not wish the police to know. Why? There is to be no attempted escape, surely?"

"I give Your Majesty my word that Madame de Rosen will not attempt to escape," I said. "I will, indeed, make myself responsible for her. The fact is that I know I have enemies among the Secret Police; hence I wish them to remain in entire ignorance of my journey."

"Enemies!" he echoed. "Who are they? Tell me, and I will quickly turn them into your friends," he said.

"Alas, Sire, I do not exactly know their identity," was my reply.

"Very well," he replied at last, selecting another cigarette from the big golden box upon the table, "I will say nothing—if you so desire. But, remember, you have made yourself responsible for the woman."

"I willingly accept the responsibility," I replied. "But, Your Majesty, there is another matter. I would suggest that Hartwig be detailed to remain with Her Highness the Grand Duchess Natalia at Brighton until my return. He is there at present, awaiting Your Majesty's orders."

At my words he rang a bell, and Calitzine, his private secretary, appeared, bowing.

"Send a telegram at once to Hartwig. Where is he?" he asked, turning to me.

"At the Hotel Métropole, Brighton," I said.

"Telegraph to him in cipher that I order him to remain with Natalia until further orders."

"Very well, Your Majesty," replied the trusted official, bowing.

"And another thing," exclaimed the Emperor. "Telegraph, also in cipher, to all Governors of Siberian provinces that Mr Colin Trewinnard, of London, is our guest during his journey across Siberia, and is to be treated as such by all authorities."

"But pardon me, Your Majesty," I ventured to interrupt, "would not that make it plain to those persons in Petersburg of whom I spoke a moment ago."

"Ah! I forgot," said the Emperor. "Write the telegram, and send a confidential courier with it to Tiumen, across the Siberian frontier. He will despatch it from there, and it will then only go over the Asiatic wires."

"I fear, Your Majesty, that a courier could not reach Omsk under six or seven days, travelling incessantly," remarked the secretary.

"In seven days will be sufficient time. Both messages are confidential."

And he dismissed Calitzine with a wave of his hand, the secretary backing out of the presence of his Imperial master.

When the door had closed the tall, muscular man before me placed his hands behind his back and slowly paced the room, saying:

"Well, Trewinnard, I must wish you a safe journey. If you find yourself in any difficulty, communicate direct with me. I must admit that I can't quite understand the object of this rather quixotic journey of yours—to see a female prisoner. I strongly suspect that you are in love with her—eh?" and he smiled knowingly.

"No, Sire," I replied, "I am not. On my return I hope to be able to show Your Majesty that I have been actuated by motives of humanity and justice—I hope, indeed, perhaps even to receive Your Majesty's commendation."

"Ah! you are too mysterious for me," he laughed. "Are you leaving at once? Or will you remain here, in the castle, until to-morrow?"

"I am greatly honoured and appreciate Your Majesty's hospitality," I said. "But I have horses ready, and I am driving back to the railway at Olevsk to-night."

"Very well, then," he said with a smile. "Good-bye, and be back again in Petersburg as soon as ever you can."

And he stretched forth his big sinewy hand and gave me such a hearty grip that I was compelled to wince.

I was backing towards the door, when it opened and the chamberlain Polivanoff, standing upon the threshold, announced:

"General Markoff begs audience of Your Majesty."

"Ah! Let him come in," the Emperor replied, smiling.

The next moment I found myself face to face with the man whom I knew to be Natalia's worst enemy and mine—that bloated, grey-faced man in military uniform, through whose instrumentality no fewer than ten thousand persons were annually being exiled to the Siberian wastes.

We met just beyond the threshold.

"Ah! my dear M'sieur Trewinnard!" he cried, raising his grey brows in evident surprise at meeting me there. "I thought you were in England. And how is your interesting young charge?"

"She is very well, I believe," was my cold reply.

I passed on, while he, crossing the threshold into the Imperial presence, bowed low, cringing before the monarch whom he daily terrorised, and yet who believed him to be the guardian of the dynasty.

"Ah! I am so glad you have come, Markoff!" I heard the Emperor exclaim as he entered. "I have several pressing matters to discuss with you."

I passed the two sentries, who presented arms, and followed Colonel Polivanoff along the corridor, full of gravest apprehension.

Ill fortune had dogged my footsteps. Markoff had seen me there. He would naturally inquire of the Emperor the reason of my audience.

His Majesty might tell him.

If so, what then?

Chapter Twenty
The Land of No Return

The day had been grey and dispiriting, the open windswept landscape a great limitless expanse of newly-fallen snow of dazzling whiteness—the same cheerless wintry tundra over which I had been travelling by sledge for the past four weary weeks to that everlasting jingle of harness-bells.

My companion, the police-agent Petrakoff, a smart, alert young man, wrapped to the tip of his nose in reindeer furs, was asleep by my side; and I, too, had been dozing, worn out by that fifteen hundred miles of road since leaving the railway at Ekaterinburg.

Suddenly I was awakened by Vasilli, our yamshick, a burly, bearded, unkempt ruffian in shabby furs, who, pointing with his whip to the grey far-off horizon, shouted:

"Tomsk! Tomsk! Look, Excellency!"

Straining my tired eyes, I discerned upon the far skyline a quantity of low, snow-covered, wood-built houses from which rose the pointed cupolas of several churches.

Yonder was the end of the first stage of my long journey. So I awoke Petrakoff, and for the next half-hour we sat with eyes fixed eagerly upon our goal, where we hoped to revel in the luxury of a hotel after a month of those filthy stancias or povarnias, the vermin-infested rests for travellers on the Great Post Road of Siberia.

The first sod of the great Trans-Siberian railway had already been cut by the Tzarevitch at Tcheliabyisk, but no portion of the line was at that time complete. Therefore all traffic across Asia, both travellers and merchandise, including the tea-caravans from China, passed along that great highway, the longest in the world.

Six weeks had elapsed since I had left the Emperor's presence, and I had accomplished by rail and road a distance of two thousand four hundred miles.

Since I had left the railway at Ekaterinburg I had only rested for a single night on two occasions, at Tiumen and at Tobolsk.

At the former place I made my first acquaintance with the inhuman exile system, for moored in the river Obi I saw several of those enormous floating gaols, in which the victims of Russia's true oppressor were transported *en route* to the penal settlements of the Far East—great double-decked barges, three hundred feet long, with a lower hold below the main deck. Along two-thirds of the barge's length ran an iron cage, reaching from the lower to the upper deck-cover, and having the appearance of a great two-storied tiger's cage. Eight of them were moored alongside the landing-stage. Five of them were crowded by wretched prisoners, each barge containing from four to five hundred persons of both sexes and the Cossack guards—a terrible sight indeed.

Provided as I was with an Imperial permit and a doubly-stamped road-passport that directed all keepers of post-stations to provide me with the mail horses, and give me the right of way on the Post Road, I had set forth again after a day's rest towards Tobolsk.

The first snow had fallen on the third day after leaving Tiumen, and the country, covered by its white mantle, presented always a dreary aspect, rendered drearier and more dispiriting by the gangs of wretched exiles which we constantly overtook.

Men, women, and children in companies from a hundred to three hundred, having left the barges, were marching forward to that far-off bourne whence none would ever return. They, indeed, presented a woeful spectacle, mostly of the criminal classes, all their heads being half, or clean-shaven. The majority of the men were in chains, and many were linked together. Not a few of the women marched among the men as prisoners, while the rest trudged along into voluntary exile, holding the hands of their husbands, brothers, lovers or children. Some of the sick, aged and young were in springless carts, but all the others toiled onward through the snow like droves of cattle, bent to the icy blast, a grey-clad, silent crowd, guarded by a dozen Cossacks, with an officer taking his ease in a tarantass in the rear.

Once we met a family of Jews—husband, wife and two children—in a tarantass, with a Cossack with bayonet fixed alongside. We stopped to change horses with them, as we were then midway between post-stations. The man, a bright, intelligent, middle-aged fellow, addressed us in French, and said he had been a wealthy fur merchant in Nijni Novgorod, but was exiled to the Yenisei country simply because he was a Jew. His eyes were clouded with regret at the bitter consciousness of his captivity. Four thousand of his townsmen had, he said, emigrated to England and America, and then pointing to his pretty, delicate wife and two chubby children, the tears rolled down his cheeks, as he faltered out: "Siberie!" Poor fellow!

That word had all the import of a hell to many—many more than him.

The distance between relays on the Great Post Road was, we found, from sixteen to thirty versts, and the speed of fresh horses about ten versts an hour.

Vasilli, the ugly bearded yamshick who had lost one eye, we had engaged in Tiumen, and he had contracted to drive me during the whole of my journey. He was a sullen fellow, who said little, but on finding that I was travelling with an Imperial permit, his chief delight was to hustle up the master of each post-station and threaten to report to the Governor of the province if I, the Excellency, were kept waiting for a single instant.

Usually, changing operations at the stations occupied anything from forty minutes to two hours, according to the temper or trickishness of the post-horse keeper and his grooms, for they were about the meanest set of knaves and rogues on the face of Asia. Yet sight of my permit caused them all to tremble and cringe and hustle, and I certainly could not complain of any undue delay.

We had set out in a tarantass from Tiumen—the town from which the Imperial courier had despatched the order to the various Governors—but as soon as the snow came I purchased a big sledge, and in this we managed to travel with far greater comfort over the snow than by cart over the deeply-rutted road.

None can know the terrible monotony of Siberian travel save those who have endured it.

Nowadays one can cover Siberia from the frontier to far Vladivostock in fifteen days in a luxurious drawing-room car, with restaurant and sleeping-berth, a bath-room and a piano, the line running for the most part near the Old Post Road. But leave the railway and strike north or south, and the same terrible greyness and monotony will grip your senses and depress you as perhaps no other journey in the world can do.

It was dusk when at last we sped, our runners hissing over the frozen snow, into the wood-built town of Tomsk, and alighted at the Hotel Million, a dismal place with corridors long and dark, and bedroom doors fastened by big iron padlocks and hasps! The full-bearded proprietor wandered along with an enormous bunch of keys, opening the doors and exhibiting his uninviting apartments; and at first I actually believed that Vasilli had mistaken my order and driven to a Siberian prison instead of conducting me to a hotel.

Upstairs, however, the rooms were much better. But there were no washing arrangements whatever, or mattresses or bedding; for every traveller in Siberia is expected to carry his own pillows and bedclothes. Here, however, we put up and ate our evening meal in true Siberian style—a single tough beefsteak—simply that and nothing more.

Afterwards I drove through the snowy, unlighted streets to the Governor's palace, a long, log-built place, and on giving my name to the Cossack sentry at the door he at once saluted. Apparently he had been warned of my coming. So had the servants, for with much bowing and grave ceremony I was shown along a corridor lit by petroleum lamps to a small reception-room at the farther end.

The furniture was of the cheap, gaudy character which in England would speak mutely of the hire-system. But it had, no doubt, come from Petersburg at enormous cost of transit, and was perhaps the best and most luxurious furniture—it was covered with red embossed velvet—in all Siberia.

Scarcely was I afforded time to look round the close, overheated place with its treble windows, when General Tschernaieff, a rather short, white-haired, pleasant-featured man in a green uniform, with the Cross of St. Anne at his throat, entered, greeting me warmly and expressing a hope that I had had a pleasant journey.

"I received word of your coming. Mr Trewinnard, some weeks ago," His Excellency said rather pompously. "I am commanded to treat you as a guest of my Imperial Master. Therefore you will, I hope, be my guest here in the palace."

I told him that I already had quarters at the Hotel Million, whereupon he laughed, saying:

"I fear that you will find it very rough and uncouth after hotels in Petersburg or in your own London."

I replied that as a constant traveller, and one who had knocked about in all corners of the world, I was used to roughing it. Then, after he had offered me a cigarette, and a lean manservant, who, I afterwards learned, was an ex-convict, had brought us each a glass of champagne, I explained to him the object of my visit.

"Madame Marya de Rosen and her daughter Luba de Rosen, politicals," repeated His Excellency, as though speaking to himself. "Of course, sir, as you know, all prisoners, both criminal or political, pass through the forwarding-prison here. It is myself who decides to which settlement they shall be sent. But—well, there are so many that the Chief of the Police puts the lists before me and I sign them away to Nerchinsk, to Yakutsk, to Sredne Kolimsk, to Verkhoiansk, to Udinsk, or wherever it may be. Their names, I

The Price of Power | 139

fear, I never notice. I have sent some politicals recently up to Parotovsk, fifty versts north of Yakutsk. The two prisoners may have been among them."

"Here, I suppose, they lose their identity, do they not?" I asked, looking at the white-headed official who governed that great Asiatic province. He was sixty-five, he had told me, and had served twenty-seven years in Siberia.

"Yes. Only across the road in the archives of the forwarding-prison are their names kept. When they leave Tomsk they are known in future—until their death, indeed—only by a registered number."

Then, rising, the white-headed Governor rang a bell, and on his secretary, a young Cossack captain, entering, he gave him certain instructions to go across to the prison and obtain the registers of prisoners during the previous month.

Afterwards, he stretched himself out in his long chair, smoking and asking me questions concerning myself and the object of my journey.

As soon as he learned that I was a British diplomat and personal friend of His Majesty, his manner became much more cordial, and he declared himself ready to do everything in his power to bring my mission to a successful issue.

Presently the secretary returned, carrying two large registers and accompanied by a tall, dark-bearded man in uniform and wearing a decoration, who I learned was the governor of the prison.

He saluted His Excellency on entering the room, and said in Russian:

"Your Excellency is, I believe, inquiring regarding the prisoner Marya de Rosen, widow, of Petersburg, deported by administrative order?"

"Yes," said the General. "Where has she been sent, and what is her number?"

"She was the woman about whom we received special instructions from the Ministry of Police in Petersburg, Your Excellency will remember," replied the prison governor.

"Special instructions!" I echoed, interrupting. "What were they?"

But His Excellency, after a moment's reflection, said: "Ah! I now remember! Of course. There was a note upon the papers in General Markoff's own handwriting to the effect that she was a dangerous person."

"Yes. She was one of those when your Excellency sent to Parotovsk," remarked the prison governor.

"To Parotovsk!" I echoed. "That is beyond Yakutsk—two thousand five hundred miles from here—far in the north, and one of the most dreaded of all the settlements!"

"All penal settlements are dreaded, I fear," remarked His Excellency, blowing the cigarette smoke from his lips. Then, turning to the prison governor, he inquired under what number the prisoner was registered.

On referring to one of the books the officer declared Madame to be now known as "Number 14956" and her daughter as "Number 14957."

I took a note of the numbers, protesting to His Excellency:

"But to compel delicate ladies to walk that great distance in the winter is surely a sentence of death!"

"And if the politicals die, the State has fewer responsibilities," he remarked. "As you see, we have received notification from Petersburg that your lady friend was a dangerous person. Now, of dangerous persons we take very special care." Then, turning to the prison governor, he asked: "How did they go?"

"By tarantass. Excellency. They were in too weak a state to walk, especially the elder prisoner. I doubt, indeed, if ever they will reach Parotovsk."

"And if they don't it will perhaps be the better for both of them," His Excellency remarked with a sigh, rising and casting his cigarette-end into the pan of the round iron stove. He was a stiff, unbending official and ruled the province with a ruthless hand, but at heart he often evinced sympathy with the female exiles.

"Were they very ill?" I inquired quickly of the prison governor.

"They were very exhausted and complained to me of ill-treatment by their guards," he answered. "But if we investigated every complaint we should have more than sufficient to do."

"How long ago did they leave here?"

"About two months," was the man's reply. "The elder prisoner implored to be sent to the Trans-Baikal, where the climate is not so rigorous as in the north, and this would probably have been done had it not been for the special memorandum of His Excellency General Markoff."

"Then he suggested her being sent to the Yakutsk settlement—in fact, to her death—eh?" I asked.

His Excellency replied:

"That seems so. The prisoners have already been on their way two months, at first by tarantass and now, no doubt, by sled. There were fifteen others, nine men and six women—all dangerous politicals, I see," he added, glancing at the order which he had signed and was now produced by the prison governor. "If it is your intention to travel and overtake them, then I fear your journey will be futile."

"Why?" I asked.

"Because I expect that long before you reach them their dead bodies will have been left upon the road," replied His Excellency. "Politicals who die here in Siberia, and especially those marked as dangerous, are not mourned, I assure you."

"There was, if I remember aright, a telegram to Your Excellency from General Markoff regarding prisoners of that name only three days ago," remarked the Cossack captain. "It inquired whether you knew if Madame de Rosen were still alive."

"Ah, yes, I remember. And I replied that I had no knowledge," the General said.

I was silent. My heart stood still.

By the fact of that telegraphic inquiry I knew that Markoff was, as I feared, aware of my journey. He would most certainly prevent my overtaking her—or, if not, he would, no doubt, contrive to seal her lips by death ere I could reach her.

Chapter Twenty One
Hot Haste across Asia

I resolved to push forward in all haste and at all hazards. I lost no time.

With only forty-eight hours' stay at the wretched Hotel Million in Tomsk we went forth again, our faces set ever eastward on that wide, straight road which first runs direct for a hundred miles to Marinsk, a poor, log-built place with a dirty verminous post-station and an old postmaster who, when I presented my Imperial permit, sank upon his knees before me. Fortunately the mail was two days behind me, hence, at every stancia I was able to obtain the best horses, though it seemed part of Vasilli's creed to curse and grumble at everything.

With the snow falling continuously our journey was not so rapid as it had been to Tomsk. Winter had now set in with a vengeance, although it still wanted a few days to the English Christmas. Yet the journey from Marinsk to Krasnoyarsk, two hundred miles, was one of wondrous beauty. It was cold, horribly cold. Often I sat beside the sleepy Petrakoff cramped and shivering, even in my furs.

But those deep, dark woods, with their little glimpses of blue sky; the dashing and jingling along under the low-reaching arms of the evergreen trees, league after league of the forest bowed down to the very earth and in places prostrated with its white weight of snow, the weird ride over hill and mountain, skirting ravine and precipice, the breaks along and across the numerous watercourses, over rude bridges or along deep gullies where rough wooden guards protect the sleds from disaster—with this quick succession of scenery, wild and strange, was I kept constantly awake and charmed.

At the stancias we met the travelling merchants from the Far East and from China with their long train of goods hauled in sleds or packed on the backs of horses. Five *pood*, we found, was the regulation load, and all packages were put up in drums bound with raw hide and so strapped that they could easily be transported by the pack-horse, which carried half a load on either side of a saddle-tree prepared for the purpose.

But those stancias were filthy, overcrowded, evil-smelling places, wherein one laid in one's sleeping-bags upon a bench amid a crowd of unwashed, vodka-drinking humanity in damp, noxious sheep-skins.

Fortunately the moon was at that moment nearly full, and often at night I went forth alone to smoke, sometimes with the snowy plain stretched on every hand about me, and at others with gigantic peaks lifting their hoary heads far into the blue night vault of heaven; silent, frigid, white. Ah! what grandeur! I rejoiced that it was night, when I could smoke and ponder. So cold and still was it that those snowy summits, bathed in the silver radiance of the Siberian moon, filled me with awe such as I had never before experienced.

Yes, those were wonderful nights which will live for ever in my memory—nights when my thoughts wandered far away to the gay promenade at Hove, wondering how fared the little madcap, and whether her peril were real or only imaginary.

Ever obsessed by the knowledge that Markoff was aware of my journey, and would endeavour to prevent its successful issue, I existed in constant anxiety and dread lest some prearranged disaster might befall Madame de Rosen ere I could reach her.

Siberia is, alas! the country where, as the exiles say: "God is nigh, and the Tzar is far away."

Thus, after three weeks more of hard travelling, I passed through the big, straggling, snow-covered town of Krasnoyarsk, and arrived at the wretchedly dirty stancia of Tulunovsk, where the road to Yakutsk—distant nearly two thousand miles—branches to the north from the Great Post Road, up the desolate valley of the Lena.

We arrived in Tulunovsk in the afternoon, and, having sent a telegram to Her Highness from Krasnoyarsk, eight days before, I was delighted to receive a charming little message assuring me that she was quite well and wishing me a continuance of good fortune on my journey.

Since I had left Tomsk no traveller had overtaken me. At Tulunovsk we found a party of politicals, about sixty men and women, in the roughly-constructed prison rest-house, being permitted a few days' respite upon their long and weary march.

Already they had been six months on the road, and were in a terrible condition, almost in rags, and most of them so weak that death would no doubt have been welcome.

And these poor creatures were nearly all of them victims of the bogus plots of His Excellency General Markoff.

To the Cossack captain in charge of the convoy I made myself known, and after taking tea with him I was permitted to go among the party and chat with them.

One tall, thin-faced man, whose hair was prematurely grey, begged me to send a message back to his wife in Tver. He spoke French well, and told me his name was Epatchieff, and that he had been a doctor in practice in the town of Tver, between Moscow and Petersburg.

"I am entirely ignorant of the reason I was arrested, m'sieur," he declared, hitching his ragged coat about him. "I have not committed any crime, or even belonged to any secret society. Perhaps the only offence was my marrying the woman I loved. Who knows?" and the sad-eyed man, whose life held more of sorrow in it than most men, went on to say:

"I had been attending the little daughter of the local chief of the police for a week, but she had recovered so far that I did not consider a further visit was necessary. One morning, six months ago, I was surprised to receive a visit from the police officer's Cossack, who demanded my presence at once at the house of his master, as the child had been seized with another attack. I told him I would go after breakfast as the matter was serious. But the Cossack insisted that I should go at once, so I agreed and went forth. Outside, the Cossack told me that I must first go to the police office, and, of course, I went wonderingly, never dreaming for a moment that anything was wrong. So I was ushered into the office, where the chief of police told me that I was a prisoner. 'A body of exiles are ready to start for Siberia,' said the heartless brute, 'and you will go with them.' I laughed—it was a good joke, but the chief of police assured me that it was a solemn fact. I was completely dumbfounded. I begged for a delay in my transportation. Why was I deprived of my liberty? Who was my accuser? What was the accusation? But I got no answer save 'administrative order.'

"I begged to be allowed to revisit my house under guard, to procure necessary articles of clothing—to say farewell to my young wife. But the scoundrel denied me everything. I waited in anguish, but they placed me in solitary confinement to await the departure of the convoy, and in six hours I was on my way here—to this living tomb!"

Of course the poor fellow was half crazed. What would become of his young wife—what would she think of him? A thousand thoughts and suspicions racked his mind, and he had already lived through an age of torture, as his whitening head plainly showed.

At my suggestion he wrote a letter to his wife informing her of his fate, and using my authority as guest of His Imperial Majesty I took it, and, in due course, posted it back to Russia.

Not until three years afterwards did I learn the tragic sequel. The poor young lady received my letter, and as quickly as she could set out to join him in his exile. With womanly wit she managed to apprise him of her coming and a light broke in upon his grief. He had been sent to Irkutsk, and daily, hourly he looked and longed for her. Yet just as he knew she must arrive, he was suddenly sent far away to the most northerly Arctic settlement of Sredne Kolimsk.

The poor young lady, filled with sweet sympathy and expectation, hoping to find him in Irkutsk, arrived there a fortnight too late. Imagine her anguish when, having travelled over four thousand miles of the worst country on the fact; of the world, she learned the cruel news. Still three thousand miles distant! But she set out to find him. Alas! however, it was too much for her. She lost her reason, raved for a little while under restraint and died at the roadside.

Is it any wonder that there were in Russia real revolutionists, revolting not against their Tzar, but against the inhuman system of the camarilla?

Petrakoff and I spent a sleepless night in that rat-eaten post-house where the food was bad, and our beds consisted only of a wooden bench. We had as companions half a dozen drivers, who had come with a big tea-caravan from China, ragged, unwashed, uncouth fellows in evil-smelling furs.

Indeed the air was so thick and intolerable that at two o'clock in the morning I took my sleeping-bag outside and lay in the sled, in preference to staying in that vermin-infested hut.

Next morning, the twenty-second of January, I signed the postmaster's book as soon as it grew light, and with three fresh horses approved of by Vasilli, we were away, leaving the Great Post Road and striking north along the Lena.

From that moment we entered an uninhabited country, the snowy dreariness of which was indescribable, and as day succeeded day and we pushed further north the climate became more rigorous, until it was no unusual thing to have great icicles hanging from one's moustache.

One day, a week after leaving Tulunovsk, we passed through an entirely deserted village of low-built huts. I asked Vasilli the reason that no one lived there.

"This is a bad place, Excellency," was the fellow's reply. "All the people died of smallpox six months ago."

And so we went on and on, and ever onward. Sometimes we would travel the whole twenty-four hours rather than rest in those horrible post-houses, and on such journeys we often covered one hundred and twenty to one hundred and forty versts, changing horses every twenty to thirty versts.

We covered seven hundred and fifty miles to Dubrovsk in sixteen days, and here, at the post-house, we met a party of Cossacks coming south after taking a convoy of prisoners to Olekminsk—half-way between Dubrovsk and Yakutsk—and handing them over to the guard sent south to meet them.

While taking our evening tea I chatted with the Cossack captain, a big, muscular giant in knee-boots who sat with his legs outstretched on the dirty floor, leaning his back against the high brick stove.

I was making inquiries regarding the prisoners he had recently brought up, whereupon he said:

"They were a batch of politicals from Tomsk. Poor devils, they've been sent to Parotovsk—and there's smallpox there. I suppose General Tschernaieff has sent them there on purpose that they shall become infected and die. Politicals are often sent into an infected settlement."

"To Parotovsk!" I gasped, for it suddenly occurred to me that the woman of whom I was in search might be of that party!

And then I breathlessly inquired if Madame de Rosen, Political Number 14956, had been with them.

"She and her daughter were ill, and were allowed a sled," I added.

"There were two ladies, Excellency, mother and daughter. One was about forty, and the other about eighteen. They came from Petersburg, and were, I believe, well connected and moved in the best society."

"You do not know their names?" I asked anxiously.

"Unfortunately, no," was his reply. "Only the numbers. I believe the lady's number was that which you mentioned. She was registered, however, as a dangerous person."

"No doubt the same!" I cried. "How is she?"

"When they left Olekminsk she was very weak and ill," he replied. "Indeed, I recollect remarking to my lieutenant that I feared she would never reach Yakutsk."

"How far are they ahead of us?" I inquired eagerly. The bearded man reflected for some minutes, making mental calculations. "They left Olekminsk a fortnight ago, therefore by this they should be nearing Yakutsk."

"And how long will it take me to reach Yakutsk?" I asked.

He again made a calculation and at last replied:

"By travelling hard, Excellency, you should reach Yakutsk, I think, in twenty-five to twenty-seven days. It would be impossible before, I fear, owing to the heavy snowdrifts and the bad state of the roads."

"Twenty-seven days!" I echoed. "And before I can reach there the ladies will already be inmates of that infected settlement of Parotovsk—the place to which they have been sent to sicken and die!"

"She was marked as 'dangerous,' Excellency. She would therefore be sent north at once, without a doubt. Persons marked as 'dangerous' are never permitted to remain in Yakutsk."

Could I reach her in time? Could I save her?

Chapter Twenty Two
In the Night

From that day and through twenty-two other dark, weary days of the black frosts of mid-winter, we travelled onward, ever onward. Sometimes we crossed the limitless snow-covered tundra, sometimes we went down into the deep valley of the frozen Lena river, changing horses every thirty versts and signing the post-horse keeper's greasy road-book.

At every stage I produced my Imperial permit, and at almost every station the ignorant peasant who kept it fell upon his knees in deep obeisance to the guest of the great Tzar.

We were now, however, off the main road, for this highway to the far-off Arctic settlements, used almost solely by the convict convoys, ran for a thousand miles through a practically uninhabited country, the only sign of civilisation being the never-ending telegraph-line which we followed, and the lonely post-stations half-buried in the snow.

Ah! those long, anxious days of icy blasts and whirling snow blizzards. My companion and I, wrapped to our eyes in furs, sat side by side often dozing for hours, our ears tired of that irritating jingle of the sled-bells, our limbs cramped and benumbed, and often ravenously hungry, for the rough fare at the post-house was very frequently uneatable.

For six dark days we met not a single soul upon the road, save a party of Cossacks coming south. But from them I could obtain no news of the last batch of "politicals" who had travelled north, and whom we were following in such hot haste.

Again I telegraphed to Hartwig in Brighton, telling him of my whereabouts, and obtaining a reply from him that Her Highness was still well and sent me her best wishes.

That in itself was reassuring.

Hard travel and bad food told, I think, upon both of us. Petrakoff dearly wished himself back in his beloved Petersburg again. Yet our one-eyed half-

Tartar driver seemed quite unconscious of either cold or fatigue. The strain of driving so continuously—sometimes for twenty hours out of the twenty-four—must have been terrible. But he was ever imperious in his dealings at post-stations, ever loud in his commands to the cringing owners of those log-built huts to bring out their best trio of horses, ever yelling to the fur-clad grooms not to keep His Excellency waiting on pain of terrible punishment.

Thus through those short, dark winter days, and often through the long, steely nights, ever following those countless telegraph-poles, we went on—ever onward—until we found ourselves in a small wretched little place of log-built houses called Olekminsk. Upon my travelling map, as indeed upon every map of Siberia, it is represented in capitals as an important place. So I expected to find at least a town—perhaps even a hotel. Instead, I discovered it to be a mere wretched hamlet, with a post-house, and a wood-built prison for the reception of "politicals."

We arrived at midnight. In the common room of the post-house, around which earth and snow had been banked to keep out the cold, was a high brick stove, and around the walls benches whereon a dozen wayfarers like ourselves were wrapped in their evil-smelling furs, and sleeping. The odour as I entered the place was foetid; the dirt indescribable. One shaggy peasant, in heavy top-boots and fur coat, had imbibed too much vodka, and had become hilarious, whereat one of the sleepers, suddenly awakened, threw a top-boot at him across the room, narrowly missing my head.

The post-house keeper, as soon as he saw my permit, sent a man to the local chief of police, a stout, middle-aged man, who appeared on the scene in his hastily-donned uniform and who invited me to his house close by. There I questioned him regarding the political prisoners, "Numbers 14956 and 14957."

Having read my permits—at which he was visibly impressed when he saw the signature of the Emperor himself—he hastened to obtain his register. Presently he said:

"The two ladies you mention have passed through this prison, Excellency. I see a note that both are dangerous 'politicals,' and that the elder lady was rather weak. Judging from the time when they left, they are, I should say, already in Yakutsk—or even beyond."

"From what is she suffering?" I asked eagerly.

"Ah! Excellency, I cannot tell that," was his reply. "All I know is that the captain of Cossacks who came down from Yakutsk to meet the convoy considered that being a dangerous political, she was sufficiently well to walk with the others. So she has gone on foot the remainder of the journey. She arrived her in a sled."

"On foot!" I echoed. "But she is ill—dying, I was told."

The chief of police shrugged his shoulders and said with a sigh:

"I fear. Excellency, that the lady was somewhat unfortunate. That particular captain is not a very humane person—particularly where a dangerous prisoner is concerned."

"Then to be marked as 'dangerous' means that the prisoner is to be treated with brutality—eh?" I cried. "Is that Russian justice?"

"We do not administer justice here in Siberia, Excellency," was the man's quiet reply. "They do that in Petersburg."

"But surely it is a scandal to put a sick woman on the road and compel her to walk four hundred miles in this weather," I cried angrily.

"Alas! That is not my affair," replied the man. "I am merely chief of police of this district and governor of the *étape*. The captain of Cossacks has entire charge of the prisoners on their journey."

What he had told me maddened me. In all that I heard I could plainly detect the sinister hand of General Markoff.

Indeed, when I carefully questioned this official, I felt convinced that the captain in question had received instructions direct from Petersburg regarding Madame de Rosen. The chief of police admitted to me that to the papers concerning the prisoners there had been attached a special memorandum from Petersburg concerning Madame and her daughter.

I smoked a cigarette with him and drank a cup of tea—China tea served with lemon. Then I was shown to a rather poorly-furnished but clean bedroom on the ground floor, where I turned in.

But no sleep came to my eyes. Such hard travelling through all those weeks had shattered my nerves.

While the bright northern moon streamed in through the uncurtained window, I lay on my back, pondering. I reflected upon all the past, the terrible fate of Madame and her daughter, the strange secret she evidently held, and the peril of the Emperor himself, so helpless in the hands of that circle of unscrupulous sycophants, and, further, of my little madcap friend, so prone to flirtation, the irrepressible Grand Duchess Natalia.

I reviewed all the exciting events of those many months which had elapsed since the last Court ball of the season at Petersburg—events which I have attempted to set down in the foregoing pages—and I was held in fear that my long journey might be in vain—that ere I could catch up with the poor wretched woman who, though ill, had been compelled to perform that last and most arduous stage of the journey through the snow, she would, alas! be no longer alive. The vengeance of her enemy Markoff would have fallen upon her.

A sense of indescribable oppression, combined with the hot closeness of the room, stifled me. For hours I lay awake, the moonlight falling full upon my head. At last, however, I must have dropped off to sleep, fagged out after twenty hours of those jingling bells and hissing of the sled-runners over the frozen snow.

A sense of coldness awakened me, and opening my eyes I saw, to my surprise, though the room was practically in darkness with only the reflected light of the snow, that the small treble window stood open. It had certainly been tightly closed when I had entered there.

I raised my eyes to peer into the darkness for the atmosphere, which when I had gone to sleep was stifling on account of the iron stove, was now at zero. Suddenly I caught sight of a dark figure moving noiselessly near where I lay. A thief had entered by the window! He seemed to be searching the pockets of my coat, which I had flung carelessly upon a chair. Surely he was a daring thief to thus enter the house of the chief of police! But in Siberia there are many escaped convicts roaming about the woods. They are called "cuckoos," on account of their increase in the spring and their return to the prisons when starved out in winter.

A "cuckoo" is always a criminal and always desperate. He must have money and food, and he dare not go near a village, as there is a price on his head. Therefore, he will not hesitate to murder a lonely traveller if by so doing he thinks he can secure a passport which will permit him to leave Siberia and re-enter European Russia, back to freedom. Some Siberian roads are in summer infested with such gentry, but winter always drives them back to the towns, and consequently into prison again. Only a very few manage to survive the rigours of the black frosts of the Siberian winter.

Rather more amused than alarmed, I lay watching the dark figure engaged in rifling my pockets. I was contemplating the best method by which to secure him and hand him over to the mercies of my host. A sudden thought struck me. Unfortunately, being guest in the house of the chief of police I had left my revolver in the sled. I never slept at a post-house without it. But that night I was unarmed.

Those moments of watching seemed hours. The man, whoever he was, was tall and slim, though of course I could not see his face. I held my breath. He was securing my papers and my money! Yet he did it all so very leisurely that I could not help admiring his pluck and confounded coolness.

I hesitated a few seconds and then at last I summoned courage to act. I resolved to suddenly spring up and throw myself upon him, so that he would be prevented from jumping out of the window with my property.

But while I was thus making up my mind how to act, the mysterious man suddenly left the chair where my coat had been lying, and turning, came straight towards me, advancing slowly on tip-toe. Apparently he was not desirous of rousing me.

Once again I waited my opportunity to spring upon him, for he fortunately was not yet aware that I was awake and watching him.

I held my breath, lying perfectly motionless, for, advancing to me, he bent over as though to make absolutely certain that I slept. I tried to distinguish his face, but in the shadow that was impossible.

I could hear my own heart beating.

He seemed to be peering down at me, as though in curiosity, and I was wondering what could be his intentions, now that he had secured both my money and my papers.

Suddenly ere I could anticipate his intention, his hand was uplifted, and falling, struck me a heavy blow in the side of the neck just beneath the left jaw.

Instantly I felt a sharp burning pain and a sensation as of the running of warm liquid over my shoulders.

Then I knew that the fluid was blood!

I had been stabbed in the side of the throat!

I shrieked, and tried to spring fiercely upon my assailant, but he was too quick for me.

My eager hand grasped his arm, but he wrenched himself free, and next instant had vaulted lightly through the open window and had disappeared.

And as for myself, I gave vent to a loud shriek for help, and then sank inertly back, next second losing consciousness.

The man had escaped with all my precious permits, signed by the Emperor, as well as my money!

My long journey was now most certainly a futile one. Without those Imperial permits I was utterly helpless. I should not, indeed, be allowed to speak with Madame de Rosen, even though I succeeded in finding her alive.

My loss was irreparable, for it had put an end to my self-imposed mission.

Such were the thoughts which ran through my overstrung brain at the moment when the blackness of insensibility fell upon me, blotting out both knowledge of the present and apprehension of the future.

Chapter Twenty Three
Identification!

When again I opened my eyes it was to find a lamp being held close to my face, and a man who apparently possessed a knowledge of surgery—a political exile from Moscow, who had been a doctor, I afterwards discovered—was carefully bathing my wound.

Beside him stood two Cossacks and the chief of police himself. All were greatly agitated that an attack should have been made upon a man who was guest to His Imperial Majesty, their Master.

To my host's question I described in a few words what had occurred, and bewailed the loss of my papers and my money.

"They are not lost," he replied. "Fortunately the sentry outside heard your scream, and seeing the intruder emerge from the window and run, he raised his rifle and shot him."

"Killed him?" I asked.

"Of course. He was an utter stranger in Olekminsk. Presently we shall discover who and what he is. Here are your papers," he added, handing back the precious documents to me. "For the present the man's body lies outside. Afterwards you shall see if you recognise him. From his passport his name would appear to be Gabrillo Passhin. Do you know anyone of that name?"

"Nobody," I replied, my brain awhirl with the crowded events of the past half-hour.

I suppose it was another half-hour before the doctor, a grey-bearded, prematurely-aged man, finished bandaging my wound and strapping my left arm across my chest. Then, assisted by my host, I rose and went forth, led by men with lanterns, to where, in the snow, as he had fallen beneath the sentry's bullet, lay the would-be assassin.

They held their lanterns against the white, dead lace, but I did not recognise him. He seemed to be about thirty-five, with thin, irregular features and shaven chin. He was respectably dressed, while his hands were soft, betraying no evidence of manual labour. The features were perfectly calm, for death had been instantaneous, the bullet striking at the back of the skull.

Near where he lay a small pool of blood showed dark against the snow.

While we were examining the body, Petrakoff, whom I had sent for from the post-house, arrived in hot haste, and became filled with alarm when he saw my neck and arm enveloped in bandages.

In a few words I told him what had occurred, and then advancing, he bent and looked upon my assailant's face. He remained bent there for quite a couple of minutes. Then, straightening himself, he asked:

"Does his passport give his name as Ivan Müller—or Gabrillo Passhin?"

"You know him!" I gasped. "Who is he?"

"Well," he replied, "I happen to have rather good reason to know him. In Odessa he was chief of a desperate gang of bank-note forgers, who, after eluding us for two years, were at last arrested—six of them in Moscow. The seventh, who called himself Müller, escaped to Germany. A year ago he was bold enough to return to Petersburg, where I recognised him one day close to the Nicholas station and followed him to the house where he lodged. I entered there alone, very foolishly perhaps, whereupon he drew a revolver and fired point-blank at me. The bullet struck me in the right shoulder, but assistance was forthcoming, and he was arrested. His sentence about eleven months ago was confinement in the Fortress of Peter and Paul for fifteen years. So he must have escaped. Ah! he was one of the most daring, astute and desperate criminals in all Russia. At his trial he spat at the judge, and contemptuously declared that his friends would not allow him to be confined for very long."

"It seems that they have not," I remarked thoughtfully. "The fact of his having dared to break into the house of the chief of police shows in itself the character of the man," Petrakoff exclaimed. "I myself had a most narrow escape when I arrested him. But what was he doing here—in Siberia?"

"He may have been exiled here and escaped," remarked the chief of police, as we were returning to the bureau at the side of the house.

"I hardly think that, Excellency," interrupted a Cossack sergeant, who had just returned from the post-station, where he had been making inquiries. "We have just arrested a yamshick, who arrived with the assassin an hour after midnight. Here he is."

A moment later a big, red-faced, shaggy, vodka-drinking driver in ragged furs was brought into the bureau between two Cossacks, and at once interrogated by the chief of police.

First he was taken out to view the body still lying in the snow; then brought back into the police office, a bare, wooden room, lit by a single petroleum lamp, and bearing on its walls posters of numbers of official regulations, each headed by the big black double eagle.

"Now," asked the chief of police, assuming an air of great severity, "where do you come from?"

"Krasnoyarsk, Excellency," answered the man gruffly.

"What do you know of the individual you have just seen dead—eh?"

"All I know of him, Excellency, is that he contracted with me to drive him to Yakutsk."

"Why? Was he quite alone?"

"Yes, Excellency. He made me hurry, driving night and day sometimes, for he was overtaking a friend."

"What friend?"

"Ah! I do not know. Only at each stancia, or povarnia, he inquired if an Englishman had passed. Therefore I concluded that it was an Englishman he was following."

Petrakoff, hearing the man's words, looked meaningly towards me.

"He was alone, you say?" I inquired. "Had he any friends in Krasnoyarsk, do you know?"

"None that I know of. He had journeyed all the way from Petersburg, and he paid me well, because he was travelling so rapidly. We heard of the Englishman at a number of stancias, and have gradually overtaken him, until we found, on arrival here, that the friend he sought had only come in an hour before us. I heard the post-house keeper tell him so."

"Then he was following this mysterious Englishman—eh?" asked the chief of police, who had seated himself at his table with some officiousness before commencing the inquiry.

"No doubt he was, Excellency. One day he told me that if he did not overtake the Englishman on his way to Yakutsk, he would remain and wait for his return."

Then I took a couple of steps forward to the official's table and said:

"I fear that I must be the Englishman whom this mysterious person has followed in such hot haste for nearly six thousand miles."

"So it seems. But why?" asked the chief of police. "I can see no reason why that escaped criminal should follow you with such sinister intent. You don't know him?"

"Not in the least. I have never even heard his name before."

"He was well supplied with money, it seems," remarked my host. "This wallet found upon him contains over ten thousand roubles in notes, together with a credit upon the branch of the National Bank in Yakutsk for a further thirty thousand." And he showed me a well-worn leather pocket-book, evidently of German manufacture.

Both Petrakoff and myself knew only too well that this daring criminal had been released from that cold citadel in the Nevi and given money, promised a free pardon in all probability, if he followed me and at all hazards prevented me from obtaining an interview with the poor, innocent, suffering woman whose dastardly enemy had marked her "dangerous."

I was about to tell the while scandalous truth, but on second thought I saw that no good could be served. Therefore I held my tongue, and allowed the officials—for the starosti of the village had now arrived—regard the affair as a complete mystery.

I had narrowly escaped death, the doctor had declared, and my friend, the chief of police of Olekminsk, kept the unfortunate yamshick under arrest while he reported the extraordinary affair to Yakutsk. He also confiscated the money found upon the man who had made that daring attack upon me.

I could see he was secretly delighted that the criminal had been killed. What, I wondered, would have happened to him if I, a guest of His Imperial Majesty, had lost my life beneath his roof?

The same thought apparently crossed his mind, for in those white winter days I was compelled to remain his guest, being unfit for travel on account of my wound, he many times referred to the narrow escape I had had.

Petrakoff, on his part, related to us some astounding stories of the man, who had been known to the coining and note-forging fraternity as Müller, *alias* Passhin, the man who had at least three murders to his record.

And this man was Markoff's hireling! What, I wondered, was the actual price placed upon my head?

For a whole week—seven weary days—I was compelled to remain there in Olekminsk. I wanted to push forward, but the exiled doctor would not allow it.

There was a small and wretched colony of political exiles in the village, and I visited them. Fancy a poet and *littérateur*, one of those rare Russian souls whose wonder-working effusions must ultimately enlighten and enfranchise the people—a Turgenieff—immured for life in that snowy desert. Yet in Olekminsk there was such a one. He lived in a wretched one-roomed, log-built cabin within a stone's-throw of the house wherein I so nearly lost my life—a tall, alert, deep-eyed man, whom even the savagery of his surroundings could not dispirit or cool the ardour of his wonderful genius. From his prolific pen flowed a ceaseless stream of learning and of light; he wrote and wrote, and in this writing forgot his wrongs and sorrows. The authorities—the local officials who wield such autocratic authority in those parts—were overjoyed to see him in this mood. They fostered his rich whim, they encouraged him to write his books, the manuscripts of which they seized and sold in Petersburg and Berlin, Paris and London.

Yet he lived in a smoky, wooden hovel, banked up by snow, and wrote his books upon a rough wooden bench, which was polished at the spot over which his forearm travelled with his pen.

No exile, I found, was allowed to carry on any business, teach in a school, till the soil, labour at a trade, practise a profession, or engage in any work otherwise than through a master. If I wanted any service, an exile would sometimes come and offer to perform it, but I would have to pay his master, upon whose bounty he must depend for remuneration.

The doctor, named Kasharofski who bandaged me was not a revolutionist, or at all intemperate in his political view's. He was one of the thousands of Markoff's victims sacrificed in order that the Chief of Secret Police should remain in favour with the Emperor. Therefore he was not in favour with many of his fellow-exiles, who held pronounced revolutionary views. He was on pleasant visiting terms with the chief of police, and I often went to his wretched, carpetless hut, around which were sleeping bunks, and spent many an hour with him listening to the cruel, inhuman wrong from which he had suffered at the hands of that marvellously alert organisation, the Secret Police.

One grey, snowy afternoon, while I sat with him in his bare wooden hut, one room with benches around for beds, and he smoked a cigar I had given him, he burst forth angrily against the exile system, declaring: "The whole government is a monstrous mistake. Russia has been striding in vain to populate Siberia for a thousand years, but she will never succeed so long as she continues in her present policy of converting the land into a vast penitentiary wherein the prisoners are prevented from making an honest livelihood, and so driven, if criminals, to a further commission of crime. Beyond doubt there are rogues of the very worst type in Russia and Siberia, but certainly it is plain that their mode of punishment will never tend to elevate or reform them; further, it is utterly impossible that Siberia, under its present system of government, should ever be populated or improved, as have been the penal colonies of the French and English."

His words were, alas! too true. What I had seen of Siberia and its exile system—those terrible prisons where men and women were herded together and infected with typhoid and smallpox; those wretched hovels of the political settlement, and those chained gangs of despairing prisoners on the roads—had indeed filled me with horror. The condition of those exiles, both socially and morally, was utterly appalling.

The day after my conversation with Doctor Kasharofski, after a week of irritating delay, in which every moment I feared that I was losing valuable time, I set forth again upon my last stage, the journey of four hundred miles of snow-covered tundra and forests of cheerless silver birch to Yakutsk.

Did Madame de Rosen still live, or had Markoff taken good care that, even though I escaped the assassin's knife, I should never meet her again in the flesh?

Ay, that was the one important question. And my heart beat quickly as, bidding farewell to my hospitable friend, the chief of police, our three shaggy horses plunged jingling away into the snow.

Chapter Twenty Four
The Journey's End

The farther north we pushed, the worse became the roads, and snow fell daily. Only by following the line of telegraph and the verst-posts could we find the road, which sometimes ran along the Lena valley, and at others crossed high hills or penetrated deep, gloomy forests of dwarfed leafless trees.

After three days we approached a high mountain range, where absolute silence reigned and the snowfall was constant and heavy. The trees were so overburdened with the white weight softly and quietly heaped upon them, that many had broken down completely and obstructed the wild road through the forest. Vasilli had furnished us with hatchets for this purpose, and we were often compelled to stop and hack and drag the fallen trees from our path.

When at last we had gained the top of the mountain pass, we at once felt a complete change in the atmosphere. Whereas to the south everything was as calm as the quiet of death, in front of us a gale was already blowing, and instead of trees bowed down and breaking with their burden of snow, to the northward of the mountain range not a single flake appeared on the shrubbery or woodland.

We had passed from the world of silence to the wild, bleak regions of the Arctic blizzard. All that day we toiled through deep snow, the mountain road rugged beyond description and the tearing wind icy and howling. It blew as though it would never calm. And the distance between the two lonely post-houses was one hundred and twenty-four English miles. Not a vestige of a habitation between. All was a great lone land.

The frost was intense, and icicles hung from Vasilli's beard and from our own moustaches—a black deadly cold, rendered the more biting by the wind straight from the Polar ice-pack.

I looked up upon that awful snow-covered road and shuddered. Luba and her mother had actually traversed it on foot. Because they had been marked as "dangerous" the Cossack captain had exposed them to that terrible suffering, hoping that they would thereby die before reaching Yakutsk—in which case he would, no doubt, receive a word of commendation from the Governor.

We were now fast approaching the dreaded Arctic penal settlements, of which the town of Yakutsk was the centre, distant over four thousand miles from the Russian frontier, every inch of which we had traversed by road.

Hour by hour, day by day, onward we went, with those irritating bells ever jingling in our ears. Petrakoff slept, his head sunk wearily upon his breast, but my mind was much too agitated for sleep. I had, by good fortune, escaped the assassin who had followed me hot-foot across Asia, and now I must soon overtake the unfortunate woman from whose lips I would seek permission for Her Highness to speak.

Pakrovskoe, a mere handful of huts, came in sight one day just as the grey light faded. It was the last village before our goal—Yakutsk. We changed horses and ate some dried fish and rye bread, washed down by a cup of weak tea. Then, after half an hour's rest, again we went forward into the grey gloom of the snow, where on our left at the edge of the plain showed the pale yellow streak of the winter afterglow.

Through that long, interminable night we toiled on and ever on in deep snowdrifts. Vasilli ever and anon uttering curses in his beard, for the horses we had obtained at Pakrovskoe were terrible screws.

At length, however, just as the first grey of dawn appeared on the horizon our driver pointed with his whip, crying excitedly:

"Yakutsk! Excellency! Yakutsk! God be thanked for a safe journey!"

At first I could see nothing, but presently, straining my eyes straight before me, I discerned at the far edge of the snow-covered plain several low towers with bulgy spires, and a long line of house roofs silhouetted against the faint horizon.

Petrakoff gazed forth sleepily, and then with a low, half-conscious grunt lapsed again into inert slumber.

But no longer could I close my eyes. I drew my furs more closely round me, and sat with eyes fixed upon my longed-for goal.

Would success crown my efforts, or had, alas! poor Marya de Rosen succumbed to the brutal treatment meted out to her by the Cossack captain.

After three eager, breathless hours, which seemed weeks to me, we at last drove into the long wide thoroughfare which is the principal street of that northerly town—a road lined by small, square wooden houses, with sloping roofs, each surrounded by its little stockade. The town seemed practically deserted, a dreary, dismal, silent place, of which half the inhabitants were exiles or the free children of exiles. The remainder were, as I afterwards discovered, free Russians—merchants who had emigrated there for the advantage of trade, together with a host of Government officials—Cossack, civil, police, revenue, church, etc.

Without much difficulty we found the Guestnitsa Hotel, a wretched place, verminous and dirty, like every other hotel in all Siberia was before the enlightening days of the great railroad. Here I established myself, and sent Petrakoff with a note to the Governor-General, asking for audience without delay.

Scarcely had I washed, shaved and made myself a trifle presentable— though I fear my unshorn hair presented a somewhat shaggy appearance— when the agent of police returned with a note from His Excellency General Vorontzoff, Governor-General of the province, expressing his regret that owing to being compelled to make a military inspection during that day he was unable to receive me until five o'clock in the evening.

Thus was I compelled to await His Excellency's pleasure.

The fame of Alexander Vorontzoff was well-known in Petersburg. He was a hard, hide-bound bureaucrat, without a spark of pity or of human feeling. And for that reason the camarilla surrounding His Majesty the Emperor had managed to obtain his appointment as Governor-General of Yakutsk. He was the catspaw of that half-dozen astute Ministers who terrorised the Emperor and his Court, and by so doing feathered their own nests. "Politicals" committed by Markoff to his tender mercies were shown little consideration, for was not his appointment as Governor-General mainly on account of his brutal treatment of offenders during his term of office at Tomsk?

Hartwig, had, more than once, mentioned this man as the most cruel, inhuman official in all Siberia. Therefore, being forewarned, I was ready to meet him on his own ground.

Many a man, and many a delicate woman, transported there from Russia, although quite as innocent of revolutionary ideas as my friend Madame de Rosen, had lived but a few short days on their arrival at the prison at Yakutsk, horrible tales of which had even filtered through back to Petersburg and Moscow.

One fact well-known was that, two years before, when smallpox had broken out at the prison, this brutal official caused a whole batch of prisoners to be placed in a room where a dozen other prisoners were lying in the last stages of that fatal disease, with the result that over two hundred exiles became infected, and of them one hundred and eighty died without receiving the least medical attention.

Such an action stood to his credit in the bureau of the Ministry of the Interior at Petersburg! He had saved the Empire the keep of a hundred and eighty prisoners—mostly the victims of Markoff and the camarilla!

When at five o'clock I was ushered into a big, gloomy room, lit by a hundred candles in brass sconces, a vulgar, thick-set man in tight-fitting, dark green uniform, his breast glittering with decorations, rose to greet me in a thick, deep voice. I judged him to be nearly sixty, with grey, steely eyes, a bloated face, short-cropped grey beard, and very square shoulders.

He apologised for his absence during the day, and after handing me a cigarette invited me to a chair covered with red plush, himself taking one opposite to me.

"I have been already notified of your coming," he said, speaking through his beard. "They sent me word from Petersburg that you were travelling to Yakutsk. I am very delighted to receive you as guest of my Imperial Master. In what way can I be of service to you?"

I treated him with considerable hauteur, as became one bearing the order of the Tzar.

From my pocket I produced the Imperial instructions to all Governors of the Asiatic provinces to do my bidding. As soon as he saw it his manner changed and he became most humble and submissive.

"I must again apologise for not receiving you—for not calling upon you instantly on your arrival, Mr Trewinnard. But, truth to tell, I had for the moment forgotten that you were the guest of His Imperial Majesty. I had quite overlooked the telegram sent to me months ago," he said; and then he read the other permits I produced. "I hope you have had a safe journey, and not too uncomfortable," he went on. "I travelled once from Moscow in winter, and I must confess I, although a Russian, found it uncommonly cold."

I gave him to understand that I had not travelled over six thousand miles merely to talk of climatic conditions.

But he strode with swagger across the big, well-furnished room, his gay decorations glittering in the candle-light. The treble windows were closed with thick, dark green curtains pulled across them. The armchairs and sofa were leather-covered, and at the farther end of the room was a big, littered writing-table set near the high stove of glazed brick.

He was a bachelor, with the reputation of being a hard drinker and a confirmed gambler. And under the iron hand of this unsympathetic and brutal official ten thousand political exiles, scattered all over the Arctic province, led an existence to which, in many cases, death would have been far preferable.

Upon the dark green walls of that sombre room—a room in which many a wretched "political" had pleaded in vain—was a single picture, a portrait of the Emperor, one of those printed by the thousand and distributed to every Government office throughout the great Empire. His Excellency General Vorontzoff, as representative of the Emperor, lived in considerable state with a large military staff, and Cossack sentries posted at all the doors. He was as unapproachable as the Tzar himself, probably knowing how hated he was among those unfortunates over whom he held the power of life and death. For the ordinary man to obtain audience of him was wellnigh impossible.

The explicit order in His Majesty's own handwriting altered things considerably in my case, and I saw that he was greatly puzzled as to who I really could be, and why his Master had been so solicitous regarding my welfare.

"I have travelled from Petersburg, Your Excellency, in order to have private interviews with two political prisoners who have recently arrived here," I explained at last.

He frowned slightly at mention of the word "political."

"I understand," he said. "They are friends of yours—eh?"

"Yes," I replied. "And I wish to have interviews with the ladies with as little delay as possible."

"Ladies—eh?" he asked, raising his grey eyebrows. "Who are they?"

"Their name is de Rosen," I said, "but their exile numbers are 14956 and 14957."

He bent to his writing-table, near which he was at that moment standing, and scribbled down the numbers. "They arrived recently, you say?"

"Yes. And I may tell you in confidence that a grave injustice has been done in exiling them. His Majesty is about to institute full and searching inquiries into the circumstances."

His bloated face fell. He grew a trifle paler, and regarded me with some concern.

"I suppose they arrived with the last convoy?" he said reflectively. "We will quickly see."

And he rang a bell, in answer to which a smart young Cossack officer appeared, saluting.

To him he handed the slip of paper with the numbers, saying in that hard, imperious voice of his:

"Report at once to me the whereabouts of these two prisoners. They arrived recently, and I am awaiting information."

The officer again saluted and withdrew. Scarcely had he closed the door when another officer, wearing his heavy greatcoat flecked with snow, entered and, saluting, handed the Governor a paper, saying:

"The prisoners for Kolimsk are ready to start, Excellency."

"How many?"

"Two hundred and seven—one hundred and twenty-six men, and eighty-one women. Your Excellency."

Sredne Kolimsk! That was the most northerly and most dreaded settlement in all the Arctic, still distant nearly one thousand miles—the living tomb of so many of Markoff's victims.

"Are they outside?" asked the Governor. To which the officer in charge replied in the affirmative.

"May I see them?" I asked. Whereupon my request was readily granted.

But before we went outside General Vorontzoff took the list from the Captain's hand and scrawled his signature—the signature which sent two hundred and seven men and women to the coldest region in the world— that frozen bourne whence none ever returned.

Outside in the dark snowy night the wretched gang, in rough, grey, snow-covered clothes, were assembled, a dismal gathering of the most hopeless and dejected wretches in the world, all of them educated, and the majority being members of the professional classes. Yet all had, by that single stroke of the Governor's pen, been consigned to a terrible fate, existence in the filthy yaurtas or huts of the half-civilised Yakuts—an unwashed race who live in the same stable as their cows, and whose habits are incredibly disgusting.

That huddled, shivering crowd had already trudged over four thousand miles on foot and survived, though how many had died on the way would never be told. They stood there like driven cattle, inert, silent and broken. Hardly a word was spoken, save by the mounted Cossack guards, who smoked or joked, several of them having been drinking vodka freely before leaving.

The Governor, standing at my side, glanced around them, mere shadows on the snow. Then he exclaimed with a low laugh, as though amused:

"Even this fate is too good for such vermin! Let's go inside."

I followed him in without a word. My heart bled for those poor unfortunate creatures, who at that moment, at a loud word of command from the Cossack captain, moved away into the bleak and stormy night.

In the cosy warmth of his own room General Vorontzoff threw himself into a deep armchair and declared that I must leave the "Guestnitsa" and become his guest, an invitation which I had no inclination to accept. He offered me champagne, which I was compelled out of courtesy to drink, and we sat smoking until presently the young Cossack officer reappeared, bearing a bundle of official papers.

"Well, where are they?" inquired the Governor quickly. "How slow you are!" he added emphatically.

"The two prisoners in question are still here in Yakutsk," was the officer's reply. "They have not yet been sent on to Parotovsk."

"Then I must go to them at once," I cried in eagerness, starting up quickly from my chair. "I must speak with them without delay. I demand to do so—in the Tzar's name."

The officer bent and whispered some low words into His Excellency's ear; whereupon the Governor, turning to me with a strange expression upon his coarse countenance, said in a quiet voice:

"I much regret, Mr Trewinnard, but I fear that is impossible—quite impossible!"

✦

Chapter Twenty Five
Luba Makes a Statement

"Impossible!" I echoed, staring at the all-powerful official. "Why?"

He shrugged his shoulders, slowly flicked the ash from his cigarette and glanced at the paper which the officer had handed to him.

I saw that beneath the candle-light his heavy features had changed. The diamond upon his finger flashed evilly.

"My pen and writing-pad," he said, addressing his aide-de-camp.

The latter went to the writing-table and handed what he required.

His Excellency rapidly scribbled a few words, then tearing off the sheet of paper handed it to me, saying:

"As you so particularly wish to see them, I suppose your request must be granted. Here is an order to the prison governor."

I took it with a word of thanks, and without delay put on my heavy fur shuba and accompanied the aide-de-camp out into the darkness. He carried a big, old-fashioned lantern to guide my footsteps, though the walk through the steadily-falling snow was not a long one.

Presently we came to a series of long, wood-built houses, windowless save for some small apertures high near the roof, standing behind a high stockade before which Cossack sentries, huddled in their greatcoats, were pacing, white, snowy figures in the gloom.

My guide uttered some password, which brought two sentries at the door to the salute, and then the great gates opened and we entered a big, open space which we crossed to the bureau, a large, low room, lit by a single evil-smelling petroleum lamp. Here I met a narrow-jawed, deep-eyed man in uniform—the prison governor, to whom I presented my permit.

He called a Cossack gaoler, a big, fur-clad man with a jingling bunch of keys at his waist, and I followed him out across the courtyard to one of the long wooden sheds, the door of which he with difficulty unlocked, unbolted, and threw open.

A hot, stifling breath of crowded humanity met me upon the threshold, a foetid odour of dirt, for the place was unventilated, and then by the single lamp high in the roof I saw that along each side of the shed were inclined plank benches crowded by sleeping or reclining women still in their prison clothes, huddled side by side with their heads against the wall, their feet to the narrow gangway.

"Prisoners!" shouted the gaoler in Russian. "Attention! Where is one four nine five seven?"

There was a silence as I stood upon the threshold.

"Come," cried the man petulantly. "I want her here."

A weak, thin voice, low and trembling, responded, and from the gloom slowly emerged a female figure in thick, ill-fitting clothes of grey cloth, unkempt and ragged.

"Move quickly," snapped the gaoler. "Here is someone to see you!"

"To see me!" repeated the weak voice slowly. Next moment, the light of the lantern revealed my face, I suppose, for she dashed forward, crying in English: "Why—you, Mr Trewinnard! Ah! save me! Oh! save me! I beg of you."

And she clung to me, trembling with fear.

It was the girl Luba de Rosen! Alas! so altered was she, so pale, haggard and prematurely-aged that I scarcely recognised her. Her appearance was dejected, ragged, horrible! Her fair hair that used to be so much admired was now tangled over her eyes, and her fine figure hidden by her rough, ill-fitting prison gown, which was old, dirty and tattered. I stared at her, speechless in horror.

She was only nineteen. In that smart set in which her mother moved her beauty had been much admired. Madame de Rosen was the widow of a wealthy Jew banker, and on account of her late husband's loans to certain high officials to cover their gambling debts, all doors had been open to her. I recollected when I had last seen Luba, the night before her arrest. She had worn a pretty, Paris-made gown of carnation chiffon, and was waltzing with a good-looking young officer of the Kazan Dragoons. Alas! what a different picture she now presented.

"Luba!" I said quietly in English, taking her hand as she clung to me. "Come outside. I am here to speak with you. I want to talk with you alone."

The gaoler, who had had his orders from the Governor, relocked and bolted the door, and taking his lantern, withdrew a respectable distance while I stood with Luba under the wooden wall of the prison wherein she had been confined.

"I have followed you here," I said, opening my capacious fur coat and throwing it around the poor shivering girl. "I only arrived to-night. Where is your mother? I must see her at once."

She was silent. In the darkness I saw that her white face was downcast.

I felt her sobbing as I held her, weak and tearful, in my arms. She seemed, poor girl, too overcome at meeting me to be able to speak. She tried to articulate some words, but they became choked by stifled sobs.

"Your mother has been very ill, I hear, Luba," I said. "Is she better?"

But the girl only drew a long sigh and slowly shook her head.

"I—I can't tell you—Mr Trewinnard!" she managed to exclaim. "It is all too terrible—horrible! My poor mother! Poor darling! She—she died this morning!"

"Dead!" I gasped. My heart sank within me. The iron entered my soul.

"Yes. Alas!" responded the unfortunate girl. "And I am left alone—all alone in this awful place! Ah! Mr Trewinnard, you do not know—you can never dream how much we have suffered since we left Petersburg. I would have preferred death a thousand times to this. And my poor mother. She is dead—at last she now has peace. The Cossacks cannot beat her with their whips any more."

"Where did she die?" I asked blankly.

"In here—in this prison, upon the bench beside where I slept. Ah!" she cried, "I feel now as though I shall go mad. I lived only for her take—to wait upon her and try to alleviate her sufferings. Now that she has been taken from me I have no other object for which to live in this dreary waste of ice and snow. In a week I shall be sent on to Parotovsk with the others. But I hope before reaching there that God will be merciful and allow me to die."

"No, no!" I exclaimed, my hand placed tenderly upon the poor girl's shoulder. "Banish such thoughts. You may be released yet. I am here, striving towards that end."

But she only shook her head again very mournfully. Nobody is released from Siberia.

As we stood together, my heavy coat wrapped about her in order to protect her a little from the piercing blast, she told me how, under the fatigue and exposure of the journey, her mother had fallen so ill that she one day dropped exhausted by the roadside. One Cossack officer, finding her unconscious, suggested that she should be left there to die, as fully half a dozen other delicate women had been left. But another officer of the convoy, a trifle more humane, had her placed in a tarantass, and by that means she had travelled as far as Tulunovsk. But the officer in charge there had compelled her to again walk, and over that last thousand miles of snow she had dragged wearily until, ill and worn out, she had arrived in Yakutsk.

From the moment of her arrival she had scarcely spoken. So weak was she, that she could only lie upon the bare wooden bench, and was ever begging to be allowed to die. And only that morning had she peacefully passed away. I had arrived twelve hours too late!

She had carried her secret to her grave!

I heard the terrible story from the girl's lips in silence. My long weary journey had been all in vain.

From the beginning to the end of poor Madame's illness no medical man had seen her. From what she had suffered no one knew, and certainly nobody cared a jot. She was, in the eyes of the law, a "dangerous political" who had died on the journey to the distant settlement to which she had been banished. And how many others, alas! had succumbed to the rigours of that awful journey!

I walked with Luba back to the Governor's bureau, and in obedience to my demand he gave me a room—a bare place with a brick stove, before which the poor sad-eyed girl sat with me.

I saw that the death of her mother had utterly crushed her spirit. Transferred from the gaiety and luxury of Petersburg, her pretty home and her merry circle of friends, away to that wilderness of snow, with brutal Cossacks as guards—men who beat exhausted women with whips as one lashes a dog—her brain was at last becoming affected. At certain moments she seemed very curious in her manner. Her deep blue eyes had an unusual intense expression in them—a look which I certainly did not like. That keen glittering glance was, I knew, precursory to madness.

Though unkempt and ragged, wearing an old pair of men's high boots and a dirty red handkerchief tied about her head, her beauty was still remarkable. Her pretty mouth was perhaps harder, and it tightened at the corners as she related the tragic story of their arrest and their subsequent journey. Yet her eyes were splendid, and her cheeks were still dimpled they had been when I had so often sat at tea with her in her mother's great salon in Petersburg, a room decorated in white, with rose-du-Barri furniture.

In tenderness I hold her hand as she told me of the brutal treatment both she and her fellow-prisoners had received at the hands of the Cossacks.

"Never mind, Luba," I said with a smile, endeavouring to cheer her, "every cloud has its silver lining. Your poor mother is dead, and nobody regrets it more than myself. I travelled in haste from England in order to see her—in order to advise her to reveal to me a certain secret which she possessed."

"A secret!" said the girl, looking straight into my face. "A secret of what?"

"Well," I said slowly, "first, Luba, let me explain that as you well know, I am an old friend of your dear mother."

"I know that, of course," she said. "Poor mother has frequently spoken of you during her journey. She often used to wonder what you would think when you heard of our arrest."

"I knew you were both the innocent victims of General Markoff," I said quickly.

"Ah! then you knew that!" she cried. "How did you know?"

"Because I was well aware that Markoff was your mother's bitterest enemy," I answered.

"He was. But why? Do you know that, Mr Trewinnard? Can you give me any explanation? It has always been a most complete mystery to me. Mother always refused to tell me anything."

I paused. I had hoped that she would know something, or at least that she might give me some hint which would serve as a clue by which to elucidate the mystery of those incriminating letters, now, alas! destroyed.

"Has your mother told you nothing?" I asked, looking earnestly straight in her face.

"Nothing."

"Immediately before her arrest she gave to Her Imperial Highness the Grand Duchess Natalia certain letters, asking her to keep them in safety. Are you aware of that?"

"Mother told me so," the girl replied. "She also believed that the letters in question must have fallen into General Markoff's hands."

"Why?"

"I do not know. She often said so."

"She believed that the arrest and exile of you both was due to the knowledge of what those letters contained—eh?" I asked.

"I think so."

"But tell me, Luba," I asked very earnestly, "did your mother ever reveal to you the nature of those letters? I am here to discover this—because—well, to tell the truth, because your friend the Grand Duchess Natasha is in deadly peril."

"In peril, why? Where is she?"

In a few brief words I told her of Natalia's *incognita* at Brighton, and of the attempt that had been made to assassinate us both, in order to suppress any knowledge of the letters that either of us might have gained.

"Our own sad case is on a par with yours," she declared thoughtfully at last. "Poor mother was, I think, aware of some secret of General Markoff's. Perhaps it was believed that she had told me. At any rate, we were both arrested and sent here, where we should never have any opportunity of using our information."

"You have no idea of its nature, Luba," I asked in a low voice, still deeply in earnest. "I mean you have no suspicion of the actual nature of the contents of those letters which your mother gave into Natalia's care?"

The girl was silent for some time, her eyes downcast in thought.

At last she replied:

"It would be untrue to say that I entertain no suspicion. But, alas! I have no corroboration. My belief is only based upon what my dear mother so often used to repeat to me."

"And what was that?" I asked.

"That she had held the life of Russia's oppressor, General Markoff, in her hand. That she could have crushed and ruined him as he so justly deserved; but that for motives of humanity she had warned him of repeating his dastardly actions, and had long hesitated to bring him to ruin and to death."

"Ah! the brute. He knew that," I cried. "He craftily awaited his opportunity, then he dealt her a cowardly blow, by arresting her and sending her here, where even in life or in death her lips would be closed for ever."

Chapter Twenty Six
Not in the Newspapers

Twelve weeks had elapsed—cold, weary weeks of constant sledging over those bleak, snow-bound plains, westward, back to civilisation.

On the twenty-seventh of April—I have, alas! cause to remember the date—at six o'clock in the evening, I alighted from the train at Brighton, and Hartwig came eagerly forward to greet me.

I had journeyed incessantly, avoiding Petersburg and coming by Warsaw and Berlin to the Hook of Holland, and that morning had apprised him of my arrival in England; but, I fear, as I emerged from the train my appearance must have been somewhat travel-worn. True, I had bought some ready-made clothes in Berlin—a new overcoat and a new hat. But I was horribly conscious that they were ill-fitting, as is every man who wears a "ready-to-wear garment"—as the tailors call it.

Yes, I was utterly fagged out after that long and fruitless errand, and a I glanced at Hartwig I detected in an instant that something unusual had occurred.

"What's the matter?" I asked quickly. "What has happened?"

"Ah! that I unfortunately do not exactly know, Mr Trewinnard," was his reply in a tone quite unusual to him.

"But what has occurred?"

"Disaster," he answered in a low, hoarse voice. "Her Highness has mysteriously disappeared!"

"Disappeared!" I gasped, halting and staring at him. "How? With whom?"

"How can we tell?" he asked, with a gesture of despair.

"Explain," I urged. "Tell me quickly. How did it happen?"

Together we walked slowly out of the station-yard down in the direction of King's Road, when he said:

"Well, the facts are briefly these. Last Monday—that is five days ago—Her Highness and Miss West had been over to Eastbourne by train to see an old schoolfellow of the Grand Duchess's, a certain Miss Finlay—with whom I have since had an interview. They lunched at Mrs Finlay's house—one of those new ones on the road to Beachy Head—and left, together with Miss Finlay, to walk back to the station at half-past seven o'clock. Her Highness would not drive, but preferred to walk along the Promenade and up Terminus Road. When close to the station, Dmitri—who accompanied them—says that Her Highness stopped suddenly before a fancy needlework shop, while the other two went on. The Grand Duchess, before entering the shop, motioned to Dmitri to walk along to the station, for his surveillance, as you know, always irritated her. Dmitri, therefore, strolled on—and—well, that was the last seen of her Highness!"

"Impossible!" I gasped.

"I have made every effort to trace her, but without avail," declared Hartwig in despair. "It appears that she purchased some coloured silks for embroidery, paid for them, and then went out quite calmly. The girl who served her recollects her customer being met upon the threshold by a man who raised his hat in greeting and spoke to her. But she could not see his face, nor could she, in the dusk, discern whether he were young or old. The young lady seemed to be pleased to meet him, and, very curiously, it struck her at the time that that meeting had been prearranged."

"Why?" I asked.

"Because she says that the young lady, while making her purchase, glanced anxiously at her gold wristlet-watch once or twice."

"She had a train to catch, remember."

-"Yes. I put that point before the girl, but she remains unshaken in her conviction that Her Highness met the man there by appointment. In any case," he added, "we have been unable to discover any trace of her since."

I was silent for a moment.

"But, surely, Hartwig, this is a most extraordinary affair!" I cried. "She may have been decoyed into the hands of Danilovitch!"

"That is, alas! what I very much fear," the police official admitted. "This I believe to be some deeply-laid plot of Markoff's to secure her silence. You have been across Siberia, and arrived too late, yet Her Highness is still in possession of the secret. She is the only living menace to Markoff. Is it not natural, therefore, that he should take steps to seal her lips?"

"We must discover her, Hartwig—we must find her, either alive or dead," I said resolutely.

This news staggered me, fagged and worn out as I was. I had been compelled to leave Luba in the hands of the Governor-General, who had promised, because I was the guest of His Majesty, that he would do all in his power to render her lot less irksome. Indeed, she had been transferred to one of the rooms in the prison hospital in Yakutsk, and was under a wardress, instead of being guarded by those brutal, uncouth Cossacks.

But this sudden disappearance of Natalia just at the very moment when her presence was of greatest importance held me utterly bewildered. All my efforts had been in vain!

Should I telegraph the alarming news to the Emperor?

Hartwig explained to me how diligently he had searched, and at once I realised the expert method with which he was dealing with the remarkable affair, and the wide scope of his inquiry. No man in Europe was more fitted to institute such a search. He had, in confidence, invoked the aid of New Scotland Yard, and being known by the heads of the Criminal Investigation Department, they had allowed him to direct the inquiry.

"At present," he said, "the papers are fortunately in entire ignorance of the matter. I have been very careful that nothing shall leak out, for the story would, of course, be a grand one for the sensational Press. The public, however, does not know whose identity is hidden beneath the name of Gottorp, and no reporter dreams that a Russian Grand Duchess has been living *incognita* in Brunswick Square," he added with a smile. "The Criminal Investigation Department have agreed with me that it would be unwise for a single word to leak out regarding the disappearance. Of course they incline to the theory of a secret lover—but—"

"You suspect young Drury—eh?" I interrupted quickly.

"I hardly know what theory to form," he said with a puzzled air: "while the shopgirl in Eastbourne describes the appearance of the man's back as exactly similar to that of Mr Drury, yet I cannot believe that he would willingly play us such a trick. I know him quite well, and I believe him to be a very honest, upright, straightforward young fellow."

"He knows nothing of Her Highness's real identity?" I asked anxiously, as we still strolled down towards the sea.

"Has no suspicion whatever of it. He believes Miss Gottorp to be the daughter of a Berlin brewer who died and left her a fortune. No," he went on, "I detect in this affair one of Markoff's clever plots. She probably believed that she was to meet young Drury, and adopted that ruse to pause and speak with him—but—!"

"But what?" I asked, turning and looking into his grave face, revealed by the light of a shop window.

"Well—she was led into a trap," he said. "Decoyed away into one of the side streets, perhaps—and then—well, who knows what might have happened?"

"You have searched Eastbourne, I suppose?"

"The Criminal Investigation Department are doing so," he said. "I am making a perfectly independent inquiry."

"You have reported nothing yet to Petersburg—eh?"

"Not a word. What can I say? I have asked Miss West to refrain from uttering a syllable—also the Finlays have promised entire secrecy."

"There is a motive in her disappearance, Hartwig," I said. "What is it?"

"Ah! That's just it, Mr Trewinnard," he replied. "Her Highness had no motive whatever to disappear. Mr Drury was always welcome at Brunswick Square, for Miss West entirely approved of him. Besides, his presence had prevented other flirtations. Therefore there was no reason that there should have been any clandestine meeting in Eastbourne."

"Then the only other suggestion is that of treachery."

"Exactly. And that is the correct one—depend upon it."

"If she has fallen into Markoff's hands then she may be already dead!" I gasped, staring at him. "If so, the secret will remain a secret for ever!"

For a moment the great detective remained silent. Then slowly he said:

"To tell the truth, that is exactly what I fear. Yes, I will try and suppress the horrible apprehension. It is too terrible."

"Danilovitch is unscrupulous," I said, "and he hates us."

"No doubt he does. He fears us, yet—" and he paused. "Yet a most curious point is the fact that Her Highness deliberately remained behind and sent Dmitri on, in order to be allowed opportunity to escape his vigilance."

"All cleverly planned by her enemies," I declared. "She was misled, and fell into some very cunningly-baited trap, without a doubt. Do you believe she is still in Eastbourne?"

"No."

"Neither do I," was my assertion. "She went to London, no doubt, for there she would be easily concealed—if death has not already overtaken her—as it has overtaken poor Madame de Rosen."

"I trust not," he said very thoughtfully. Then he added: "I have been thinking whether we might not again approach Danilovitch?"

"He is our enemy and hers. He will give us no satisfaction," I said. "Certainly, whatever plot suggested by Markoff arose in his fertile brain. And his plots usually have the same result—the death of the victim. It may be so in this case," I added reflectively; "but I sincerely trust not."

Hartwig drew a long breath. His face clouded.

"Remember," he said, "it is to Markoff's advantage—indeed to him her death means the suppression of some disgraceful truth. If she lives— then his fall is imminent. I have foreseen this all along, hence my constant precaution, which, alas! was relaxed last Monday, because I had to go to London to consult the Ambassador. They evidently were aware of that."

I explained the failure of my errand, whereat he drew a long breath and said:

"It almost seems, Mr Trewinnard, that our enemies have secured the advantage of us, after all. I really feel they have."

"You fear that the trap into which Her Highness has fallen is a fatal one—eh?" I asked, glancing at him quickly.

"What can I reply?" he said in a low tone. "Every inquiry I can devise is in progress. All the ports are watched, and observation is kept night and day upon the house in Lower Clapton from a house opposite, which Matthews, of New Scotland Yard, has taken for the purpose. Her Highness has not been there—up to now. Markoff is in Petersburg."

The great detective—the man whose cleverness in the detection of crime was perhaps unequalled in Europe—drew a long, thoughtful face as he halted with me beneath a street-lamp.

People hurried past us, ignorant of the momentous question we were discussing.

"Where is Drury?" I asked suddenly.

"Ah! That is yet another point," answered Hartwig. "He, too, is missing—he has disappeared!"

Chapter Twenty Seven
At Tzarskoie-Selo.

Just before eleven o'clock that night, accompanied by Hartwig, I called at Richard Drury's cosy artistic flat in Albemarle Street, and in answer to my questions his valet, a tall, thin-faced young man, informed me that his master was not at home.

"I understand that you have had no news of him since last Monday?" I said. "The fact is, this gentleman is a detective, and we are endeavouring to elucidate the mystery of Mr Drury's disappearance."

The valet recognised Hartwig as having called before, and invited us into the small bachelor sitting-room, over the mantelpiece of which were many photographs of its owner's friends—the majority being of the opposite sex.

"Well, sir, it's a complete mystery," the man replied. "My master slept here on Sunday night, and left for the country on Monday afternoon. He had a directors' meeting at Westminster on Tuesday, and told me that he should be back at midday. But he has never returned. That's all. They sent round from the office to know if he was in town, and of course I told them that he had not come back."

"Have there been any callers lately?" I asked. "Has a lady been here?"

"Only one lady ever calls, sir—a foreign lady named Gottorp."

"And has she been here lately?" I inquired quickly. "She called on the Friday, and they went out together to lunch at Jules's. She often calls. She's a very nice young lady, sir."

"She hasn't called since Monday?" I asked.

"No, sir. A stranger—a foreigner—called on Tuesday afternoon and inquired for Mr Drury."

"A foreigner!" I exclaimed. "Who was he? Describe him."

"Oh! he was a dark, middle-aged man, dressed in a shabby brown suit. He wanted to see Mr Drury very particularly."

Hartwig and I exchanged glances. Was the caller an agent of Secret Police.

"What did he say when you told him of your master's absence?"

"He seemed rather puzzled, and went away expressing his intention of calling again."

"He was a stranger?"

"I'd never seen him before, sir."

"And this Miss Gottorp—is your master very attached to her?"

"He worships her, as the sayin' is, sir," replied the man frankly. "She lives down at Brighton, and he spends half his time there on her account."

"You say your master left London for the country on Monday afternoon. What was his destination?"

"Ah, I don't know. I only know he drove to Victoria, but whether he left by the South Eastern or the South Coast line is a mystery."

I had already formed a theory that Drury had travelled down to Eastbourne and had met his well-beloved outside the shop in Terminus Road. Afterwards both had disappeared! My amazement was mingled with annoyance and chagrin. Natalia had, alas! too little regard for the *convenances*. She had acted foolishly, with that recklessness which had always characterised her and had already scandalised the Imperial Family. Now it had resulted in her becoming victim of some dastardly plot, the exact nature of which was not yet apparent.

For half an hour we both questioned Drury's valet, but could learn little of further interest. Therefore we left, and strolled along Piccadilly as far as St. James's Club, where, until a late hour, we sat discussing the sensational affair.

Was it an elopement, or had they both fallen victims of some cleverly-conceived trap in which we detected the sinister hand of His Excellency General Serge Markoff?

Next day I returned to Brighton and closely questioned Miss West, the maid Davey, and the puzzled Dmitri. I saw the manager of the hotel where Drury was in the habit of staying, and, discovering that Drury's friend, Doctor Ingram, lived in Gower Street, I resumed to London and that same night succeeded in running him to earth.

He was perfectly frank.

"Dick has disappeared as suddenly as if the earth has swallowed him," he declared. "I can't make it out, especially as he told me he had a most important directors' meeting last Tuesday, and that he must travel up to Greenock on Thursday to be present at the launch of a new cruiser which his firm is building for the Admiralty. He certainly would have kept those two appointments had he been free to do so."

"You knew Miss Gottorp, I believe?" I asked of the quiet-mannered, studious young man in gold-rimmed glasses.

"Quite well. Dick's man told me yesterday that the young lady has also disappeared," he said. "It is really most extraordinary. I can't make it out. Dick is not the kind of man to elope, you know. He's too straightforward and honourable. Besides, he was always made most welcome at Brunswick Square—though, between ourselves, the young lady though inexpressibly charming, was always a very great mystery to me. I went with Dick twice to her house, and on each occasion saw men, foreigners they seemed, lurking about the hall. They eyed one suspiciously, and I did not like to visit her on that account."

I pretended ignorance, but could see that he held Natalia in some suspicion. Indeed, he half hinted that for aught they knew, the pretty young lady might be some clever foreign adventuress.

At that I laughed heartily. What would he think if I spoke the truth?

Next day I put into the personal columns of several of the London newspapers an advertisement which read:

"Gottorp.—Have returned: very anxious; write club—Uncle Colin."

Then for four days I waited for a reply, visiting the club a dozen times each day, but all in vain.

I called at Chesham House one afternoon and had a chat with His Excellency the Russian Ambassador. He was unaware of Her Imperial Highness's disappearance, and I did not inform him. I wanted to know what knowledge he possessed, and whether Markoff was still in Petersburg. I discovered that he knew nothing, and that at that moment the Chief of Secret Police was with the Emperor at the military manoeuvres in progress on that great plain which stretches from the town of Ivanovo across to the western bank of the broad Volga.

Hartwig was ever active, night and day, but no trace could we find of the missing couple. Drury's friends, on their part, were making inquiry in every direction, but all to no avail. The pair had entirely disappeared.

The house of the conspirators in Lower Clapton was being watched night and day, but as far as it could be observed there was little or no activity in that quarter. Danilovitch was still living there in retirement, going out only after dark, and though he was always shadowed it could not be found that he ever called at any other place than a little shop kept by a Russian cigarette-maker in Dean Street, Soho, and a small eight-roomed villa in North Finchley, where lived a compatriot named Felix Sasonoff, the London correspondent of one of the Petersburg daily newspapers.

Our warning had, it seemed, had its effect. Much as we desired to approach the mysterious head of the so-called Revolutionary Organisation — the man known as "The One," but whose identity was veiled in mystery — we dared not do so, knowing that he was our bitterest enemy.

One morning, in despair at obtaining no trace of the missing pair, I resolved to travel to Petersburg and there make inquiry. I realised that I must inform the Emperor, even at risk of his displeasure, for, after all, I had been compelled by my journey to Siberia to relax my vigilance, though I had left the little madcap under Hartwig's protection.

What if they had actually eloped! Alas! I knew too well the light manner in which Natalia regarded the conventions of old-fashioned Mother Grundy. Indeed, it had often seemed her delight to commit breaches of the Imperial etiquette and to cause horror in her family.

Yet surely she would never commit such an unpardonable offence as to elope with Richard Drury!

Again, was she already dead? That was, I confess, my greatest fear, knowing well the desperate cunning of Serge Markoff, and all that her decease meant to him.

So, with sudden resolve, I took the Nord Express once more back across Europe, and four days later found myself again in my old room at the Embassy, where Stoyanovitch brought me a command to audience from the Emperor.

How can I adequately describe the interview, which took place in a spacious room in the Palace of Tzarskoie-Selo.

"So your friend Madame de Rosen was unfortunately dead before you reached Yakutsk," remarked His Majesty gravely, standing near the window in a brilliant uniform covered with glittering decorations, for he had just returned from an official function. "I heard of it," he added. "The Governor-General Vorontzoff reported to me by telegraph. Indeed, Trewinnard, I had frequent reports of your progress. I am sorry you undertook such a journey all in vain."

"I beg of Your Majesty's clemency towards the dead woman's daughter Luba," I asked.

But he only made a gesture of impatience, saying:

"I have already demanded a report on the whole case. Until that comes, I regret I cannot act. Vorontzoff will see that the girl is not sent farther north, and no doubt she will be well treated."

In a few brief words I described some of the scenes I had witnessed on the Great Post Road, but the Emperor only sighed heavily and replied:

"I regret it, I tell you. But how can I control the loyal Cossacks sent to escort those who have made attempts upon my life? I admit most freely that the exile system is wrong, cruel—perhaps inhuman. Yet how can it be altered?"

"If Your Majesty makes searching inquiry, he will find some terrible injustices committed in the name of the law."

"In confidence, I tell you, I am having secret inquiry made in certain quarters," he replied. "And, Trewinnard, I wish you, if you will, to make out for me a full and confidential report on your journey, and I will then have all your allegations investigated."

I thanked him. Though an autocrat, he was yet a humane and just ruler—when he was allowed to exercise justice, which, unfortunately, was but seldom.

"My journey had a tragic sequel in Yakutsk, Sire," I said presently, "and upon my return to England I was met with still another misfortune—a misfortune upon which I desire to consult Your Imperial Majesty."

"What?" he asked, opening his eyes widely. "A further misfortune?"

"I regret to be compelled to report that her Imperial Highness the Grand Duchess Natalia has disappeared," I said in a low voice.

His dark, heavy brows narrowed, his cheeks went pale, and his lips compressed.

"Disappeared!" he gasped. "What do you mean? Describe this latest escapade of hers—for I suppose it is some ridiculous freak or other?"

"I fear not, Sire," was my reply. Then, having described to him the facts as I have related them here to you, my reader, omitting, of course, all reference to Richard Drury, I added: "What I fear is that Her Highness has fallen victim to some revolutionary plot."

"Why? What motive can the revolutionary party have in making an attempt upon her—a mere giddy girl?"

"The fame motive which incited the attempt in Petersburg, in which her lamented father lost his life," was my quiet reply.

His Majesty touched a bell, and in answer Stoyanovitch appeared upon the threshold and saluted.

"If General Markoff is still here I desire to see him immediately."

The Captain saluted, backed out and withdrew.

I held my breath. This was, indeed, a misfortune. I had no wish that Markoff should know of the inquiries I was instituting.

"May I venture to make a request of Your Majesty?" I asked in a low, uncertain voice.

"What is it?" he asked with quick irritation.

"That General Markoff shall be allowed to remain in ignorance of Her Highness's disappearance?"

"Why?" asked the Emperor, looking across at me in surprise.

"Because—well, because, for certain reasons, I believe secrecy at present to be the best course," I replied somewhat lamely.

"Nonsense!" was his abrupt response. "Natalia is missing. You suspect that she has fallen victim to some conspiracy. Therefore Markoff must know, and our Secret Police must investigate. Markoff knows of every plot as soon as it is conceived. His organisation is marvellous. He will probably know something. Fortunately, he had only just left me on your arrival."

His Excellency probably left the Emperor's presence because he did not wish to meet me face to face.

Again I tried to impress upon His Majesty that, as Hartwig had commenced an investigation in England, the matter might be left to him. But he only replied:

"Hartwig is head of the criminal police. He therefore has little, if any, knowledge of the revolutionaries. No, Trewinnard. This is essentially a matter for Markoff."

I bit my lips, for next second the white-enamelled steel door of that bomb-proof room in which we were standing was thrown open, and a chamberlain announced:

"His Excellency General Serge Markoff!"

Chapter Twenty Eight
The Emperor's Favourite

For a second the famous chief of Secret Police turned his cunning, steel-blue eyes upon mine and bowed slightly, after making obeisance to His Majesty.

"Why, I believed, Mr Trewinnard, that you were still in Siberia!" he said with a crafty smile. Though my bitterest enemy, he always feigned the greatest friendliness.

"Trewinnard has just revealed a very painful and serious fact, Markoff," exclaimed the Emperor, in a deep, earnest voice. "Her Highness the Grand Duchess Natalia has disappeared."

The General gave no sign of surprise.

"It has already been reported to us," was his calm answer. "I have not reported it, in turn, to Your Majesty, fearing to cause undue alarm. Both here and in England we are instituting every possible inquiry."

"Another plot," I remarked, with considerable sarcasm, I fear.

"Probably," was His Excellency's reply, as he turned to His Imperial Master, and in that fawning voice of his, added: "Your Majesty may rest assured that if Her Highness be alive she will be found, wherever she may be."

Hatred—hatred most intense—arose within my heart as I glanced at the sinister face of the favourite before me, the man who had deliberately ordered the commission of that crime which had resulted in the death of the Emperor's brother, the Grand Duke Nicholas. To his orders had been due that exciting episode in which I had so nearly lost my life in Siberia; at his orders, too, poor Marya de Rosen had been deliberately sent to her grave; and at his orders had been planned the conspiracy against the Grand Duchess which Danilo Danilovitch had intended to carry into execution, and would no doubt have done, had he not been prevented by Hartwig's boldness.

I longed to turn and denounce him before his Imperial Master. Indeed, hot, angry words were upon my lips, but I suppressed them. No! The time was not yet ripe. Natalia herself had promised to make the revelations, and to her I must leave them.

I must find her—and then.

"Ah!" exclaimed His Majesty, well pleased. "I knew that you would be already informed, Markoff. You know everything. Nothing which affects my family ever escapes you."

"I hope not, Sire. I trust I may ever be permitted to display my loyalty and gratitude for the confidence which Your Majesty sees fit to repose in me."

"To your astuteness, Markoff, I have owed my life a score of times," the Emperor declared. "I have already acknowledged your devoted services. Now make haste and discover the whereabouts of my harebrained little niece, Tattie, for the little witch is utterly incorrigible."

Markoff, pale and hard-faced, was silent for a moment. Then with a strange expression upon his grey, deceitful countenance he said:

"Perhaps I should inform Your Majesty of one point which to-day was reported to us from England—namely, that it is believed that Her Highness has fled with—well, with a lover—a certain young Englishman."

"A lover!" roared the Emperor, his face instantly white with anger. "Another lover! Who is he, pray?"

"His name is Richard Drury," His Excellency replied.

"Then the girl has created an open scandal! The English and French newspapers will get hold of it, and we shall have detailed accounts of the elopement—eh?" he cried excitedly. "This, Markoff, is really too much!" Then turning to me he asked: "What do you know of this young Drury? Tell me, Trewinnard."

"Very little, Sire, except that he is her friend, and that he is in ignorance of her true station."

"But are they in love with each other?" he demanded in a hard voice. "Have you neglected my instructions and allowed clandestine meetings—eh?"

"Unfortunately my journey across Siberia prevented my exercising due vigilance," I faltered. "Yet she gave me her word of honour that she would form no male attachment."

"Bosh!" he cried angrily, as he crossed the room. "No girl can resist falling in love with a man if he is good-looking and a gentleman—at least, no girl of Tattie's high spirits and disregard for the *convenances*. You were a fool, Trewinnard, to accept the girl's word."

"I believed in the honour of a lady," I said in mild reproach, "and especially as the lady was a Romanoff."

"The Romanoff women are as prone to flirtation as any commoner of the same sex," he declared hastily. "Markoff knows of more than one scandal which has had to be faced and crushed out during the last five years. But this fellow Drury," he added impatiently, "who is he?"

In a few brief sentences I told him what I knew concerning him.

"You think they have fallen in love?"

"I am fully convinced of it, Sire."

"Therefore they may have eloped! Tattie's disappearance may have no connection with any revolutionary plot—eh?"

"It may not. But upon that point I am quite undecided," was my reply.

"Let me hear your views, Markoff," said the Emperor sharply.

"I believe that Her Highness has fallen the victim of a plot," was his quick reply. "The man Drury may have shared the same fate."

"Fate!" he echoed. "Do you anticipate, then, that the girl is dead?"

"Alas, Sire! If she has fallen into the hands of the revolutionists, then without doubt she is dead," was the cunning official's reply.

Was he revealing to his Imperial Master a fact that he knew? Was he preparing the Emperor for the receipt of bad news?

I glanced at his grey, coarse, sphinx-like countenance, and felt convinced that such was the case. Had she, after all, fallen a victim of his craft and cunning, and were her lips sealed for ever?

I stood there staring at the pair, the Emperor and his all-powerful favourite, like a man in a dream. Suddenly I roused myself with the determination that I would leave no stone unturned to unmask this man and reveal him in his true light to the Sovereign who had trusted him so complacently, and had been so ingeniously blinded and misled by this arch-adventurer, to whose evil machinations the death of so many innocent persons were due.

"Then you are not certain whether, after all, it is an elopement?" asked the Emperor, glancing at him a few moments later. And turning impatiently to me he said in reproach: "I gave her into your hands, Trewinnard. You promised me solemnly to exercise all necessary vigilance in order to prevent a repetition of that affair in Moscow, when the madcap was about to run away to London. Yet you relaxed your vigilance and she has escaped while you have been on your wild-goose chase through Siberia."

"With greatest respect to your Majesty, I humbly submit that my mission was no wild-goose chase. It concerned a woman's honour and her liberty," and I glanced at Markoff's grey, imperturbable countenance. "But the unfortunate lady was sent to her death—purposely killed by exhaustion and exposure, ere I could reach Yakutsk."

"She was a dangerous person," the General snapped, with a smile of sarcasm.

"Yes," I said in a hard, bitter voice. "She was marked as such upon the list of exiles—and treated as such—treated in a manner that no woman is treated in any other country which calls itself Christian!"

I saw displeasure written upon the Emperor's face, therefore I apologised for my outburst.

"It ill becomes you, an Englishman, to criticise our penal system, Trewinnard," the Emperor remarked in quiet rebuke. "And, moreover, we are not discussing it. Madame de Rosen conspired against my life and she is dead. Therefore the question is closed."

"I believe when Your Majesty comes to ascertain the truth—the actual truth," I said, glancing meaningly at Markoff, who was then standing before the Sovereign, his hands clasped behind his back, "that you will discover some curious connection between the death of Marya de Rosen in the Yakutsk prison and the disappearance and probable death of Her Imperial Highness the Grand Duchess Natalia."

"What do you mean?" he asked, staring at me in surprise.

"For answer," I said, "I must, with great respect, direct Your Majesty to His Excellency General Markoff, who is aware of all that concerns the Imperial family. He probably knows the truth regarding the strange disappearance of the young lady, and what connection it has with Madame de Rosen's untimely end."

"I really do not understand you," cried the renowned chief of Secret Police, drawing himself up suddenly. "What do you infer?"

"His Majesty is anxious to learn the truth," I said, looking straight into those cunning blue eyes of his. "Your Excellency, a loyal and dutiful subject, will, I trust, now make full revelation of what has really happened during the past twelve months, and what secret tie existed between Her Highness and Marya de Rosen." His face went white as paper. But only for a single second. He always preserved the most marvellous self-control.

"I do not follow your meaning," he declared. "Madame de Rosen's death was surely no concern of mine. Many other politicals have died on their way to the Arctic settlements."

"You speak in enigmas, Trewinnard. Pray be more explicit," the Emperor urged.

I could see that my words had suddenly aroused his intense curiosity, although well aware of the antagonism in which I held the dreaded oppressor of Holy Russia.

"I regret, Your Majesty, that I cannot be more explicit," I said. "His Excellency will reveal the truth—a strange truth. If not, I myself will do so. But not, however, to-day. His Excellency must be afforded an opportunity of explaining circumstances of which he is aware. Therefore I humbly beg to withdraw."

And I crossed to the door and bowed low.

"As you wish, Trewinnard," answered the Emperor impatiently, as with a wave of the hand he indicated that my audience was at an end.

So as I backed out, bowing a second time, and while Markoff stood there in statuesque silence, his face livid, I added in a clear voice:

"Ask His Excellency for the truth—the disgraceful truth! He alone knows. Let him find Her Imperial Highness—if he can—if he dare!"

Then I opened the door and made my exit, full of wonder at what might occur when the pair were alone.

Chapter Twenty Nine
Presents another Problem

On returning to Petersburg that evening and entering the Embassy, I found a telegram from Hartwig, summoning me back to London immediately. There were no details, only the words: "Return here at once." All my letters to the club I had ordered to be sent to him during my absence, so I wondered whether he had received any communication from the missing pair. With the knowledge that any telegrams to me would be copied and sent to the Bureau of Secret Police, he had wisely omitted any reason for my return to London. I sent him, through the Bureau of Detective Police, the message to wire me details to the Esplanade Hotel in Berlin, and at midnight left by the ordinary train for the German frontier.

Four eager anxious days I spent on that never-ending journey between the Neva and the Channel. At Berlin, on calling at the hotel, I received no word from him, only when I entered the St. James's Club at five o'clock on the afternoon of my arrival at Charing Cross did I find him awaiting me.

"Well," I asked anxiously, as I entered the square hall of the club, "what news?"

"She's alive," he said. "She saw your advertisement and has replied!"

"Thank heaven!" I gasped. "Where is she?"

"Here is the address," and he drew from his pocket-book a slip of paper, with the words written in Natalia's own hand: "Miss Stebbing, Glendevon House, Lochearnhead, Perthshire." And with it he handed the note which had come to the club and which he had opened—a few brief words merely enclosing her address and telling me to exercise the greatest caution in approaching her. "I have been watched by very suspicious persons," she added, "and so I am in hiding here. When you can come, do so. I am extremely anxious to see you."

"What do you make of that?" I asked the famous police official.

"That she scented danger and escaped," he replied. "My first intention was to go up to Scotland to see her, but on reflection I thought, sir, that you might prefer to go alone."

"I do. I shall leave Euston by the mail to-night and shall be there to-morrow morning. She has, I see assumed another name."

"Yes, and she has certainly gone to an outlandish spot where no one would have thought of searching for her."

"Drury suggested it, without a doubt. He knows Scotland so well," I said.

Therefore yet another night I spent in a sleeping-car between Euston and Perth, eating scones for breakfast in the Station Hotel at the latter place, and leaving an hour later by way of Crieff and St. Fillans, to the beautiful bank of Loch Earn, lying calm and blue in the spring sunshine.

At the farther end of the loch the train halted at the tiny station of Lochearnhead, a small collection of houses at the end of the picturesque little lake, where the green wooded banks sloped to the water's edge. Quiet, secluded, and far from the bustle of town or city it was. I found a rural little lake-side village, with a post-office and general shop combined, and a few charming old-world cottages inhabited by sturdy, homely Scottish folk.

Of a brown-whiskered shepherd passing near the station I inquired for Glendevon House, whereupon he pointed to a big white country mansion high upon the hill-side, commanding a wide view across the loch and surrounding hills; a house hemmed in by tall firs, fresh in their bright spring green.

A quarter of an hour later, having climbed the winding road leading to it, I entered the long drive flanked by rhododendrons, and was approaching the house when, across the lawn a slim female figure, in a white cotton gown, with a crimson flower in the corsage, came flying toward me, crying:

"Uncle Colin! Uncle Colin! At last!"

And a moment later Natalia wrung my hand warmly, her cheeks flushed with pleasure at our encounter.

"Whatever is the meaning of this latest escapade?" I asked. "You've given everybody a pretty fright, I can tell you."

"I know, Uncle Colin. But you'll forgive me, won't you? Say you do," she urged.

"I can't before I know what has really happened."

"Let's go over to that seat," she suggested, pointing to a rustic bench set invitingly on the lawn beneath a spreading oak, "and I'll tell you everything."

Then as we walked across the lawn she regarded me critically and said: "How thin you are! How very travel-worn you look!"

"Ah!" I sighed. "I've been a good many thousand miles since last I saw Your Highness."

"I know. And how is poor Marya? You found her, of course."

"Alas!" I said in a low voice, "I did not. My journey was of no avail. She died a few hours before my arrival in Yakutsk!"

"Died in Yakutsk," she echoed in a hoarse whisper halting and looking at me. "Poor Marya dead! And Luba?"

"Luba is well, but still in prison."

"Dead!" repeated the girl, speaking to herself, "and so your long winter journey was all in vain!"

"Utterly useless," I said. "Then, on returning to London a fortnight ago, I learned that you had mysteriously disappeared. I have been back to Petersburg and informed the Emperor."

"And what did he say? Was he at all anxious?" she asked quickly.

"It is known that Drury has also disappeared, and therefore His Majesty believes that you have fled together."

"So we did, but it was not an elopement. No, dear old Uncle Colin, you needn't be horribly scandalised. Mrs Holbrook, the owner of this place, is Dick's aunt, and he brought me here so that I might hide from my enemies."

"Then where is he?"

"Staying at the hotel over at St. Fillans, at the other end of the loch, under the name of Gregory. Fortunately his aunt has only recently bought this place, so he has never been here before. She is extremely kind to me."

"Then you often see Drury—eh?"

"Oh, yes, we spend each day together. Dick comes over by the eleven o'clock train. It is such fun—much better than Brighton."

"But the London police are searching everywhere for you both," I said.

"This is a long way from London," she replied with a bright laugh; "they are not likely to find us, nor are those bitter enemies of ours."

"What enemies?"

"The revolutionists. There is a desperate plot against me. Of that I am absolutely convinced," she said as she sank upon the rustic garden seat beneath the tree. The sunny view over loch and woodland was delightful, and the pretty garden and fir wood surrounding were full of birds singing their morning song.

"But you told neither Hartwig nor Dmitri of your fears," I remarked. "Why not?" and I looked straight into her beautiful face, lit by the brilliant sunshine.

"Well, I will tell you, Uncle Colin," she said, leaning back, putting her neat little brown shoe forth from the hem of her white gown, and folding her bare arms as she turned to me. "Dick one day discovered that wherever we went we were followed by Dmitri, and, as you may imagine, I had considerable difficulty in explaining his constant presence. But Dick loves me, and hence believes every word I tell him. He—"

"I know, you little minx," I interrupted reprovingly, "you've bewitched him. I only fear lest your mutual love may lead to unhappiness."

"That's just it. I don't know exactly what will happen when he learns who I really am."

"He must be told very soon," I said; "but go on, explain what happened."

"Ah! no," cried the girl in quick alarm; "you must not tell him. He must not know. If so, it means our parting, and—and—" she faltered, her big, expressive eyes glistened with unshed tears. "Well—you know, Uncle Colin—you know how fondly I love Dick."

"Yes, I know, my child," I sighed. "But continue, tell me all about your disappearance and its motive." Now that I had found her I saw to what desperate straights Markoff must be reduced. He had, after all, no knowledge of her whereabouts.

"It was like this," she said. "One evening we had walked along the cliffs to Rottingdean together. Dmitri had not followed us, or else he had missed us before we left Brighton. But just as we were coming down the hill, after passing that big girls' college, Dick noticed that we were being followed by a man, who he decided was a foreigner. He was, I saw, a thin-faced man with a black moustache and deeply-furrowed brow, and then I recognised him as a man whom I had seen on several previous occasions. I recollected that he followed us that night on the pier when you first saw Dick walking with Doctor Ingram."

"A man of middle height, undoubtedly a Russian," I cried. "I remember him distinctly. His name is Danilo Danilovitch—a most dangerous person."

"Ah!" she exclaimed, "I see you know him. Well, at the moment I was not at all alarmed, but next day I received an anonymous letter telling me to exercise every precaution. There was a revolutionary plot to kill me.

It was intended to kill both Dick and myself. I showed him the letter. At first he was puzzled to know why the revolutionary party should seek to assassinate a mere girl like myself, but again he accepted my explanation that it was in revenge for some action of my late father, and eventually we resolved to disappear together and remain in hiding until you returned. Then, according to what Marya de Rosen had told you, I intended to act."

"Alas! I learnt nothing."

"Ah!" she sighed. "That is the unfortunate point. I am undecided now how to act."

"Explain how you managed to elude Dmitri's vigilance in Eastbourne."

"Well, on that evening in Eastbourne I induced Miss West, Gladys Finlay and Dmitri to walk on to the station, and I entered a shop. When I came cut, Dick joined me. We slipped round a corner, and after hurrying through a number of back streets found ourselves again on the Esplanade. We walked along to Pevensey, whence that night we took train to Hastings, and arrived in London just before eleven. At midnight we left Euston for Scotland, and next morning found ourselves in hiding here. I was awfully sorry to give poor Miss West such a fright, and I knew that Hartwig would be moving heaven and earth to discover me. But I thought it best to escape and lie quite low until your return. I telegraphed to you guardedly to the British Consulate in Moscow, hoping that you might receive the message as you passed through."

"I was only half an hour in Moscow, and did not leave the station," I replied. "Otherwise I, no doubt, should have received it."

"To telegraph to Russia was dangerous," she remarked. "The Secret Police are furnished with copies of all telegrams coming from abroad, and Markoff is certainly on the alert."

"No doubt he is," I said. "As you well know, he is desperately anxious to close your lips. Now that poor Marya is dead, you alone are in possession of his secret—whatever it may be."

"And for that reason," she said slowly, her fine eyes fixed straight before her across the blue waters of the loch, "he has no doubt decided that I, too, must die."

"Exactly; therefore it now remains for Your Highness to reveal to the Emperor the whole truth concerning those letters and the secret which resulted in Marya de Rosen's arrest and death. It is surely your duly! You have no longer to respect the promise of secrecy which you gave her. Her death must be avenged—and by you—*and you alone*," I added very quietly and in deep earnestness. "You must see the Emperor—you must tell him the whole truth in the interests of his own safety—in the interests, also, of the whole nation." My dainty little companion remained silent, her eyes still fixed, her slim white fingers toying nervously with her skirt.

"And forsake Dick?" she asked presently in a low voice which trembled with emotion. "No, Uncle Colin. No, don't ask me!" she urged. "I really can't do that—I really can't do that. I—I love him far too well."

I sighed. And of a sudden, ere I was aware of it the girl, torn by conflicting emotions, burst into a flood of tears.

There, at her side I sat utterly at a loss what to say in order to mitigate her distress; for too well I knew that the pair loved each other truly, nay, madly. I knew that the love of an Imperial Grand Duchess of the greatest family in Europe is just as intense, just is passionate, just as fervent as that of a commoner, be she only a typist, a seamstress, or a serving-maid. The same feelings, the same emotions, the same passionate longings and tenderness; the same loving heart bests beneath the corsets of the patrician as beneath those of the plebeian.

You, my friendly readers, each of you—be you man or woman, love to-day, or have loved long ago. Your love is human, your affection firm, strong and undying, differing in no particular to the emotions experienced by the peasant in the cottage or the princess of the blood-royal.

I looked at the little figure on the rustic seat at my side, and all my sympathy went out to her.

I have loved once, just as you have, my reader; and I knew, alas! what she suffered, and how she foresaw opened before her the grave of all her hopes, of all her aspirations, of all her love.

She was committing the greatest sin pronounced by the unwritten law of her Imperial circle. She loved a commoner! To go forward, to speak and save her nation from the depredations of that unscrupulous camarilla, the Council of Ministers, would mean to her the abandonment of the young Englishman she loved so intensely and devotedly—the sacrifice, alas! of all she held most dear in life by the betrayal of her identity.

Chapter Thirty
Reveals the Gulf

Having been introduced to Mrs Holbrook—a pleasant-fated old lady in a white-laced cap with mauve ribbons—I made excuse to "Miss Stebbing" to leave, and took train a quarter of an hour later back to St. Fillans. From the village post-office I sent an urgent wire to Hartwig to go again to Lower Clapton, see Danilovitch, explain how Her Highness had discovered the plot against her, and assure him that if any attempt were male, proof of his treachery would be placed at once before his "comrades."

I called at the hotel and inquired for Mr Gregory, but was informed that he was out fishing. But though I lunched there and waited till evening, yet he did not return.

So again I took train back to Lochearnhead, and with the golden sunset flashing upon the loch, climbed the hill path towards Glendevon House—a nearer cut than by the carriage road.

Suddenly, as I turned the corner, I saw two figures going on before me—Natalia and Richard Drury. She wore a darker gown than in the morning, with simple, knockabout country hat, while he had on a rough tweed jacket and breeches. I drew back quickly when I recognised them. His arm was tenderly around her waist as they walked, and he was bending to her, speaking softly, as with slow steps they ascended through the hill-side copse.

Yes, they were indeed a handsome, well-matched pair. But I held, my breath, foreseeing the tragic grief which must ere long arise as the result of that forbidden affection.

Standing well back in the hedge, I gazed after their as with halting steps they went up that unfrequented Scotch by-way, rough and grass-grown. Suddenly they paused, and the man, believing that they were alone, took his well-beloved in his strong embrace, pushed back her hat, and imprinted a warm, passionate kiss upon her white, open brow.

Perhaps it was impolite to watch. I suppose it was; yet my sympathy was entirely with them. I, who had once loved and experienced a poignant sorrow as result, knew well all that they felt at that moment, especially now that the girl, even though an Imperal Princess, was compelled to decide between love and duty.

Unseen, I watched them cling to each other, exchanging fond, passionate caresses. I saw him tenderly push the dark hair from her eyes and again place his hot lips reverently to her brow. He held her small hand, and looking straight into her wonderful eyes, saw truth, honesty and pure affection mirrored there.

They had halted. While the evening shadows fell he had placed his hand lightly upon her shoulder and was whispering in her ear, speaking words of passionate affection, in ignorance that between them, alas! lay a barrier of birth which could never be bridged.

I felt myself a sneak and an eavesdropper; but I assure you it was with no idle curiosity—only because what I had witnessed aroused within me the most intense sorrow, because I knew that only a man's great grief and a woman's broken heart could accrue from that most unfortunate attachment.

In all the world I held no girl in greater respect than Natalia, the unconventional daughter of proud Imperial Romanoffs. Indeed, I regarded her with considerable affection, if the truth were told. She had charmed me by her natural gaiety of heart, her disregard for irksome etiquette and her plain outspokenness. She was a typical outdoor girl. What the end of her affection for Dick Drury would be I dreaded to anticipate.

Again he bent, and kissed her upon the lips, her sweet face raised to his, aglow in the crimson sunset.

He had clasped her tenderly to his heart, holding her there in his strong arms, while he rained his hot, fervent kisses upon her, and she stood in inert ecstasy.

Soon the shadows declined, yet the pair still stood there in silent enjoyment of their passionate love, all unconscious of observation. I drew a long breath. Had I not myself long ago drunk the cup of happiness to the very dregs, just as Dick Drury was now drinking it—and ever since, throughout my whole career in those gay Court circles in foreign cities, I had been obsessed by a sad and bitter remembrance. She had married a peer, and was now a great lady in London society. Her pretty face often looked out at me from the illustrated papers, for she was one of England's leading hostesses, and mentioned daily in the "personal" columns.

Once she had sent me an invitation to a shooting-party at her fine castle in Yorkshire. The irony of it all! I had declined in three lines of formal thanks.

Ah! yes. No man knew the true depths of grief and despair better than myself, therefore, surely, no man was more fitted to sympathise with that handsome couple, clasped at that moment in each other's arms.

I turned back; I could endure it no longer, foreseeing tragedy as I did.

Descending the hill to the loch-side again, I found the carriage road, and approached the big white house.

I was standing alone in the long, old-fashioned drawing-room, with its bright chintzes and bowls of potpourri, awaiting Mrs Holbrook, when the merry pair came in through the long French windows, from the sloping lawn.

"Why, Uncle Colin!" she gasped, starting and staring at me. "How long have you been here?"

"Only a few moments," I replied, and then, advancing, I shook Drury's hand. He looked a fine, handsome fellow in his rough country tweeds.

"So glad to meet you again, Mr Trewinnard," he said frankly, a smile upon his healthy, bronzed face. "I've heard from Miss Gottorp of your long journey across Siberia. You've been away months—ever since the beginning of the winter! I've always had a morbid longing to see Siberia. It must be a most dreadful place."

"Well, it's hardly a country for pleasure-seeking," I laughed; then changing my tone, I said: "You two have given me a nice fright! I returned to find you both missing, and feared lest something awful had happened to you."

"Fear of something happening caused us to disappear," he answered; then he practically repeated what Natalia had told me earlier in the day. "My aunt very kindly offered to put Miss Gottorp up, and I have since lived down at St. Fillans under the name of Gregory."

I told him of the search in progress in order to discover him. But he declared that a Scotch village or the back streets of a manufacturing town were the safest places in which to conceal oneself.

"But how long do you two intend causing anxiety to your friends?" I asked, glancing from one to the other.

Natalia looked at her lover with wide-open eyes of admiration.

"Who knows?" she asked. "Dick has to decide that."

"But Miss West and Davey, and all of them at Hove are distracted," I said, and then, turning to Drury, added, "Your man in Albemarle Street and the people at your offices in Westminster are satisfied that you've met with foul play. You certainly ought to relieve their minds by making some sign."

"I must, soon," he said. "But meanwhile—" and he turned his eyes upon his well-beloved meaningly.

"Meanwhile, you are both perfectly happy—eh?"

"Now don't lecture us, Uncle Colin!" cried the little madcap, leaning over the back of a chair and holding up her finger threateningly; and then to Dick she added: "Oh! you don't know how horrid my wicked uncle can be when he likes. He says such caustic things."

"When my niece deserves them—and only then," I assured her lover.

Though Dick Drury was in trade a builder of ships, as his father before him, he was one of nature's gentlemen. There was nothing of the modern young man, clean-shaven, over-dressed, with turned-up trousers and bright socks. He was tall, lithe, strong, well and neatly dressed as became a man in his station—a man with an income of more than ten thousand a year, as I had already secretly ascertained.

Had not Natalia been of Imperial birth the match would have been a most suitable one, for Dick Drury was decidedly one of the eligibles. But her love was, alas! forbidden, and marriage with a commoner not to be thought of.

They stood together laughing merrily, he bright, pleasant, and all unconscious of her true station, while she, sweet and winning, stood gazing upon him, flushed with pleasure at his presence.

I was describing to Drury the fright I had experienced on arrival in Brighton to find them both missing, whereupon he interrupted, saying:

"I hope you will forgive us in the circumstances, Mr Trewinnard. Miss Gottorp resolved to go into hiding until you returned to give her your advice. Therefore, with my aunt's kind assistance, we managed to disappear completely."

"My advice is quickly given," I said. "After to-night there will be no danger, therefore return and relieve the anxiety of your friends."

"But how can you guarantee there is no danger?" asked the young man, looking at me dubiously. "I confess I'm at a loss to understand the true meaning of it all—why, indeed, any danger should arise. Miss Gottorp is so mysterious, she will tell me nothing," he said in a voice of complaint.

For a moment I was silent.

"There was a danger, Drury—a real imminent danger," I said at last. "But I can assure you that it is now past. I have taken steps to remove it, and hope to-morrow morning to receive word by telegraph that it no longer exists."

"How can you control it?" he queried. "What is its true nature? Tell me," he urged.

"No, I regret that I cannot satisfy your curiosity. It is—well—it's a family matter," I said; "therefore forgive me if I refuse to betray a confidence reposed in me as a friend of the family. It would not be fair to reveal anything told me in secrecy."

"Of course not," he said. "I fully understand, Mr Trewinnard. Forgive me for asking. I did not know that the matter was so entirely confidential."

"It is. But I can assure you that, holding the key to the situation as I do, and being in a position to dictate terms to Miss Gottorp's enemies, she need not in future entertain the slightest apprehension. The danger existed, I admit; but now it is over."

"Then you advise us to return, Uncle Colin?" exclaimed the girl, swaying herself upon the chair.

"Yes—the day after to-morrow."

"You are always so weirdly mysterious," she declared. "I know you have something at the back of your mind. Come, admit it."

"I have only your welfare at heart," I assured her.

"Welfare!" she echoed, and as her eyes fixed themselves upon me she bit her lips. I knew, alas! the bitter trend of her thoughts. But her lover stood by, all unconscious of the blow which must ere long fall upon him, poor fellow. I pitied him, for I knew how much he was doomed to suffer, loving her so fondly and so well. He, of course, believed her to be a girl of similar social position to himself—a dainty little friend whom he had first met as a rather gawky schoolgirl at Eastbourne, and their friendship had now ripened to love.

"I feel that you, Mr Trewinnard, really have our welfare at heart," declared the young man earnestly. "I know in what very high esteem Miss Gottorp holds you, and how she has been awaiting your aid and advice."

"I am her friend, Drury, as I am yours," I declared. "I am aware that you love each other. I loved once, just as deeply, as fervently as you do. Therefore—I know."

"But we cannot go south—back to Brighton," the girl declared. "I refuse."

"Why?" he asked. "Mr Trewinnard has given us the best advice. You need not now fear these mysterious enemies of yours who seem to haunt you so constantly."

"Ah!" she cried in a low, wild voice, "you do not know, Dick! You don't know the truth—all that I fear—all that I suffer—for—for your sake! Uncle Colin knows."

"For my sake!" he echoed, staring at her. "I don't quite follow you. What do you mean?"

"I mean," she exclaimed in a low, hoarse voice, drawing herself up and standing erect, "I mean that you do not know what Uncle Colin is endeavouring to induce me to do—you do not realise the true tragedy of my position."

"No, I don't," was his blunt response, his eyes wide-open in surprise.

"Oh, Dick," she cried in despair, her voice trembling with emotion, "he speaks the truth when he urges me for my own sake to go south—to return again to Hove. But, alas! if I followed his advice, sound though it is, it would mean that—that to-morrow we should part for ever!"

"Part!" gasped the young man, his face becoming white in an instant. "Why?"

"Because—well, simply because all affection between us is forbidden," she faltered in a hoarse, half whisper, her beautiful face ashen pale, "because,"—she gasped, still clinging to the back of the chintz-covered chair, "because, although we love each other as passionately and as dearly as we do, we can never marry—never! Between us there exists a barrier—a barrier strong but invisible, that can never be broken—never—until the grave!"

Chapter Thirty One
The Painful Truth

With Her Highness's permission I had despatched a reassuring telegram in the private cipher to the Emperor prefixed by the word "Bathildis"—a message which, I think, greatly puzzled the local postmaster at Lochearnhead. Another I had sent to Miss West, and then returned to the small hotel at the loch-side where I intended to spend the night.

I had left the pair together, and strolled out across the lawn. Of what happened afterwards I was in ignorance. The girl had come in search of me a quarter of an hour later, pale, trembling and tearful, and in a broken voice told me that they had parted.

I took her soft little hand, and looking straight into her eyes asked:

"Does he know the truth?"

She shook her head slowly in the negative.

"I—I have resolved to return to Russia," she said simply, in a faltering voice.

"To see the Emperor?" I asked eagerly. "To tell him the truth—eh?"

Her white lips were compressed. She only drew a long, deep breath.

"Dick has gone," she said at last, in a strange, dreamy voice. "And—and I must go back again to all the horrible dreariness and formality of the life to which, I suppose, I was born. Ah! Uncle Colin—I—I can't tell you how I feel. My happiness is all at an end—for ever."

"Come, come," I said, placing my hand tenderly upon the girl's shoulder. "You will go back to Petersburg—and you will learn to forget. We all of us have similar disappointments, similar sorrows. I, too, have had mine."

But she only shook her head, bursting into tears as she slowly disengaged herself from me.

Then, with head sunk upon her chest in blank despair and sobbing bitterly, she turned from me, and in the clear, crimson afterglow, went slowly back up the garden-path to the house.

I stood gazing upon her slim, dejected figure until it was lost around the bend of the laurels. Then I retraced my steps towards the little lake-side village.

At ten o'clock that night, while writing a letter in the small hotel sitting-room, Richard Drury was shown in.

His face was paler than usual, hard and set.

He apologised for disturbing me at that hour, but I offered him a chair and handed him my cigarette-case. His boots were very dusty, I noticed; therefore I surmised that since leaving his well-beloved he had been tramping the roads.

"I am much puzzled, Mr Trewinnard," he blurted forth a moment later. "Miss Gottorp has suddenly sent me from her and refused to see me again."

"That is to be much regretted," I said. "Before I left I heard her declare that there were certain circumstances which rendered it impossible for you to marry. I therefore know that your interview this evening must have been a painful one."

"Painful!" he echoed wildly. "I love her, Mr Trewinnard! I confess it to you, because you are her friend and mine."

"I honestly believe you do, Drury. But," I sighed, "yours is, I fear, an unfortunate—a very unfortunate attachment."

I was debating within myself whether or not it were wise to reveal to him Natalia's identity. Surely no good could now accrue from further secrecy, especially as she had resolved to return at once to Russia.

I saw how agitated the poor fellow was, and how deep and fervent was his affection for the girl who, after all, was sacrificing her great love to perform a duty to her oppressed nation and to avenge the lives of thousands of her innocent compatriots.

"Yes. I know that my affection for her is an unfortunate one," he said, in a thick voice. "She has talked strangely about this barrier between us, and how that marriage is not permitted to her. It is all so mysterious, so utterly incomprehensible, Mr Trewinnard. She is concealing something. She has some secret, and I feel sure that you, as an intimate friend of her family, are aware of it." Then after a slight pause he grew calm and, looking me straight in the face, asked: "May I not know it? Will you not tell me the truth?"

"Why should I, Drury, when the truth must only cause you pain?" I queried. "You have suffered enough already. Why not go away and forget? Time heals most broken hearts."

"It will never heal mine," he declared, adding: "Her words this evening have greatly puzzled me. I cannot see why we may not marry. She has no parents, I understand. Yet how is it that she seems eternally watched by certain suspicious-looking foreigners? Why is her life—and even mine—threatened as it is?"

For a few moments I did not speak. My eyes were fixed upon his strong, handsome face, tanned as it was by healthy exercise.

"If you wish to add to your grief by ascertaining the truth, Drury, I will tell you," I said quietly.

"Yes," he cried. "Tell me—I can bear anything now. Tell me why she refuses any longer to allow me at her side—I who love her so devotedly."

"Her decision is only a just one," I replied. "It must cause you deep grief, I know, but it is better for you to be made aware of the truth at once, for she knew that a great and poignant sorrow must fall upon you both one day."

"Why?" he asked, still puzzled and leaning in his chair towards me.

"Because the woman you love—whom you know as Miss Gottorp—has never yet revealed her true identity to you."

"Ah! I see!" he cried, starting to his feet. "I guess what you are going to say. She—she is already married!"

"No."

"Thank God for that!" he gasped. "Well, tell me."

Again I paused, my eyes fixed steadily upon his.

"Her true name is not Gottorp. She is Her Imperial Highness the Grand Duchess Natalia Olga Nicolaievna of Russia, niece of His Majesty the Emperor!"

The man before me stared at me with open mouth in blank amazement.

"The Grand Duchess Natalia!" he echoed. "Impossible!"

"It is true," I went on. "At Eastbourne, in her school-days, she was known as Miss Gottorp—which is one of the family names of the Imperial Romanoffs—and on her return to Brighton she resumed that name. The suspicious-looking foreigners who have puzzled you by haunting her so continuously are agents of Russian police, attached to her for her personal protection; while the threats against her have emanated from the Revolutionary Party. And," I added, "you can surely now see the existence of the barrier between you—you can discern why, at last, foreseeing tragedy in her love for you, Her Highness has summoned courage and, even though it has broken her heart, has resolved to part from you in order to spare you further anxiety and pain."

For some moments he did not speak.

"Her family have discovered her friendship, I suppose," he murmured at last, in a low, despairing voice.

"Her family have not influenced her in the least," I assured him. "She told me the truth that she could not deceive you any longer, or allow you to build up false hopes, knowing as she did that you could never become her husband."

"Ah! my God! all this is cruel, Mr Trewinnard!" he burst forth, with clenched hands. "I have all along believed her to be a girl of the upper middle-class, like myself. I never dreamed of her real rank or birth which precluded her from becoming my wife! But I see it all now—I see how—how utterly impossible it is for me to think of marriage with Her Imperial Highness. I—I—"

He could not finish his sentence. He stretched out his strong hand to me, and in a broken breath murmured a word of thanks.

In his kind, manly eyes I saw the bright light of unshed tears. His voice was choked by emotion as, turning upon his heel, poor fellow! he abruptly left the room, crushed beneath the heavy blow which had so suddenly fallen upon him.

Chapter Thirty Two
At What Cost!

Colonel Paul Polivanoff, Marshal of the Imperial Court, gorgeous in his pale-blue and gold uniform of the Nijni-Novgorod Dragoons, with many decorations, tapped at the white-enamelled steel door of His Majesty's private cabinet in the Palace of Tzarskoie-Selo, and then entered, announcing in French:

"Her Imperial Highness the Grand Duchess Natalia and M'sieur Colin Trewinnard."

Nine days had passed since that parting of the lovers at Lochearnhead, and now, as we stood upon the threshold of the bomb-proof chamber, I knew that our visit there in company was to be a momentous event in the history of modern Russia.

As we entered, the Emperor, who had been busy with the pile of State documents upon his table, rose, settled the hang of his sword—for he was in a dark green military uniform, with the double-headed eagle of Saint Andrew in diamonds at his throat—and turned to meet us.

Towards me His Majesty extended a cordial welcome, but I could plainly detect that his niece's presence caused him displeasure.

"So you are back again in Russia—eh, Tattie?" he snapped in French, speaking in that language instead of Russian because of my presence. "It seems that during your absence you have been guilty of some very grave indiscretions and more than one scandalous escapade—eh?"

"I am here to explain to Your Majesty," the girl said quite calmly, and looking very pale and sweet in her half-mourning.

"Trewinnard has furnished me with reports," he said hastily, motioning her to a chair. "What you have to say, please say quickly, as I have much to do and am leaving for Moscow to-night. Be seated."

"I am here for two reasons," she said, seating herself opposite to where he had sunk back into his big padded writing-chair, "to explain what you are pleased to term my conduct, and also to place your Majesty in possession of certain facts which have been very carefully hidden from you."

"Another plot—eh?" he snapped. "There are plots everywhere just now."

"A plot—yes—but not a revolutionary one," was her answer.

"Leave such things to Markoff or to Hartwig. They are not women's business," he cried impatiently. "Rather explain your conduct in England. From what I hear, you have so far forgotten what is due to your rank and station as to fall in love with some commoner! Markoff made a long report about it the other day. I have it somewhere," and he glanced back upon his littered table, whereon lay piled the affairs of a great and powerful Empire.

Her cheeks flushed slightly, and I saw that her white-gloved hand twitched nervously. We had travelled together from Petersburg, and upon the journey she had been silent and thoughtful, bracing herself up for an ordeal.

"I care not a jot for any report of General Markoff's," she replied boldly. "Indeed, it was mainly to speak of him that I have asked for audience to-day."

"To tell me something against him, I suppose, just because he has discovered your escapades in England—because he has dared to tell me the truth—eh, Tattie?" he said, with a dry laugh. "So like a woman!"

"If he has told you the truth about me, then it is the first time he has ever told Your Majesty the truth," she said, looking straight at the Emperor.

The Sovereign glanced first at her with quick surprise and then at myself.

"Her Imperial Highness has something to report to Your Majesty, something of a very grave and important nature," I ventured to remark.

"Eh? Eh?" asked the big bearded man, in his quick, impetuous way. "Something grave—eh? Well, Tattie, what is it?"

The girl, pale and agitated, held her breath for a few moments. Then she said:

"I know, uncle, that you consider me a giddy, incorrigible flirt. Perhaps I am. But, nevertheless, I am in possession of a secret—a secret which, as it affects the welfare of the nation and of the dynasty, it is, I consider, my duty to reveal to you."

"Ah! Revolutionists again!"

"I beg of you to listen, uncle," she urged. "I have several more serious matters to place before you."

"Very well," he replied, smiling as though humouring her. "I am listening. Only pray be brief, won't you?"

"You will recollect the attempt planned to be made in the Nevski on the early morning of our arrival from the Crimea, and in connection with that plot a lady, a friend of mine and of Mr Trewinnard's, named Madame de Rosen, and her daughter Luba were arrested and sent by administrative process to Siberia?"

"Certainly. Trewinnard went recently on a quixotic mission to the distressed ladies," he laughed. "But why, my dear child, refer to them further? They were conspirators, and I really have no interest in their welfare. The elder woman is, I understand, dead."

"Yes," the Grand Duchess cried fiercely; "killed by exposure, at the orders of General Serge Markoff."

"Oh!" he exclaimed, "then you have come here to denounce poor Markoff as an assassin—eh? This is really most interesting."

"What I have to relate to Your Majesty will, I believe, be found of considerable interest," she said, now quite calm and determined. "True, I have charged Serge Markoff with the illegal arrest and the subsequent death of an innocent woman. It is for me now to prove it."

"Certainly," said His Imperial Majesty, settling himself in his big chair, and placing the tips of his strong white fingers together in an attitude of listening.

"Then I wish to reveal to you a few facts concerning this man who wields such wide and autocratic power in our Russia—this man who is the real oppressor of our nation, and who is so cleverly misleading and terrorising its ruler."

"Tattie! What are you saying?"

"You will learn when I have finished," she said. "I am only a girl, I admit, but I know the truth—the scandalous truth—how you, the Emperor, are daily deceived and made a catspaw by your clever and unscrupulous Chief of Secret Police."

"Speak. I am all attention," he said, his brows darkening.

"I have referred to poor Marya de Rosen," said the girl, leaning her elbow upon the arm of the chair and looking straight into her uncle's face. "If the truth be told, Marya and Serge Markoff had been acquainted for a very long time. Two years after the death of her husband, Felix de Rosen, the wealthy banker of Odessa and Warsaw, Serge Markoff, in order to obtain her money, married her."

"Married her!" echoed the Emperor in a loud voice. "Can you prove this?"

"Yes. Three years ago, when I was living with my father in Paris, I went alone one morning to the Russian Church in the Rue Daru, where, to my utter amazement, I found a quiet marriage-service in progress. The contracting parties were none other than General Markoff and the widow, Madame de Rosen. Beyond the priest and the sacristan, I was the only person in possession of the truth. They both returned to Petersburg next day, but agreed to keep their marriage secret, as the General was cunning enough to know that marriage would probably interfere with his advancement and probably cause Your Majesty displeasure."

"I had no idea of it!" he remarked, much surprised. "Marya de Rosen — or Madame Markoff, as she really was — frequently went to her husband's house, but always clandestinely and unknown to Luba, who had no suspicion of the truth," the girl went on. "According to the story told to me by Marya herself, a strange incident occurred at the General's house one evening. She had called there and been admitted, by the side entrance, by a confidential servant, and was awaiting the return of the General, who was having audience at the Winter Palace. While sitting alone, a young woman of the middle-class — probably an art-student — was ushered into the room by another servant, who believed Marya was awaiting formal audience of His Excellency. The girl was highly excited and hysterical, and finding Marya alone, at once broke out in terrible invective against the General. Marya naturally took Markoff's part, whereupon the girl began to make all sorts of charges of conspiracy, and even murder, against him — charges which Marya declared to the girl's face were lies.

"Suddenly, however, the girl plunged her hand deep into the pocket of her skirt and produced three letters, which, with a mocking laugh, she urged Marya to read and then to judge His Excellency accordingly. Meanwhile, the manservant, having heard the girl's voice raised excitedly, entered and promptly ejected her, leaving the letters in Marya's hands. She opened them. They were all in Serge Markoff's own handwriting, and were addressed to a certain man named Danilo Danilovitch, once a shoemaker at Kazan, and now, in secret, the leader of the Revolutionary Party.

"From the first of these Marya saw that it was quite plain that the General — the man in whom Your Majesty places such implicit faith — had actually bribed the man with five thousand roubles and a promise of police protection to assassinate Your Majesty's brother, the Grand Duke Peter Michailovitch, from whom he feared exposure, as he had been shrewd enough to discover his double-dealing and the peculation of the public funds of which Markoff had been guilty while holding the office of Governor of Kazan. Six days after that letter," Her Highness added in a hard, clear voice, "my poor Uncle Peter was shot dead by an unknown hand while emerging from the Opera House in Warsaw."

"Ah! I remember!" exclaimed His Majesty hoarsely, for the Grand Duke Peter was his favourite brother, and his assassination had caused him the most profound grief.

"Of the other two letters—all of them having been in my possession," Her Highness went on, "one was a brief note, appointing a meeting for the following evening at a house near the Peterhof Station, in Petersburg, while the third contained a most amazing confession. In the course of it General Markoff wrote words to the following effect: 'You and your chicken-hearted friends are utterly useless to me. I was present and watched you. When he entered the theatre you and your wretched friends were afraid—you failed me! You call yourself Revolutionists—you, all of you, are without the courage of a mouse! I thought better of you. When you failed so ignominiously, I waited—waited until he came out. Where you failed, I was fortunately successful. He fell at the first shot. Arrests were, of course, necessary. Some of your cowardly friends deserve all the punishment they will get. Forty-six have been arrested to-day. Meet me to-morrow at eight p.m. at the usual rendezvous. You shall have the money all the same, though you certainly do not deserve it. Destroy this.'"

"Where is that letter?" demanded His Majesty quickly.

"It has unfortunately been destroyed—destroyed by its writer. Marya was aghast at these revelations of her husband's treachery and double-dealing, for while Chief of Secret Police and Your Majesty's most trusted adviser he was actually aiding and abetting the Revolutionists! She placed the letters which had so opportunely come into her possession into her pocket, and said nothing to Markoff when he returned. But from that moment she distrusted him, and saw how ingenious and cunning were his dealings with both yourself and with the leader of the Revolutionists. He, assisted by his catspaw, Danilo Danilovitch, formed desperate plots for the mere purpose of making whole sale arrests, and thus showing you how active and astute he was. Danilo Danilovitch—who, as 'The One,' the leader whose actual identity is unknown by those poor deluded wretches who believe they can effect a change in Russia by means of bombs—is as cunning and crafty as his master. It was he who threw the bomb at our carriage and who killed my poor dear father. He—"

"How can you prove that?" demanded the Emperor quickly.

"I myself saw him throw the bomb," I said, interrupting. "The outrage was committed at Markoff's orders."

"Impossible! Why do you allege this, Trewinnard? What motive could Markoff have in killing the Grand Duke Nicholas?"

"The same that he had in ordering the arrest and banishment of his own wife and her daughter," was my reply. "Her Highness will make further explanation."

"The motive was simply this," went on the girl, still speaking with great calmness and determination. "A few days before I left with Your Majesty on the tour of the Empire, I called upon Marya de Rosen to wish her good-bye. On that occasion she gave me the three letters in question—which had apparently been stolen from Danilovitch by the girl who had handed them to her. Marya told me that she feared lest her husband, when he knew they were in her possession, might order a domiciliary visit for the purpose of securing possession of them. Therefore she begged me, after she had shown me the contents and bound me to strictest silence, to conceal them. This I did.

"While we were absent in the south nothing transpired, but Danilovitch had arranged an attempt in the Nevski on the morning of our return to Petersburg. The plot was discovered at the eleventh hour, as usual and among those arrested was Madame de Rosen and Luba. Why? Because Your Majesty's favourite, Serge Markoff, having discovered that the incriminating letters had been handed to his wife, knew that she, and probably Luba, were aware of his secret. He feared that the evidence of his crime must have passed into other hands, and dreading lest his wife should betray him, he ordered her arrest as a dangerous political. After her arrest he saw her, and, hoping for her release, she explained how she had handed the letters to me for safe-keeping, and confessed that I was aware of the shameful truth. She was not, however, released, but sent to her grave. For that same reason Markoff ordered his agent Danilovitch to throw the bomb at the carriage in which I was riding with my poor father and Mr Trewinnard."

"But I really cannot give credence to all this!" exclaimed the Emperor, who had risen again and was standing near the window which looked out upon the courtyard of the palace, whence came the sound of soldiers drilling and distant bugle-calls.

"Presently Your Majesty shall be given a complete proof," his niece responded. "Danilovitch has confessed. At Markoff's orders—which he was compelled to carry out, fearing that if he refused the all-powerful Chief of Secret Police would betray him to his comrades as a spy—he, at imminent risk of being shot by the sentries, visited our palace on four occasions, and succeeded at last, after long searches, in discovering the letters where I had hidden them for safety in my old nursery, and, securing them, he handed them back to his master."

"Then this Danilovitch is a Revolutionist paid by Markoff to perform his dirty work—eh?" asked the Emperor angrily.

"He is paid, and paid well, to organise conspiracies against Your Majesty's person," I interrupted. "The majority of the plots of the past three years have been suggested by Markoff himself, and arranged by Danilovitch, who finds it very easy to beguile numbers of his poor deluded comrades into believing that the revolution will bring about freedom in Russia. A list of these he furnishes to Markoff before each attempt is discovered, hence the astute Chief of Secret Police is always able to put his hand upon the conspirators and to furnish a satisfactory report to Your Majesty, for which he receives commendation."

"Apparently a unique arrangement," remarked the sovereign reflectively.

"In order to close the lips of Madame de Rosen, he contrived that she should receive such brutal and inhuman treatment that she died of the effects of cold, hardship and exposure," I went on. "One of Markoff's agents made a desperate attempt upon myself while in Siberia, fearing that Her Highness had revealed the truth to me, and well knowing that I was aware of Danilovitch's true *métier*. The attempt fortunately failed, as did another recently formed by Danilovitch in London at Markoff's orders. Therefore—"

"But this Danilovitch!" interrupted His Majesty, turning to me. "Has he actually confessed to you?"

"He has, Sire," I replied. "The sole reason of my journey to Yakutsk was in order to see Marya de Rosen on Her Highness's behalf and obtain permission for her to speak and reveal to Your Majesty all that the Grand Duchess has now told you. Her Highness had promised strictest secrecy to her friend, but now that the lady is dead I have at last induced her to speak in the personal-interests of Your Majesty, as well as in the interests of the whole nation."

"Yes, yes, I quite understand," said His Majesty very gravely.

"By returning here, by abandoning my *incognita*, I—I have been compelled to sacrifice my love," declared the girl in a low, faltering voice, her cheeks blanched, her mouth drawn hard, and her fine eyes filled with tears.

"Ah! Tattie! If what you have revealed to me be true, then the reason of Markoff's unsatisfactory reports concerning, you is quite apparent," His Majesty said, slowly folding his arms as he stood in thought, a fine commanding figure with the jewelled double eagle at his throat flashing with a thousand fires.

"And so, Trewinnard," he added, turning to me, "all this is the reason why, more than once, you have given me those mysterious hints which have set me pondering."

"Yes, Sire," I replied. "You have been blinded by these clever adventurers surrounding you—that circle which, headed by Serge Markoff, is always so careful to prevent you from learning the truth. The intrigue they practise is most ingenious and far-reaching, ever securing their own advancement with fat emoluments at the expense of the oppressed nation. Their basic principle is to terrorise you—to keep the bogy of revolution constantly before Your Majesty, to discover plots, and by administrative process to send hundreds, nay thousands, into exile in those far-off Arctic wastes, or fill the prisons with suspects, more than two-thirds of whom are innocent, loyal and law-abiding citizens."

He turned suddenly and, pale with anger, struck his fist upon his table.

"There shall be no more exile by administrative process!" he cried, and seating himself, he drew a sheet of official paper before him, and for a few moments his quill squeaked rapidly over the paper.

Thus he wrote the ukase abolishing exile by administrative process— that law which the camarilla had so abused—and signed it with a flourish of his pen.

The first reform in Russia—a reform which meant the yearly saving of thousands of innocent lives, the preservation of the sanctity of every home throughout the great Empire, and which guaranteed to everyone in future, suspect or known criminal or Revolutionist, a fair and open trial—had been achieved.

Surely the little Grand Duchess, the madcap of the Romanoffs, had not sacrificed her great love in vain, even though while that Imperial ukase was being written she sat with bitter tears rolling slowly down her white cheeks.

Chapter Thirty Three
Describes a Momentous Audience

A dead silence fell in that small, business-like room, wherein the monarch, the hardest-working man in the Empire, transacted the complicated business of the great Russian nation.

Outside could be heard a sharp word of command, followed by the heavy tramp of soldiers and the roll of drums. The sentries were changing guard.

Slowly—very slowly—His Majesty placed a sheet of blotting-paper over the document he had written, and then turning to the tearful girl, asked:

"Will not this individual, Danilo Danilovitch, furnish me with proofs? He is a Revolutionist, yet that is no reason why I should not see him. From what you tell me, Markoff holds him in his power by constantly threatening to betray him to his comrades as a police-spy. I must see him. Where is he?"

"He has accompanied us from London, Your Majesty," was my reply. "I had some difficulty in assuring him that he would obtain justice at Your Majesty's hands."

"He is an assassin. He killed my brother Nicholas; yet it seems—if what you tell me be true—that Markoff compelled him to commit this crime."

"Without a doubt," was my reply.

"Then, Revolutionist or not, I will see him," and he touched the electric button placed in the side of his writing-table.

A sentry appeared instantly, and at my suggestion His Majesty permitted me to go down the long corridor, at the end of which the dark, thin-faced man, in a rather shabby black suit, was sitting in a small ante-room, outside which stood a tall, statuesque Cossack sentry.

A few words of explanation, and somewhat reluctantly Danilovitch rose and followed me into the presence of the man he was ever plotting to kill.

The Emperor received him most graciously, and ordered him to be seated, saying:

"My niece here and Mr Trewinnard have been speaking of you, Danilo Danilovitch, and have told me certain astounding things."

The man looked up at his Sovereign, pale and frightened, and His Majesty, realising this, at once put him at his ease by adding: "I know that, in secret, you are the mysterious 'One' who directs the revolutionary movement throughout the Empire, and the constant conspiracies directed against my own person. Well," he laughed, "I hope, Danilovitch, you will not find me so terrible as you have been led to expect, and, further, that when you leave here you will think a little better of the man whose duty it is to rule the Russian nation than you hitherto have done. Now," he asked, looking straight at the man, "are you prepared to speak with me openly and frankly, as I am prepared to speak to you?"

"I am, Your Majesty," he said.

"Then answer me a few questions," urged the Imperial autocrat. "First, tell me whether these constant conspiracies against myself—these plots for which so many hundreds are being banished to Siberia—are genuine ones formed by those who really desire to take my life?"

"No, Sire," was the answer. "The last genuine plot was the one in Samara, nearly two years ago. Your Majesty escaped only by a few seconds."

"When the railway line was blown up just outside the station; I remember," said the Emperor, with a grim smile. "Four of your fellow-conspirators were killed by their own explosives."

"That was the last genuine plot. All the recent ones have been suggested by General Markoff, head of the Secret Police."

"With your assistance?"

The man nodded in the affirmative.

"Then you betray your fellow-conspirators for payment—eh?"

"Because I am compelled. I, alas! took a false step once, and His Excellency the General has taken advantage of it ever since. He forces me to act according to his wishes, to conspire, to betray—to murder if necessity arises—because he knows how I dread the truth becoming known to the secret revolutionary committee, and how I fully realise the terrible fate which must befall me if the actual facts were ever revealed. The Terrorists entertain no sympathy with their betrayer."

"I quite understand that," remarked the Sovereign. And then, in gracious words, he closely questioned him regarding the assassination of the Grand Duke Peter outside the Opera House in Warsaw, and heard the ghastly truth of Markoff's crime from the witness's own lips.

"I read the letters which I secured from the Palace of the Grand Duke Nicholas," he admitted. "They were to the same effect as Your Majesty has said. In one of them His Excellency the General confessed his crime."

"You threw the bomb which killed my brother, the Grand Duke Nicholas?"

"It was intended to kill Her Highness the Grand Duchess," and he indicated Natalia, "and also the Englishman, Mr Trewinnard. The General was plotting the death of both of them, fearing that they knew his secret."

"And in England there was another conspiracy against them—eh?"

"Yes," replied the man known as the Shoemaker of Kazan. "But Mr Trewinnard and the Chief of Criminal Police, Ivan Hartwig, discovered me, and dared me to commit the outrage on pain of betrayal to my friends. Hence I have been between two stools—compelled by Markoff and defied by Hartwig. At last, in desperation, I sent an anonymous letter to Her Highness warning her, with the fortunate result that both she and her lover—a young Englishman named Drury—disappeared, and even the Secret Police were unable to discover their whereabouts. I did so in order to gain time, for I had no motive in taking Her Highness's life, although if I refused to act I knew what the result must inevitably be."

"All this astounds me," declared the Emperor. "I never dreamed that I was being thus misled, or that Markoff was acting with such cunning and unscrupulousness against the interests of the dynasty and the nation. I see the true situation. You, Danilo Danilovitch, are a Revolutionist—not by conviction, but because of the drastic action of the Secret Police, the real rulers of Russia. Therefore, read that," and he took from his table the Imperial ukase and handed it to him.

When he had read it he returned it to the Emperor's hand, and murmured:

"Thank God! All Russia will praise Your Majesty for your clemency. It is the reform for which we have been craving for the past twenty years— fair trial, and after conviction a just punishment. But we have, alas! only had arrest and prompt banishment without trial. Every man and woman in Russia has hitherto been at the mercy of any police-spy or any secret enemy."

"My only wish is to give justice to the nation," declared the Sovereign, his dark, thoughtful eyes turned upon the dynamitard whose word was law to every Terrorist from Archangel to Odessa, and from Wirballen to Ekaterinburg.

"And, Sire, on behalf of the Party of the People's Will I beg to thank you for granting it to us," said the man, whose keen, highly-intelligent face was now slightly flushed.

"What I have heard to-day from my niece's lips, from Mr Trewinnard and from yourself, has caused the gravest thoughts to arise within me," His Majesty declared after a slight pause. "Injustice has, I see, been done on every hand, and the Secret Police has been administered by one who, it seems, is admittedly an assassin. It is now for me to remedy that—and to do so by drastic measures."

"And the whole nation will praise Your Majesty," Danilovitch replied. "I am a Revolutionist, it is true, but I have been forced—forced against my will—to formulate these false plots for the corrupt Secret Police to unearth. I declare most solemnly to Your Majesty that my position as leader of this Party and at the same time an *agent-provocateur* has been a source of constant danger and hourly terror. In order to hide my secret, I was unfortunately compelled to commit murder—to kill the woman I loved. She discovered the truth, and would have exposed me to the vengeance which the Party never fails to mete out to its betrayers. Markoff had given me my liberty and immunity from arrest in exchange for my services to him. He held me in his power, body and soul, and, because of that, I was forced to strike down the woman I loved," he added, with a catch in his voice. "And—and—" he said, standing before the Emperor, "I crave Your Majesty's clemency. I—I crave a pardon for that act for which I have ever been truly penitent."

"A pardon is granted," was the reply in a firm, deep voice. "You killed my brother Nicholas under compulsion. But on account of your open confession and the service rendered to me by these revelations, I must forgive you. I see that your actions have, all along, been controlled by Serge Markoff. Now," he added, "what more can you tell me regarding this maladministration of the police?"

Danilovitch threw himself upon his knees and kissed the Emperor's hand, thanking him deeply and declaring that he would never take any further part in the revolutionary movement in the future, but exercise all his influence to crush and stamp it out.

Then, when he had risen again to his feet, he addressed His Majesty, saying:

"The Secret Police, as at present organised, manufacture revolutionaries. I was a loyal, law-abiding Russian before the police arrested my brother and my wife illegally, and sent them to Siberia without trial. Then I rose, like thousands of others have done, and fell into the trap which Markoff's agents so cleverly prepared. No one has been safe from arrest in Russia—"

"Until to-day," the Emperor interrupted. "The ukase I have written is the law of the Empire from this hour."

"Ah! God be thanked!" cried the man, placing his hands together fervently. "Probably no man can tell the many crimes and injustices for which General Markoff has been responsible. You want to know some of them—some within my own knowledge," he went on. "Well, he was responsible for the great plot in Moscow a year ago when the little Tzarevitch so narrowly escaped. Seventeen people were killed and twenty-three were injured by the six bombs which were thrown, and nearly one hundred innocent persons were sent to Schusselburg or to Siberia in consequence."

"Did you formulate that plot?" the Emperor asked.

"I did. Also at Markoff's orders the one at Nikolaiev where the young woman, Vera Vogel, shot the Governor-General of Kherson and two of his Cossacks. Again at Markoff's demand, I formed the plot whereby, near Tchirskaia, the bridge over the Don was blown up; fortunately just before Your Majesty's train reached it. It was I who pressed the electrical contact—I pressed it purposely a few moments too quickly, as I was determined not to be the cause of that wholesale loss of life which must have resulted had the train fallen into the river. Another attempt was the Zuroff affair, when an infernal machine charged with nitro-glycerine was not long ago actually found within the Winter Palace—placed there by an unknown hand in order to terrify Your Majesty. But I tell you the hand that placed it where it was found was that of Serge Markoff himself—the same hand which killed His Imperial Highness the Grand Duke Peter in order to prevent His Highness telling Your Majesty certain ugly truths which he had accidentally discovered. And," he went on, "there were many other conspiracies of various kinds conceived for the sole purpose of keeping the Empire ever in a state of unrest and the arrest of hundreds of the innocent of both sexes. Indeed, explosives—picric acid, nitro-glycerine, mélinite and cordite—were supplied to us from a secret source. Sometimes, too, when I furnished a list of, say, ten or a dozen of those implicated in a plot, the police would arrest them with probably thirty others besides, people taken haphazard in the streets or in the houses. Whole families have been banished, men dragged from their wives, women from their husbands and children, and though innocent were consigned to those terrible oubliettes beneath the level of the lake at Schusselburg, or in the Fortress of Peter and Paul. To adequately describe all the fierce brutality, the gross injustice and the ingenious plots conceived and financed by Serge Markoff would be impossible. I only speak of those in which I, as his unwilling catspaw, have been implicated."

Her Highness and myself had listened to this amazing confession without uttering a word.

The Emperor, intensely interested in the man's story, put to him many questions, some concerning the demands of the Party of the People's Will, others in which he requested further details concerning Markoff's crimes against persons, and against the State.

"This man in whom for years I have placed such implicit confidence has played me false!" cried the ruler presently, his face pale as he struck the table fiercely in his anger. "He has plotted with the Terrorists against me! He has been responsible for several attempts from which I have narrowly escaped with my life. Therefore he shall answer to me—this cunning knave who is actually my brother's assassin! He shall pay the penalty of his crimes!"

"All Russia knows that at Your Majesty's hands we always receive justice," the Revolutionist said. "From the Ministry, however, we never do. They are our oppressors—our murderers."

"And you Revolutionists wish to kill me because of the misdeeds of my Ministers!" cried the Emperor in reproach.

"If Your Majesty dismisses and punishes those who are responsible, then there will be no more Terrorism in Russia. I am a leader; I have bred and reared the serpent of the Revolution, and I myself can strangle it—and I promise Your Majesty that as soon as General Markoff is removed from office—I will do so."

Chapter Thirty Four
The Emperor's Command

Again the Emperor turned to his table and scribbled a few lines in Russian, which he handed to the man.

It was an impressive moment. What he had written was the dismissal in disgrace of his favourite, the most powerful official in the Empire.

"I shall receive him in audience to-night, and shall give this to him," he said. "The punishment I can afterwards consider."

Then, after a pause, he added:

"I have to thank you, Danilo Danilovitch, for all that you have revealed to me. Go and tell your comrades of the Revolution all that I have said and what I have done. Tell them that their Emperor will himself see that justice is accorded them—that his one object in future shall be to secure, by God's grace, the peace, prosperity and tranquillity of the Russian nation."

Then the Emperor bowed as sign that the audience was at an end, and the man, unused to the etiquette of Court, bowed, turned, and wishing us farewell, walked out.

"All this utterly astounds me, Trewinnard," said His Majesty, when Danilovitch had gone. He was speaking as a man, not as an Emperor. "Yet what Tattie has revealed only confirms what I suspected regarding the death of my poor brother Peter," he went on. "You recollect that I told you my suspicions—of my secret—on the day of the fourth Court ball last year. It is now quite plain. He was ruthlessly killed by the one man in my *entourage* whom I have so foolishly believed to be my friend. Ah! How grossly one may be deceived—even though he be an Emperor!" and he sighed, drawing his strong hand wearily across his brow.

After a pause he added: "I have to thank you, Trewinnard, for thus tearing the scales from my eyes. Indeed, I have to thank you for much in connection with what I have learned to-day."

"No, Sire," was my reply. "Rather thank Her Imperial Highness. To her efforts all is due. She has sacrificed her great love for a most worthy man in the performance of this, her duty. Had she not resolved to return to Russia and speak openly at risk of giving you offence, she might have remained in England—or, rather, in Scotland, still preserving her *incognita*, and still retaining at her side the honest, upright young Englishman with whom she has been in love ever since her school-days at Eastbourne."

"I quite realise the great sacrifice you have made, Tattie," said the Emperor, turning to her kindly, and noting how pale was her beautiful countenance and how intense her look. "By this step you have, in all probability, saved my life. Markoff and his gang of corrupt Ministers would have no doubt killed me whenever it suited their purpose to do so. But you have placed your duty to myself and to the nation before your love, therefore some adequate recompense is certainly due to you."

The great man of commanding presence strode across the room from end to end, his bearded chin upon his breast, deep in thought. Suddenly he halted before her, and drawing himself up with that regal air which suited him so well, he looked straight at her, placed his hand tenderly upon her shoulder as she sat, and said:

"Tell me, Tattie; do you really and truly love this Englishman?"

"I do, uncle," the girl faltered, her fine eyes downcast. "Of course I do. I—I cannot tell you a lie and deny it."

"And—well, if Richard Drury took out letters of naturalisation as a Russian subject, and I made him a Count—and I gave you permission to marry—what then—eh?" he asked, smiling merrily as he stood over her.

She sprang to her feet and grasped both his big hands.

"You will!" she cried. "You really will! Uncle, tell me!"

The Emperor, smiling benignly upon her—for, after all, she was his favourite niece—slowly nodded in the affirmative.

Whereupon she turned to me, exclaiming:

"Oh! Uncle Colin. Dear old Uncle Colin! I'm so happy—so very happy! I must telegraph to Dick at once—at once!"

"No, no, little madcap," interrupted the Emperor; "not from here. The Secret Police would quickly know all about it. Send someone to the German frontier with a telegram. One of our couriers shall start to-night. Drury will receive the good news to-morrow evening, and, Tattie,"—he added, taking both her little hands again, "I have known all along, from various reports, how deeply and devotedly you love this young Englishman. Therefore, if I give my consent and make your union possible, I only hope and trust that you will both enjoy every happiness."

In her wild ecstasy of delight the girl raised her sweet face to his heavy-bearded countenance, that face worn by the cares of State, and kissed him fervently, thanking him profoundly, while I on my part craved for the immediate release of poor Luba de Rosen.

The Emperor at once scribbled something upon an official telegraph form, and touching a bell, the sentry carried it out.

"The young lady so cruelly wronged will be free and on her way back to Petersburg within three hours," the Monarch said quietly, after the sentry had made his exit.

"Oh! Uncle Colin!" cried Her Highness excitedly to me, "what a red-letter day this is for me!"

"And for me also, Tattie," remarked His Majesty in his deep, clear voice. "Owing to your efforts, I have learned some amazing but bitter truths; I have at last seen the reason why my people have so cruelly misjudged me, and why they hate me. I realise how I have, alas! been blinded and misled by a corrupt and unscrupulous Ministry who have exercised their power for their own self-advancement, their methods being the stirring-up of the people, the creation of dissatisfaction, unrest, and the actual manufacture of revolutionary plots directed against my own person. I now know the truth, and I intend to act—to act with a hand as strong and as relentless as they have used against my poor, innocent, long-suffering subjects." Her Highness was all anxiety to send a telegram by courier over the frontier to Eydtkuhnen. If he left Petersburg by the night train at a quarter-past ten, he would, she reckoned, be at the frontier at six o'clock on the following evening. It was half an hour by train from Tzarskoie-Selo to Petersburg, and she was now eager to end the audience and be dismissed.

But His Majesty seemed in no hurry. He asked us both many questions concerning Markoff, and what we knew regarding his dealings with the bomb-throwers.

Natalia explained what had occurred in Brighton, and how she had been constantly watched by Danilovitch, while I described the visit of Hartwig and myself to that dingy house in Lower Clapton. That sinister, unscrupulous chief of Secret Police had been directly responsible for the death of Natalia's father; and Her Highness was bitter in her invectives against him.

"Leave him to me," said the Emperor, frowning darkly. "He is an assassin, and he shall be punished as such."

Then, ringing his bell again, he ordered the next Imperial courier in waiting to be summoned, for at whatever palace His Majesty might be there were always half a dozen couriers ready at a moment's notice to go to the furthermost end of the Empire.

"I know, Tattie, you are anxious to send your message. Write it at my table, and it shall be sent from the first German station. Here, in Russia, the Secret Police are furnished with copies of all messages sent abroad or received. We do not want your secret disclosed just yet!" he laughed.

So the girl seated herself in the Emperor's chair, and after one or two attempts composed a telegram containing the good news, which she addressed to Richard Drury at his flat in Albemarle Street.

Presently the courier, a big, bearded man of gigantic stature, in drab uniform, was ushered into the Imperial presence, and saluted. To him, His Majesty gave the message, and ordered him to take it by the next train to Eydtkuhnen. Whereupon the man again saluted, backed out of the door, and started upon his errand. What, I wondered, would Dick Drury think when he received her reassuring message?

Natalia's face beamed with supreme happiness, while the Emperor himself for the moment forgot his enemies in the pleasure which his niece's delight gave to him.

Again His Majesty, with darkening brow, referred to the brutal murder of his favourite brother, the Grand Duke Peter, saying:

"You will recollect, Trewinnard, the curious conviction which one day so suddenly came upon me. I revealed it to you in strictest secrecy—the ghastly truth which seemed to have been forced upon me by some invisible agency. It was my secret, and the idea has haunted me ever since. And yet here to-day my suspicion that poor Peter was killed by some person who feared what secret he might reveal stands confirmed; and yet," he cried, "how many times have I, in my ignorance, taken the hand of my brother's murderer!"

Colonel Polivanoff, the Imperial Marshal; my old friend, Captain Stoyanovitch, equerry-in-waiting, both craved audience, one after the other, for they bore messages for His Majesty. Therefore they were received without ceremony and impatiently dismissed. The subject the Sovereign was discussing with us was of far more importance than reports from the great military camps at Yilna and at Smolensk, where manoeuvres were taking place.

The Emperor turned to his private telephone and was speaking with Trepoff, the Minister for Foreign Affairs in Petersburg, when the Marshal Polivanoff again entered, saying:

"His Excellency General Markoff petitions audience of Your Majesty."

Natalia and I exchanged quick glances, and both of us rose.

For a second the Emperor hesitated. Then, turning to us, he commanded us to remain.

"I will see him at once," he said very calmly, his face a trifle paler.

Next moment the man whose dismissal in disgrace was already lying upon the Emperor's desk stood upon the threshold and bowed himself into the Imperial presence.

Chapter Thirty Five
"From Our Own Correspondent"

That moment was indeed a breathless one.

The Emperor's countenance was grey with anger. Yet he remained quite calm and firm. He was about to deal with an enemy more bitter and more dangerous than the most relentless firebrand of the whole Revolutionary Party.

"I was not aware that Your Majesty was engaged with Her Imperial Highness," the sinister-faced official began. "I have a confidential report to make—a matter of great urgency."

"Well, I hope it is not another plot," remarked the Sovereign with bitter, weary sarcasm. "But whatever report you wish to make, Markoff, may be made here—before my niece and Mr Trewinnard."

He glanced at us suspiciously and then said:

"This afternoon the Moscow police have unearthed a most desperate plot to wreck Your Majesty's train early to-morrow morning at Chimki. I furnished them with information, and twenty-eight arrests have been made."

"Indeed," remarked his Imperial Master, raising his eyebrows, quite unmoved. "Have you the list of names?"

In answer, the General produced a yellow official paper, which he placed upon His Majesty's table. Then, with but a casual glance, the Emperor took up his quill and scribbled some words across the sheet and handed it back.

Markoff glanced at the words written, then, much puzzled, looked at His Majesty.

"Yes," the latter said. "I order their immediate release. And, let me tell you, Serge Markoff, that this afternoon I have given audience to a very intimate friend of yours; your *agent-provocateur*, Danilo Danilovitch!"

The General's countenance went white as paper. Such a reception was entirely unexpected.

"Ah!" exclaimed His Majesty, with a bitter smile, "I see what surprise and apprehension my talk with Danilovitch causes you. Well, I will not give utterance to the loathing I feel towards you—the man in whose hands I have placed such supreme power, and whom I have so implicitly trusted. Suffice it to say that he has revealed to me the ingenious manner in which plots have been formed in order to terrorise me, and your inhuman method of sending hundreds of innocent ones into exile, merely in order to obtain my favour."

"I have never done such a thing!" cried the man in uniform, standing at attention as his master spoke. "The fellow lies."

"Enough," said the Emperor, in a loud, commanding voice. "Hear me! You are an assassin. You killed my brother the Grand Duke Peter with your own dastardly hand in order to hide your disgraceful tactics. You sent your own wife to her grave, and you paid your catspaw to kill the Grand Duke Nicholas. To-day there is a plot afoot to close the lips of my niece and my good friend Trewinnard! These are only a few of your disgraceful crimes. No; do not attempt to deny them, brute and liar that you are. Rather reflect upon the terrible fate of the thousands of poor wretches who have been sent to the Arctic settlements by your relentless, inhuman hand. The souls of all those who have been worn out by the journey and died like dogs upon the Great Post Road, or in other ways have fallen innocent victims of your plots, call loudly for vengeance. And I tell you, Serge Markoff," he said, his dark, heavy brows narrowing in fierce anger, "I tell you that I shall find means by which adequate punishment will be awarded to you. Here is your dismissal!" he added, taking the document from his table. "It will be gazetted to-morrow. Go back to Petersburg at once and there remain. Do not attempt to leave Russia, or even to leave Petersburg, or you will at once be placed under arrest and sent to the fortress. Go home, place your affairs in order, and await until I send for you again."

The Emperor had not yet decided what form his punishment should take.

"But—but surely Your Imperial Majesty will allow me to—" he gasped with difficulty.

"I will allow you nothing—nothing! You are my enemy, Serge Markoff—a crafty, cunning enemy, who now stands revealed as a brutal assassin! Ah! I shall avenge my brother Peter's death—depend upon it! Go!

Get from my presence!" he commanded, and raising his hand, he pointed with his finger imperiously to the door. I had never before seen such a look upon His Majesty's strong face.

And the man whose evil actions had spread terror into every corner and every home throughout the Russian Empire, thus receiving his sudden *congé*, slowly crossed the room, his head bowed, his face ashen.

He was unable to speak or to protest.

For a second he stood still, then, opening the door, he passed out in silence.

Extract from the second edition of *The Times* issued on the following day:

"From Our Own Correspondent.

"St. Petersburg, May 16th.

"A startling tragedy occurred just after seven o'clock last evening in front of the barracks in the Zagarodny Prospect in St. Petersburg, just outside the Tzarskoie-Selo Station. According to the journal *Novosti*, His Excellency General Serge Markoff, Chief of Secret Police, and one of the Emperor's most trusted officials, who had been to Tzarskoie-Selo for audience with His Majesty, had arrived at the station unexpectedly on his return to Petersburg, and his carriage not being there, he resolved to walk down into the city. He had turned out of the station, when he was followed by an unknown man, who had, it seems, arrived by the same train. In front of the barracks the pair apparently recognised each other, and, according to a bystander, His Excellency drew a revolver and fired point-blank at the stranger, who next instant drew his own weapon and shot the General dead.

"All took place in the space of a few seconds, so suddenly, indeed, that the stranger, who certainly fired in self-protection, was able to get clear away before any of the passers-by could stop him. The General's body was removed by the military ambulance to his residence facing the Summer Gardens, and the strange affair created the greatest sensation throughout the city.

"It is believed that the man so suddenly recognised by His Excellency must have been a prominent Terrorist from whom the General feared assassination; but it is proved by an onlooker—a butcher who was walking only a few feet from them—that His Excellency, who appeared seized by sudden anger, fired the first shot.

"The police are making every inquiry, and it is believed that the assassin of the well-known official will be arrested.

"Another curious feature in connection with the strange affair is that the same journal in another column publishes in the 'Official Gazette' the announcement that His Majesty the Emperor only two hours before the tragic occurrence dismissed his favourite official in disgrace. No reason is given, but it is rumoured in the diplomatic circle that certain grave administrative scandals have been discovered, and this dismissal is the first of several which are to follow. In fact, in certain usually well-informed quarters it is persistently declared that the whole Cabinet will be dismissed.

"The Emperor left with the Tzarina for Moscow last evening. The Grand Duchess Natalia accompanied them, and Mr Colin Trewinnard, of the British Embassy, travelled by the same train."

Chapter Thirty Six
Describes To-day

Three months later.

It was hot August in Russia—the month of drought and dust.

Luba de Rosen had returned to her mother's house in Petersburg, where her property and her dead mother's handsome income, which had been confiscated by the State, had been returned to her. Several times both Her Highness and myself had visited her, while one afternoon she had been received in private audience at Gatchina by the Emperor, who had sympathised with her and promised to make amends in every way for the injustice she had suffered.

The camarilla who had so long ruled Russia, placing the onus of their oppression upon the Emperor, had, thanks to Natalia, been broken up, and a new and honest Cabinet established in its place.

Danilo Danilovitch, on the day following Markoff's assassination, had telegraphed openly from Germany to His Majesty, announcing that he had rid Russia of her worst enemy. And probably that message did not cause the Emperor much displeasure. It was the carrying out of the old Biblical law of an eye for an eye. And as the catspaw was beyond the frontier, and the crime a political one, its perpetrator was immune from arrest.

Five weeks later, however, the Supreme Council of the People's Will, held in an upstairs room in Greek Street, Soho, and presided over by Danilovitch in person, heard from him a long and complete statement, in which he described his audience at Tzarskoie-Selo, and delivered the message sent by the Emperor to the Revolutionists.

Unanimously it was then decided to put an end to all militant measures, now that the Emperor knew the truth, and to trust the assurances given from the throne. A loyal reply was drafted to His Majesty's message, and this was duly despatched by a confidential messenger to Russia and placed in the Emperor's own hands—a declaration of loyalty which gave him the greatest gratification.

Diplomatic Europe, in ignorance of what was actually in progress, was surprised at the sudden turn of events in Russia, and on account of the unexpected dismissal of Ministers and the establishment of the Duma, felt that open revolution was imminent. From the official busybodies at the various Embassies the truth was carefully concealed. It was, of course, known that General Markoff had all along been the worst enemy of Russia, and in consequence the Revolutionary Party made open rejoicing at the news of his death. Yet the actual facts were ingeniously suppressed, both from the diplomatic corps and from the correspondents of the foreign newspapers.

The entire change in the Emperor's policy and the granting of many much-needed reforms were regarded abroad as the natural reaction after the drastic autocracy. But nobody dreamed of the truth, how the Emperor, after all a humane man and a benign ruler, had at last learned the bitter truth, and had instantly acted for the welfare and safety of his beloved people.

Many of the London journals published leading articles upon what they termed "the new era in Russia," attributing it to all causes except the right one, the popular opinion being that His Majesty had at last been terrorised into granting justice and a proper representation to the people. Exile of political prisoners to Siberia had been suddenly abolished by Imperial ukase, together with the major powers vested in the Secret Police. The safety and sanctity of the home was guaranteed, and no person could in future be consigned to a dungeon or exiled without fair and open trial.

All this, it was said, was a triumph of the Revolution. Journalists believed that the Emperor had been forced to accord the people their demand. Little, indeed, did the world dream the actual truth, the secret of which was so well kept that only the British Foreign Minister at Downing Street was aware of it, for by the Emperor's express permission I was able to sit one day in that sombre private room in the Foreign Office and there in confidence relate the strange events, the shadows of a throne, which I have endeavoured to set down in the foregoing pages.

Since the day of the dismissal of Serge Markoff with five members of the Cabinet, and the breaking up of that disgraceful camarilla which had surrounded the Sovereign, suppressing the truth, preventing reforms, and ruling Holy Russia with a hand of iron, the nation had indeed entered upon an era of financial and social progress. Russia has become a nation of enlightenment, prosperity and industry, even, perhaps, against the will of her upper classes.

I was present on that August day in the handsome private church attached to the great Palace of Peterhof, and there witnessed the marriage of Her Imperial Highness the Grand Duchess Natalia to Richard Drury, Count of Ozerna, who had become a naturalised Russian subject and been ennobled by the Emperor.

It was a brilliant function, for all the Ministers, foreign Ambassadors and the whole Imperial Court, including the Emperor and Empress, were present. The Court now being out of mourning for the Grand Duke Nicholas, the display of smart gowns, uniforms and decorations was more striking than even at a State ball at the Winter Palace.

Standing beside Captain Stoyanovitch, I was near Natalia, the incorrigible little madcap of the Romanoffs, when with her husband she knelt before the altar while the priest, in his gorgeous robes, bestowed upon them his blessing. And when they rose and passed out, their handsome faces reflected the supreme joy of the triumph of their mutual love.

Some years have now passed.

His Imperial Majesty, alas! lies in his great sarcophagus in Moscow, and the Tzarevitch reigns in his stead. But in Russia the Revolutionary movement is no longer a militant one, for the people know well that their ruler's aims and aspirations are those of his father, and patiently await the reforms which, though perhaps slow in progress, nevertheless do from time to time become law and bestow the greatest benefits upon the many millions of souls from the German frontier to the Sea of Japan.

Ivan Hartwig, the Anglo-Russian, still lives on the outskirts of Petersburg as Otto Schenk, and is still head of the Russian Sûreté, and from him I only recently heard that Danilo Danilovitch had been discovered in Chicago, leading the life of a highly-respected citizen. He had changed his name into Daniels, and was the proprietor of one of the largest boot factories in that progressive city. Miss West has been pensioned and remains in Brighton, but Davey, the English maid, is still in the Grand Duchess's service.

As for myself—well, I am still a diplomat, and still a bachelor.

After service as Councillor of Embassy in Berlin, Washington and Paris, I was appointed by the late King Edward his *Envoy extraordinaire et Ministre plénipotentiaire* to a certain brilliant Court in the South of Europe, where I still reside in the great white Embassy as chief of a large and brilliant staff.

Sometimes when I go on leave, I manage to snatch a week or two with Count Drury and his pretty wife, at the Grand Ducal Palace in Petersburg, where they live together in perfect idyllic happiness, and where splendid receptions are given during the winter season. More than once, too, I have been guest at their great Castle of Ozerna, a gloomy mediaeval fortress, near Orel in Central Russia, to enjoy the excellent boar-hunting in the huge forests surrounding.

And often as I have sat at their table, waited on by the gorgeous flunkeys in the blue-and-gold Grand Ducal livery, headed by old Igor, I have looked into Natalia's pretty face and reflected how Little the Russian people ever dream that for the liberty which has recently come to them they are indebted solely to a woman—to the girl who was once declared to be an incorrigible flirt, and who had scandalised the Imperial family—the little Grand Duchess, who, at the sacrifice of her own great love, boldly exposed and denounced that unscrupulous and powerful official, Markoff, the one-time Chief of Secret Police, the man who had sacrificed so many innocent lives as the Price of Power.